W9-BEX-577

TRIBE, CASTE, AND NATION

PAN musicians at a wedding.

TRIBE, CASTE, AND NATION

A study of political activity and political change
in highland Orissa

by

F. G. BAILEY

*University of California
San Diego*

MANCHESTER UNIVERSITY PRESS

© 1960 F. G. Bailey
Published by the University of Manchester at
THE UNIVERSITY PRESS
316–324 Oxford Road, Manchester M13 9NR
First published 1960
Repinted 1966, 1971

ISBN 0 7190 0250 8

Distributed in the U.S.A. by
Humanities Press, Inc.
303 Park Avenue South, New York, N.Y. 10010

Printed in Great Britain by Butler & Tanner Ltd., Frome and London

To
MARY

PREFACE

IN putting the names of castes into English and using capital letters I have followed here the same conventions as I did in *Caste and the Economic Frontier* (1957, pp. xv–xvi). An exception is 'Boad OUTCASTES' who are here presented in their vernacular name 'PAN'. I made a land survey in Baderi similar to that in Bisipara, and the size of estates is presented in the same way (*ibid.*, pp. 279–84).

Bisipara is the name of an actual village. But elsewhere in this book I have used pseudonyms for the names of all persons and some places. Many of these pseudonyms are not Kui words, but my own invention. For this reason I have not tried to say how these names should be pronounced. For the pronunciation of Kui words see W. W. Winfield, 1928, pp. 1–7.

Cases written in inverted commas are translations of vernacular texts, or quotations from published works. Other cases are summaries in my own words of conversations with informants, or descriptions of incidents which I witnessed.

Most of the material was gathered in 1955, although I have also drawn upon material collected between 1952 and 1954, when I lived in Bisipara. Both these visits were made possible by a Treasury Studentship in Foreign Languages and Cultures. I again thank members of the Treasury Committee, and I remember with gratitude the help given me by Mr. C. R. Allen.

I began to write this book in the autumn of 1957 and the manuscript was completed early in 1958. Four papers, outlining the argument, were read in the summer of 1957 at seminars in the Department of Social Anthropology in Manchester University. I am grateful to the members of this seminar for their careful criticisms, and in particular I wish to thank Professor Max Gluckman, by whom I was first guided into examining problems of social change. I also thank, for their constructive criticisms of my manuscript, Professor C. von Fürer-Haimendorf, Dr. Adrian Mayer, Dr. Colin Rosser, Dr. Elizabeth Colson, Dr. H. H. Meinhard, and Dr. Bernard Cohn.

Publication has been made possible by a grant from the School of Oriental and African Studies, University of London. I wish to thank the members of the Publications Committee, in particular the secretary, Mr. J. R. Bracken.

I am grateful to Dr. R. L. Rooksby who compiled an index for this book, and to Professor Aiyappan of Utkal University for his assistance in correcting the proofs, and for many acts of kindness.

Lastly, while recalling my gratitude to the people of Bisipara, I also thank the Konds and other people who live in the village here called Baderi.

Bhubaneswar,   F. G. BAILEY
   October, 1959

CONTENTS

PART ONE: THE KONDS

ix

LIST OF CASES

LIST OF TABLES

LIST OF MAPS

LIST OF PLATES

PART ONE
THE KONDS

CHAPTER I

PROBLEMS AND METHODS

BISIPARA AND BADERI

BADERI village, around which this book is written, is less than an hour's walk from Bisipara, about which I wrote *Caste and the Economic Frontier*. The people of the two villages know one another. The Bisipara Oriyas visit Baderi in search of turmeric, which they buy from the Konds of Baderi and sell to middlemen in their own village. The head (Sirdar) of Balimendi, the administrative division (*mutha*) in which Baderi lies, is an Oriya of WARRIOR caste from Bisipara: the schoolmaster in the Lower Primary School in Baderi is also a Bisipara WARRIOR. Baderi Konds patronize the shops, attend fairs and festivals, and are sometimes invited to take part in the singing and drum-playing contests which are held in Bisipara.

The two villages lie in the same geographical region. Their climate and rainfall are similar. Both villages depend primarily upon irrigated rice for subsistence. They are also part of the same 'historical' region, which was isolated from metropolitan India for many centuries by poverty of resources, inaccessibility, the ferocity of the Kond inhabitants, and by the rigours of the climate, which even to-day afflict men from the plains of Orissa. In the middle of the nineteenth century the region was brought under effective control by the East India Company in the campaigns called the Meriah Wars. Since then the Administration has taken on more and more functions of government, which previously either were not fulfilled at all, or were performed by indigenous institutions: at the same time there has been a slow expansion of an economic frontier, which gradually incorporates the people of the Kond hills into the wider economy of India. The Administration and the growth of a diversified economy have changed the existing patterns of social relations both in Bisipara and in Baderi. The two villages are close to one another: they share a common geographical and historical background: and they have been affected by the same outside factors. But Baderi and Bisipara were

3

different before the process of social change began, and in this change they have followed different courses. By sketching out this difference I can show the purpose and scope of the present monograph.

The people of Bisipara are Oriya-speaking Hindus. The people of Baderi are Konds, and formerly they would have appeared in the Census Lists as 'Animists' or 'Tribalists' and not as 'Hindus'. The Konds to-day say that they are Hindus like everyone else, but they make a sharp distinction between themselves and the Oriyas who live in their midst. Usually they phrase the contrast between 'Kond' and 'Oriya' custom: but I have heard them make the contrast between their own culture and the 'Hindu' culture, and this way of phrasing the difference has appeared in texts which Konds have written for me. The category of 'Tribes' became the subject of an acrimonious debate in Indian politics,[1] but it need not concern this analysis for the present. If we grant the Konds their desired 'Hindu' status, then we will have to add that they are Hindus of a different kind from their Oriya neighbours, and both the Konds themselves and the Oriyas would be anxious to make this distinction. There are many cultural differences between the two peoples. The Konds speak Kui, a language which belongs to the great Dravidian family of south India: while the Oriya language is part of the Sanskritic group of northern India. The traditional Kond house is different from the Oriya house: their traditional dress is different: their rites and ceremonies are very different: their method of greeting one another is different: and although both depend on rice cultivation and use the same techniques, the Konds also cultivate axe-fields on the mountainside, while the Oriyas do not. These differences are recognized and emphasized by both parties, and the Konds are proud of their status as Adibasis (lit.: 'aboriginals' or 'first settlers'), a word which has become an acceptable substitute in modern India for 'tribes'.

Besides these cultural differences there are also social differences between Bisipara and Baderi. Bisipara is a nucleated village containing nearly 700 people. Baderi consists of a number of hamlets dispersed throughout a valley, and the aggregate population of these hamlets is less than 500. Bisipara is a multi-caste village containing a score of castes, none of which is larger than one-fifth of the total population. Baderi is virtually a one-caste village, in

[1] G. S. Ghurye, 1943, Chapter 5.

which the Konds form 70 per cent of the population. Bisipara is a village of part-time middlemen, while the men of Baderi partici-pate in the modern commercial economy as the producers of a cash-crop and never act as middlemen or traders.

The activities of the Administration and the spread of a diversi-fied economy changed the political structure of Bisipara. Wealth and power, formerly monopolized by the WARRIOR caste, was distributed more evenly throughout the village, and castes which formerly were dependent upon the WARRIORS asserted their inde-pendence and rebelled against WARRIOR dominance. At the same time effective political action came to be taken more and more outside the system of relationships within one village, and the men of Bisipara, of whatever caste, gained their end more frequently by appeal to the Administration rather than within the caste system in the village, and in some cases, notably the Harijan untouchables, by concerted action in the framework of a widespread caste organization.

I was able to isolate Bisipara from its surroundings and to con-sider it as a social system in itself. This does not mean that Bisipara was in fact isolated: the changes which occurred were the result of external factors, and had the village been truly isolated, they would never have taken place. But the factors which brought about change in the village were considered only in so far as they intruded into the village. I did not analyse the systems in which these factors were themselves elements (with the partial exception of political developments among the Harijans). In other words I focused attention mainly on the political system of the village, because this seemed a significant and important arena for political action.

Baderi village is an arena for political action, but for two reasons I have not concentrated only upon Baderi. In the traditional political system the Kond village is a unit in a larger corporate group, the clan, whereas Bisipara stood on its own as a maximal unit of corporate political activity. The political changes among the Konds, which correspond to the change in Bisipara, occcured not at the level of the village but at clan level, and these changes cannot be analysed without surveying a political arena much larger than one village. The second reason lies not in the material but in the purpose of this book, which is intended to be not so much a comparison between political change in a Kond and in an Oriya village, but rather to provide a complementary account,

B

which, taken together with *Caste and the Economic Frontier*, will give a general view of political activity and political change in one part of the Kond hills. The first book made a study of political action within a single village. Some events which affected the course of political development were the result of the peculiar situation of Bisipara, as a sophisticated commercially-minded community in the middle of a Kond area. But this fact was noticed only incidentally. In this book I concentrate on a wider political field, in which important political cleavages are not only within Kond villages and within the Kond tribe, but also between Konds and other castes. The first book was a study of an Oriya village and of the decay of caste as a political institution within that village: this is a study of a region, and of the rise and fall of political institutions not only in the caste system, but also in a tribal system, in a modern bureaucracy, and in a representative democracy.

STRUCTURE AND SYSTEM

I might have called this book 'The political structure of the Konds'. I have not done so, although I lean heavily on the concept of 'structure'. A structural analysis emphasizes the regularity, the continuity, the permanence of certain forms of social interaction, and of groups of persons. It also emphasizes system: that is to say, it assumes that the various roles (or institutions) in which persons or groups are engaged are connected with one another in such a way that what happens in one institution, or role, will regularly affect what happens in others.

I have distinguished between 'structure' and 'sub-structure'. A 'sub-structure' is made up of groups and institutions which are classified by their content—by what they are about. There are sub-structures which concern primarily politics or economics or ritual or kinship, and so forth. I have not used 'sub-structure' often because the phrase is clumsy, and because the relevant adjective is sufficient to distinguish the meaning of the noun. The word 'structure', strictly used, refers to a higher level of analysis at which interconnections are sought not *within* a political or ritual sub-structure but *between* them. 'Structure' thus carries with it the idea of 'total social structure', while 'sub-structure' refers to divisions classified on the basis of the 'referent' or 'content' of social relations.

In making a structural analysis the elements of social activity which are abstracted are those of coherence and continuity. The relationship between the different roles is necessarily one of *ultimate* consistency. These roles are part of one structure only in so far as they either re-inforce one another or at least do not *in the end* contradict one another. A structure, as I am using the word, cannot be self-destroying.[1] This emphatically does not mean that where there is conflict, there a structural analysis cannot be made. The structure itself will contain rules for the resolution of conflict, and conflict will even play a crucial part in maintaining the structure. The law, as often is said, is strengthened in the breach.[2] In another sense, conflict in one group may bring into action a larger group and so maintain its existence, as when caste councils meet to settle conflicts between lineages. It is these situations which I have in mind when I use the words 'ultimately' and 'in the end'. It may be impossible for one individual to fulfil the roles of father and mother's brother to the satisfaction both of his own sons and his sister's sons, and there may arise conflicts: yet these roles may still be part of a single sub-structure, in that both parties are members of a larger group within which the conflict can be contained and which provides machinery for its resolution without abolishing one or the other role.[3]

It is helpful to make a distinction between conflict and contradiction. 'Conflict', as I use it, is contained and 'sealed off' within a structure. 'Contradiction'—between roles or institutions—is not, and is symptomatic of social change. Contradictions of this kind are most readily apparent at the level of 'structure' rather than 'sub-structure'. It was, for instance, very obvious in Bisipara that the ritual sub-structure in which the WARRIORS and the untouchables interacted was in many respects inconsistent with their political and economic relationships. There was an irresolvable contradiction between these two sub-structures, and taken together they did not add up to one consistent structure. There were neither rules nor institutions nor roles within the caste system designed to cope with such a situation. The same was true in Baderi (Case 35: p. 128). The presence in any situation of irresolvable contradiction between different roles indicates that the total situation cannot be

---

[1] These are definitions which I have found useful. I do not claim that they are the only useful definitions.

[2] Llewellyn and Hoebel, 1941, p. 20.

[3] M. Gluckman, 1955, *passim*: especially Chapter III.

understood within the framework of a single omnicompetent structure. If the analysis is to be continued within the framework of one structure, then one or the other side of the contradiction must be ignored. This is not satisfactory since it removes the analysis further from reality. Alternatively it may be assumed that there is not one structure to be analysed, but there are two or more structures operating in a single social field.

The signs of irresolvable contradiction between roles and between institutions were quickly obvious in the field, but it was not until a comparatively advanced stage of the analysis that I could take account of the presence of more than one structure. My analysis moves from the simpler to the more complex, and it will be necessary to explain some of the words which designate the various stages of complexity in the analysis. These words are 'static' and 'dynamic', 'synchronic' and 'diachronic'.

It is important to point out, particularly with a word like 'static', that these adjectives apply not to societies, but to the analysis of them. Putting it crudely, the simplest analysis is that which can take account of the fewest facts, and which has to hold equal the largest number. As the analysis moves to more complicated stages, a relatively larger number of facts is taken into account, and the number of variables assumed to be steady diminishes.

I begin with a 'static' analysis. Roughly speaking such an analysis holds two things equal. Firstly it does not concern itself with variations in the content of relationships: that is to say, with variations in the thing concerning which social interaction is taking place. For instance, land tenure relationships would be described without references to changes in the land-population ratio, or to variations in the fertility of the land. Secondly such an analysis takes into account not actors but only persons. The role of a chief may be described, but the fact that the actors who fill this role pass from the cradle to the grave, and that in infancy or senility they may be unable to fulfil their chiefly functions, is ignored. A static analysis is of necessity synchronic and it is to be compared to a chart of roles or statuses, describing their mutual relationships either in terms of 'ought' or of 'usually do'. In brief, a static analysis, while not of course denying that social relationships are about something, ignores the fact that this 'something' may vary independently of the social relations, and may make it difficult for the relationship described by the static chart to be fulfilled.

I cannot think of any examples of a purely static analysis of a society. For most people this is a preliminary stage in their analysis. In the dynamic analysis which follows some external factors are taken into account, and they are allowed to vary. The chart is, so to speak, set in motion.[1] The life cycle of the actors is considered. The analysis comes to be concerned with the flexibility of the structure and the way it can 'cope with' disturbances originated outside it. Various rules and institutions which are specifically designed to meet periodic crises are described—examples being the rules of succession and inheritance, and the procedures brought into action against actors who deviate from their appropriate role. In this category also fall the institutions which serve to 'seal off' or resolve conflicts arising from structural ambiguities.

A dynamic analysis is necessarily diachronic. But these two words are not interchangeable. The 'dynamic' analysis, as I use the word in this book, is still the analysis of one structure, and it is concerned with elements of continuity and permanence. The whole effort is directed to showing that in spite of possible variations in 'outside' factors, the chart of structure continues unchanged. Those rules and institutions are described which restore the *status quo* and often which dramatize, in one way or another, the structure, which—paradoxically—becomes strongest when it is attacked. Although a dynamic analysis is diachronic in one sense, in another sense—that of history—it is timeless, and it is to indicate this fact that the phrase 'structural time' is used.[2]

In a dynamic analysis one can deal with conflict and apparent contradictions. Every conflict needs to be examined to see how far it brings into play redressive mechanisms and how far it is contained within one structure. It is clearly a mistake to leap at once to the conclusion that every conflict is evidence of irresolvable contradiction and therefore of change. Some conflicts are temporary disturbances of a structure which has its own means of finding a way back to equilibrium. It is only after this question has been asked that one is justified in concluding that the analysis can only be saved from undue 'unreality' by postulating the presence in the

[1] I frequently use the word 'system' or the phrase 'structures in action' to refer to structure in its dynamic aspects.

[2] E. E. Evans-Pritchard, 1940, Chapter 3.

social field of more than one structure, and thus moving into a more complex stage in the analysis.

The second, third, etc., structures in themselves do not differ theoretically from the first, but their joint presence in a single field raises a host of theoretical questions. At the broadest level the question is what relations exist between these different structures. This question is not unlimited for one possibility has already been ruled out: there are between these structures (or between their several sub-structures, or between the institutions belonging to different sub-structures) irresolvable contradictions, so that, whatever else is the relationship between the different structures, it is not itself a structure.

I take up these questions again in the concluding chapter. I do not think that I have any conclusive answer to the problem posed at the end of the last paragraph and I have been content to elaborate the idea of several structures, incompatible with one another, existing in the same field. These introductory remarks are given so that the reader may know what I have in mind when I use words like structure, system, sub-structure, static, dynamic, and so forth.

POLITICAL ACTIVITY

Through political activity a man achieves command over resources, or power over men, or both these things. Political relationships are those through which he achieves the same ends. These definitions are used widely and are offered not so much as criteria of relevance, but to show the assumptions which underlie my approach to political problems. Society is an arena (or 'field') in which men compete for prizes: to control one another; to achieve command over property and resources (in the Kondmals this has generally meant land): and, negatively, to avoid being controlled by others and to retain such resources as they already possess. In order better to achieve these ends (and, of course, for other reasons which are not specifically political) men combine into groups, and competition lies not only between individuals but also between groups. I assume that the individual's motive in giving or continuing to give his allegiance to a political group is that in this way he expects to gain his ends and retain or achieve command over men and resources. If, by experience, he finds that he can retain or better achieve command by giving his allegiance elsewhere, then he will do so: and if sufficient people do this, then one type of group is likely to disappear and be replaced by groups of a different kind.

I am aware that this is a crude view both of human nature and of social process.[1] Men do not always know how to achieve their ends, even if they are thoroughly self-interested. Often men are not self-interested, are not interested in achieving power and wealth, and for an ideal or a principle will willingly destroy themselves. But this is neither here nor there. In enquiring why men abandon one kind of allegiance and prefer another, one needs to ask of every incident: Whose was the profit?

The relationships in any structure are not purely and simply mandatory upon the actors: if they were, and the structure were to survive, then it would have to be perfect and exhaustive, laying down a course of action for every possible eventuality. I have regarded the structure not so much as made up of relationships which are obligatory upon the various actors, but rather as imposing some kind of limit on possible action, while leaving within these limits an area of discretion and choice, which the actors can manipulate in order to achieve their ends. This is not a 'meta-anthropological' statement about free will and social determinism: it is rather a statement about the way I have analysed my material. The starting-point of the analysis is the actor, certainly as a child of his social environment and bridled by training and sanctions, but also as an active person who makes use of this social environment, and who exploits its uncertainties and ambiguities, and who is able to profit particularly when the structure is set out of balance by outside factors.

These 'organizational' [2] elements—the region of choice and uncertainty—exist within any system. But choice, in the society which I studied, lies not only within one system of political relations, but also between systems. The actors have roles not only within one political system but within several systems which can be clearly defined and analysed separately from one another. The Kond has a role in a tribal system, in the caste system, and in the complex system of the Administration and the representative democracy. To achieve his political ends, or to prevent others from exploiting him, he can call upon allegiances in all three systems. He can employ one system to redress a weakness in another. 'The political structure of

[1] See p. 255.
[2] R. Firth, 1951, 1954, 1955.

the Konds' would properly refer to the tribal system alone: but if we attempt to understand the motives and actions of the protagonists in any incident to-day, then within the framework of the tribal structure alone a very limited understanding can be achieved. It is not possible to analyse political activity in the Kondmals and get anywhere near to reality in the framework of a single structure. This book, therefore, is not about the political *structure* of the Konds so much as about political *activity* (by Konds and other categories of persons) in several different structures. In other words, I describe rather a political field than a political structure.

Nor do I attempt to cover the entire organizational field—the entire field of choice. I have neglected choice within a single structure and I have concentrated on choice between structures, in particular where this seems to be relevant to social change. I have tried to describe the process by which one type of allegiance is dropped in favour of another.

To manipulate a social system, to exercise choice between several structures, to be active rather than passive, requires energy, foresight, intelligence, and cunning. In concentrating upon this side of political life I may well have presented the Konds and the other inhabitants of the Kond Hills as self-centred opportunists, with a well-developed entrepreneurial sense, a Machiavellian grasp of political alternatives, and a Machiavellian cynicism in making use of these alternatives. If the reader gets this impression, then I apologize both to him and to the Konds. Kond society contains an average proportion of people who are politically passive, simple, honest, and easy-going. Indeed, in the social myths which are current about Konds both among themselves and among outsiders, they have more than an average proportion of people who lack political energy and cunning.[1] But there are among them men who are conspicuously gifted with these qualities (Case 38: p. 197), and even those who are by nature passive are sometimes forced by circumstances to exert themselves. Necessity becomes the mother of social invention. In the manoeuvres of those who are energetic, ambitious, cunning, and perhaps unscrupulous, and in the activities of those who are jerked by necessity out of their customary lethargy and their customary reliance on the established rules of society, the process of social change is to be perceived.

[1] See p. 185.

METHOD OF PRESENTATION

A political structure can be described as regularities in behaviour between persons or between groups concerning power over men and resources. One method of doing this is to state the rule, and give examples of particular individuals either within one's own experience, or within the experience of one's informants, behaving in this way. A more rigorous presentation is achieved by giving the rule numerically, if that is possible. One counts the ← number of situations in which a particular rule of behaviour is appropriate, and then states on how many of these occasions the actors did in fact behave in the prescribed way. The method of presentation by example alone is often the only one available. Sometimes not even that is available and the informant's statement of what should happen is presented and left to stand alone. But even an example is a meagre presentation, because it might be a selected example, because negative examples might have been overlooked, or because what is presented as an example is in fact a random occurrence and not a regularity at all. A numerical presentation overcomes these difficulties, but often there is not sufficient material to make this kind of presentation possible: and in any case a numerical statement of a rule cannot effectively convey its mandatory aspect. It cannot show that this kind of behaviour is part of the manifest structure, and not of the latent structure: that it is part of the 'ought' rather than part of the 'usually do'. This can best be done by describing the occasions on which the rule is challenged, on which the would-be deviants are brought into conformity, and on which the rule is publicly stated and proved effective. A numerical presentation and the use of case material are not, of course, alternatives: they complement one another and check one another.

A social structure can be described without any reference whatsoever to particular individuals and without the use of specific cases.[1] A description of this kind, if well done, makes a strong appeal to the intellect: it is elegant, sparing in detail, rounded and complete, and has a sharp, tidy, thoroughly 'scientific' exactness. It is a work of logic: the various parts of the structure agree with one another and all fit together to make a neat whole. On the other hand, the more exact is the structure the more difficult it

[1] P. Kaberry, 1957, p. 88.

becomes to fit it to reality. The presentation of the material at a high level of abstraction makes it impossible for the reader to measure its adequacy as a description of the society which it is supposed to explain, and to see whether this is the only possible interpretation. Indeed, it would be unfair to question the interpretation in this way, for the only accepted criticism is one which shows an internal inconsistency in the structure. An analysis of this kind makes sparing use of case material, and we are presented not with the actors, but with the system or structure, which we assume governs all their actions.

Such a description is the more easily made, and the canons of intellectual elegance are least violated, the more the writer is prepared to ignore the dynamic aspects of social life. The mild disorders which occur and are solved by succession and inheritance, and the problem of growth in general, are treated within the perspective of structural time, but the larger disorders which rearrange whole groups are presented, if at all, in a highly mechanical fashion. Much of the primary material is discarded. If, on the other hand, the writer tries to take into fuller consideration the dynamic aspects of the social structure, and still endeavours to present them as regularities without the use of case material, then the result is likely to be less elegant, less exact and nearer to reality. Such writing, however, usually puts a strain on the language and the literary ingenuity of the writer, leads him into tortuous metaphors which are often drawn from the more exact sciences (and are therefore specious), and in the end, although it conveys in its own intricacies some of the complexities of social life, is apt to be confusing. The internal inconsistencies[1] are still the weaknesses for which the critic must look: the basic question which he asks himself is still whether the system would work, given the conditions which the writer postulates. He still has little knowledge of

[1] It is still, of course, true that this book, in itself, can only be checked by the consistency of the material which I offer in the thirty-eight cases presented. It is also true that these cases are themselves selective and do not present the complete raw material which was available to me in the field. But for two reasons most of these cases, in particular the longer ones, cannot be considered merely extended examples, used to illustrate a point of theory. Firstly, the point of theory is itself deduced from the material presented in that case. Secondly the cases mostly concern the village of Baderi, involve the same actors, and thus provide some kind of cross-check upon one another. Neither of these two statements could be made about examples used only as illustrations.

the actual instances from which the writer made his first abstractions, and he still is unable to find out—except by guesswork and
material got from other sources—whether, even if the system
would work, conditions are appropriate for it to do so.

In parts of this book I have made analyses of this kind, because
the material I gathered was a statement of the rules or regularities,
and not instances. I was told, for example, that in the wars between
Kond clans women were never attacked, and I have had to repro-
duce this as a regularity in social life, because wars came to an end a
hundred years ago and neither I nor my informants had seen a
Kond war. But whenever possible I have tried to present a case or
a dispute, and to use it as a text, to comment upon it, and from the
commentary to extract regularity and structure. Two whole chapters hinge upon single cases of this kind and there are numerous
cases in other parts of the book.

A low level of generalization is less exact, less elegant, and
infinitely more untidy and incomplete than high abstraction. Its
advantage is that it can present data from which generalizations
are made and it allows the reader some kind of check on these
abstractions, not by the test of internal consistency only, but also
by relating the analysis to what goes on. It is particularly necessary
to make use of case material in studying social change, because our
theoretical apparatus for the study of change scarcely exists. The
beginnings must be empirical. A second reason is that in any incident there will be activities which belong not to one structure, but
to several different structures, some of which are decaying and
some of which are growing. There is no reason why one should
not present these structures as wholes in themselves: but such a
presentation will give only the two ends of a process of change—
the before and the after—and will not show what point the
society has reached in the course of change. In order to do this we
need case material. The third reason is that just as change becomes
apparent in the activities and stratagems of the ambitious or of the
hard-pressed, so also it is most apparent in situations of crisis. Crisis
situations have a diagnostic value. In disputes an established rule
may be proclaimed, publicly stated, and uttered as a warning to
would-be deviants: but a dispute may also proclaim that an
established rule of behaviour can now be flouted with impunity
(Case 35: p. 128), it may encourage other would-be deviants, and
it may announce that a particular type of relationship or allegiance

is no longer an effective means of gaining one's end. In other words, while it may sanction one system of political relationships, it may at the same time proclaim another system bankrupt. In dealing with social change we are not dealing with whole structures, but with the decay of some and with the genesis and growth of others.

In the following four chapters I present the Kond[1] political structure in its dynamic aspects, and I show in what respects it has changed in the last hundred years. I discuss the relationship of the Konds with their dependent castes in Chapter VI. Chapter VII is largely an historical survey of the protracted conflict between Konds and Oriyas, and an analysis of the different alignments which both sides have at different times found effective. In the last part of the book I show how the actors make use of the different alternatives which the multiplicity of political structures presents to them, and finally I discuss the relevance of my material to some problems in Indian sociology.

[1] The Konds are a 'tribe' only in respect of a common culture and a common language, and even within these two categories there are many differences of usage and dialect, often arising from variations in the degree to which the Oriya (or Telugu) language and customs have been adopted. (See W. W. Winfield, 1929, pp. viii and x. See also W. W. Winfield, 1928, and F. V. P. Schulze, 1911 and 1913.)

In the 1941 Census of India the Konds were numbered at 690,365 and in the 1951 Census there is a guess that they might be 750,000 (Census of India, 1951, Vol. XI, Part 1, Report, p. 422). Their greatest concentration is in the present Phulbani District, in particular within the Kondmals sub-division and in Baliguda. They are also found in Boad, which is part of Phulbani District, and in the Districts of Puri (Nayagarh sub-division), Koraput, Kalahandi, and Bolangir. A few Konds are found outside Orissa.

I emphasize that I have not attempted a descriptive ethnography of 'the Kond tribe'. This book is an analysis of political development as it has occurred in the eastern part of the Kondmals sub-division (see p. 85). For the people of the rest of the Kond hills my explanations are to be treated rather as an analytical framework within which *their* particular history may be examined.

1. Baderi Valley.

CHAPTER II

THE VILLAGE

(Case 1)   (Time: *c*. 1945)

About ten years ago a man from Rupamendi, a clan territory which lies to the south of Baderi village, bought a field in Baderi. It was a large irrigated paddy field lying to the west of the road (Map 1). He had great difficulty in cultivating this field, since his home lay five miles away, and the journey to and fro not only took up much of his time, but also tired his oxen. When the field was under water he had more difficulties, because someone kept coming in the night and breaking a hole in the lower dyke, so that the water flowed away, and he several times nearly lost his crop. The Rupamendi man then approached the Baderi Konds and asked if his younger brother might be permitted to build a house on the waste land that lay alongside the field. The Baderi people refused, not because they had any use for the waste land, but because they wanted to keep the Rupamendi man away. After some years the man from Rupamendi gave up and sold the field to a Baderi man.

The conflict in this case is not merely between the people of Baderi and the Rupamendi landowner, but also between two systems of land-holding. The Rupamendi man had bought the field and had registered his title in the Record of Rights kept by the Administration. His title under this system was unassailable, and the people of Baderi could have had no grounds for complaint before the courts, But that same field, the land around it, and indeed the whole of the Baderi valley belongs, under a different system of land-holding, to the Baderi people. In the idiom of the country, while the Rupamendi man owned the field, the people of Baderi owned the earth, and they made use of this right in the earth to regain control of the field. They could not do so directly: a proprietary right entered in the Record would be upheld in the courts against a claim made on the grounds of ownership of the earth. But waste land is not entered into the Record of Rights and is assumed to belong to the local community: the Baderi people were therefore within the law in refusing land to build a house:

and they were in this way able to prevent the Rupamendi man from making efficient use of the field which he had bought.

By the law of the Government the right to hold cultivated land derives ultimately from itself, and the Government is (with certain exceptions) not concerned with the place of residence or social affiliations of the owner. Under the tribal system a right to land involves membership of the local community and acceptance of duties within that community. The action of the people of Baderi is an assertion of the tribal system and a denial of the Government system. They rejected the Rupamendi man because he belongs to a group which is by tradition at enmity with the Baderi people, and because he would be disqualified in many other ways from playing his part as a full member of Baderi village.

Proprietary right in land and a market for land have developed since the British took over the Kondmals. The ownership of community land by people who were not compelled to take on community obligations would tend to break down the unity of the village. But in Baderi the community possessed sufficient unity to resist change and to preserve its own integrity. In this chapter I shall begin to examine the relationships which make up that unity.[1]

THE MAIN LINEAGE

Baderi consists of nine hamlets in a valley which rises eastwards from the Salki river. The valley is shown in Map 1 and the names of the hamlets, together with their population by caste are shown in Table 1.

Baderi is the name both of this cluster of hamlets and of the largest hamlet within it. I shall use the word 'village' or 'village cluster' to refer to the larger group, and 'hamlet' for the smaller.

[1] The analysis in Part Two has been made possible by work on lineage systems in Africa by Professor Evans-Pritchard, Professor Fortes, and their colleagues and successors, whose names are listed at the end of this book. Partly because of social change, and partly because my interests lie elsewhere, my synchronic analysis of Kond lineages and clans does not measure up in fulness and detail to the standard expected of an Africanist at the present day. But my purpose has been not to make a deeper internal exploration of this kind of social system, but to relate it to other systems, and to describe what happens to it in situations of social change.

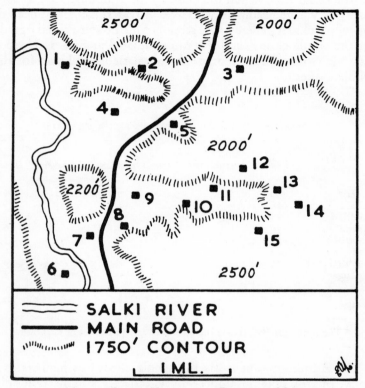

MAP 1.—BADERI VILLAGE AND BALIMENDI MUTHA

Balimendi mutha
1. Manipara
2. Birabhui
3. Damopara
4. Gomapara
5. Punuripara

Baderi village cluster
6. Majisai
7. Atisai
8. Baderi
9. Kamopara
10. Pandrisai
11. Dudopara
12. Dobenisai
13. Kinisuga
14. Kendrisai

Other village
15. Bandibari

The people of the village cluster are known as 'Baderi people' to outsiders, and the names of the other hamlets tend to be used only for discrimination within the cluster. The Administration recognizes one village headman, who lives in Baderi hamlet, as head of the whole cluster. There is one school of the Lower Primary grade for the whole cluster, and this too is situated in Baderi. There is also one Government-recognized and salaried watchman for the whole cluster.

TABLE 1

POPULATION OF HAMLETS IN BADERI CLUSTER BY CASTE

Hamlet	Konds	Kond SMITHS	Kond HERDSMEN	Oriya HERDSMEN	Untouchables	Total
Baderi* . .	100	18	9	7	72	206
Atisai . . .	28	—	—	—	5	33
Pandrisai . .	88	2	—	4	—	94
Majisai . .	36	—	—	6	4	46
Dobenisai .	41	—	4	—	—	45
Dudopara .	24	—	7	—	—	31
Kendrisai . .	15	—	—	4	—	19
Kinisuga . .	2	—	—	—	—	2
Total	334	20	20	21	81	476

* The figure for Baderi here includes the adjacent hamlet of Kamopara

The Administration treats the whole cluster of hamlets as a unity. But this does not impose unity: rather it is a reflection of it. Many activities in which the Baderi people meet one another are typically the activities of neighbours. They gossip together: the men take their recreation together, hunting and fishing in one another's company: the women gather leaves and other wild products from the forest together: they visit the markets at Phulbani and Phiringia in company with other people from their own village: and the men have a village council which meets to decide upon the dates and organization of joint activities, and to settle disputes which arise within the village. But the unity of the village derives from a bond which is stronger than that of neighbourhood. Baderi is a religious community and the people join together in propitiating many deities, principally those of the Mountain (*soru penu*) and of the Earth (*tana penu*).[1] Fellow villagers are required to help at marriages and at funerals and at times of crisis—during illness, in a dispute in which a man is involved with people from other villages, or when he is in trouble with the Administration.

The obligation to help and the right to receive aid from one's fellows pertain to everyone in the village, irrespective of caste: but the nucleus of the village, its hard core, is the group of Konds. They form 70 per cent of the village. They own the village and the land on which it is built. They are the true citizens, while other castes enjoy only second-class citizenship, deriving their membership from dependency on the Konds.

The relationship within the group of Baderi Konds is one of brotherhood, not in the vague sense in which any fellow-villager of the same age is called a 'village-brother', but more literally. Of the 334 Konds who live in Baderi, 79 per cent can be shown on one agnatic genealogy.[2] I shall call this group a lineage. The Baderi lineage is divided into four segments, B1, B2, B3, and B4. The first three are descended through seven generations from three brothers, Kelura, Ramo, and Bruska, respectively, and B4 is believed to be connected further back in the genealogy. For the first three the genealogy can be shown complete. The linking of B4 with the others is putative, but is not doubted.

Sexual relations within this group are incestuous, and pollute the Earth, putting the whole group (both Konds and persons of different caste) into ritual danger. The rains will fail: the earth will lose its fertility: the women of the group will lose their fertility and children will die: the people will go hungry: and they will be attacked by wild beasts in the forest. These disasters can be averted by a proper ritual atonement and by ending the liaison which has polluted the Earth, either by separating the offenders and making the man sponsor a ceremony of atonement, or by driving them outside the territory of the village and of the clan to which the village belongs.

(Case 2)   (Time: *c.* 1950)

A young man of B2 segment, who was living in Dobenisai in the house of his elder brother, impregnated a girl of B3 segment

---

[1] 'Earth' as a divinity is written with a capital letter.

[2] These figures include the wives of the men of the Baderi lineage, who were, of course, born into other lineages. Women of Baderi lineage who have married out are not included.

c

who lived in Baderi hamlet. When the girl named her lover the
men of Baderi went to Dobenisai and attacked the flock of goats
which belonged to that village. They chased the goats and cut down
two of them as the herd ran. One goat belonged to the offender's
elder brother and the other belonged to a man of the B4 segment
who lived in Dobenisai. This man received compensation from the
offender's elder brother.

A meeting was then summoned and attended by men from all
the hamlets of the Baderi cluster. They demanded that the young
man should provide money to hold a ceremony of purification,
but he chose instead to leave. He went to the Tea Gardens of
Assam.

Killing goats from the herd of the hamlet in which the offender
resides serves two purposes. It makes public the offence, and
ensures that the village council will have to take cognizance.
Secondly the manner of cutting down the goats ensures that the
Earth receives a minimum purificatory offering of blood, even if
the offender subsequently refuses to pay for the full ceremony and
prefers to go away. In former days cattle were attacked and a cow
or a buffalo slaughtered. At the present day, under the influence
of Hindu reformers, this is no longer done.

Only those who observe correctly the obligations of agnatic
brotherhood are entitled to receive the benefits conferred by the
ritual powers of the Earth. An offender not only foregoes these
benefits, but puts everyone else in danger, so that they are impelled
to take action against him. Brotherhood is in this way connected
with the cult of the Earth. But this connection is not with the
Earth in its all-pervading aspect, so much as with particular
stretches of territory, politically defined. These territories are
wider than the village and embrace the clan. Baderi belongs to the
Balimendi clan (see Chapter III).

ADOPTION INTO THE MAIN LINEAGE

Agnatic brotherhood automatically involved ritual relationships
which were connected with a particular stretch of territory. If two
Baderi persons commit incest somewhere else than in Baderi
territory (and the territory of the clan to which it belongs), then
no pollution falls upon the village and no ritual expiation need be
undertaken unless the offending couple come to the village.

Conversely the village is cleared of pollution with a minimum of ceremonial providing the offenders remove themselves. In other words the relationships of the Earth cult are limited territorially.

The same is true of agnatic brotherhood in so far as it has a political function. Those Konds who come from outside to settle in Baderi territory must take on some degree of agnatic obligation. Those who leave the territory and settle elsewhere, although they do not cease to be brothers so far as exogamy is concerned (so long as the link is remembered), do abandon their rights and obligations as brothers in the territory in which they were formerly settled. The system works in such a way that it is impossible to be at the same time a full member of two localized agnatic brotherhoods. Full understanding of this will have to wait until I have discussed the clan.

A political system can be viewed, as I have suggested earlier, as a means of distributing power and scarce resources and regulating competition for these things. The resource to be distributed is the land, and the land cannot support an infinite number of people. When there arises an imbalance between people and land, there must be some means of restoring a balance. The balance is not guaranteed under the ordinary process of internal recruitment, by which the members of the brotherhood are succeeded by their sons: there may be too many sons in one place and too few in another. For the system to survive there is required some process of external recruitment by which people who have moved from an overpopulated to an underpopulated area do not enter into any new *type* of political relationship.

Those who are recruited externally are not an homogeneous category. In some cases their different origin is continually referred to and made use of: in others assimilation seems almost complete. I shall begin with those who appear to be most completely assimilated and work outwards to those who have not acquired full citizenship in Baderi village, but who are members of the Baderi lineage to a greater degree than they are members of any other lineage.

The status of true agnates was conferred by my informants upon segments B2, B4, and a sub-segment of B3. They were said to be the true owners of the earth, and were believed in fact to be descended from a common ancestor. When I first recorded the Baderi genealogy, the B1 segment was given the same status as the rest and it was only later that an informant of the B2 segment told me this story:

(Case 3)   (Time: *c.* 1940)

    'About fifteen years ago Tuka Kohoro (B1) of Baderi village had his eye on a girl from Rampara. He persuaded me (B2) and a few others to go there and sound the parents. When we arrived at Rampara and told them why we had come and where we came from, they said, 'Ho! And are you Druba's line (B2) or Dibi's (B1)?' I said I was Druba's line. They then asked what line was the man who wanted the girl. I told them he was of Dibi's line. They became angry at once and said, 'Then be off with you! You know very well that we can't give one of our girls in marriage to that line. Why do you come here raising an affair like that?' Now of course I know what was wrong. But I didn't know then. I was young then, and although I was always good at talking, I really knew nothing. Now I know all about it and I wouldn't go on such an errand.'

    The B1 segment in fact came from Rampara, and thence from another village called Alari, and was adopted into the Baderi lineage.

(Case 4)   (Time: traditional)

    Many years ago the people of Alari grew too numerous for their land and some of them migrated to Rampara. In Rampara there was a youth called Goli who had leprosy. He was driven out of the village and he wandered about for some time and then came to Punuripara—a village about a mile from Baderi—where he found employment as a goatherd. He stayed there some years and later he came to Baderi, where he was taken on as a farm servant by Kelura (B1). Kelura had no sons, and he adopted Goli. From Goli the whole of the B1 segment are descended.

    The story of Goli and the origin of the B1 segment in Baderi is well known. Whenever I have heard it the story has been told with relish, but in confidence. It is a skeleton in the cupboard of the B1 segment. The secret has to emerge from time to time, when people blunder upon it as Tuka and his friends did (Case 3: p. 24), and as I did later. But the story is scandal, to be whispered and not to be proclaimed, for fear of giving public offence.

    An important reason why this story should be regarded as scandal is not immediately obvious. Certainly it is no credit to be descended of a man who had leprosy, a dreaded and defiling disease, and believed to be a supernatural punishment for theft. Leprosy is believed to be hereditary, and the fact that in every generation someone of the B1 segment suffers from it, was cited as additional proof of their origin. It is also a discredit to be descended from a man so humble as Goli. He was a goatherd, an occupation which to-day is often relegated to inferior castes, even to untouchables. He then became a menial in the house of a Baderi man. Had the B1 people remained menials then the story might be told more readily. But in the last two generations they have been the largest of the four segments in Baderi, and at one time the richest. The segment also contained, in the last generation, a man of commanding personality and resource, who would have taken a sharp revenge on anyone who traded the story in public.

The stigmata of leprosy and poverty are not the main reasons for the element of scandal in this story. Goli's origin reflects on the status of all the men of the B1 segment as full members of the community and owners of the earth. Their rights are safeguarded, of course, by the fact that title to the most valuable form of land, the rice field, rests not with the community but with the Government. Even in the story they are given an unassailable title by Goli's adoption into the lineage. In practice their different origin cannot be used to weaken their title to land. Their assimilation as citizens of Baderi is almost complete, but their origin remains a bar sinister. Some years ago a man of Majisai hamlet, which is populated exclusively by B2 people, sold one of his fields to a B1 man. His neighbours upbraided him: 'Why did you go and sell Baderi earth to him? It's Baderi earth. You could have sold it to one of us.' The story gives other segments in Baderi no tangible weapon against B1 people, but rather a chance for malicious comment and spite against the all-too-successful members of B1 at the present day.

A sub-segment of B3 is also descended from an outsider, but their story is less discreditable and is not told with the same relish. But I did hear the story from Liringa (B2) who is not on good terms with the head of this sub-segment.

(Case 5)   (Time: traditional)

'Many years ago a young man came as a fugitive from Mandi-padeari, where the distant agnates of the Baderi people live to-day.

He had been in trouble and his leg was cut and as he ran he left a trail of blood. He came to the hamlet where B4 were living, and they gave him shelter and food. Some hours later pursuers arrived, following the trail of blood. They demanded the young man. The men of B4 said that no young man had come. The pursuers pointed to the trail of blood. The men of B4 said, "But to-day we are holding sacrifices to our ancestors. Many cows have been slaughtered and the streets are flowing with blood." So they were, and the pursuers retired baffled. The young man stayed and eventually he became a farm servant in the house of Bruska (B3).

'Bruska became an old man and still had no sons to succeed him, and so he adopted the young man, whose name was Tunde. Later a son was born to Bruska, so that the B3 segment to-day consists of the descendants both of Bruska's own son and of his adopted son, Tunde.'

Like Goli the young man made his entry in poverty and as a suppliant. There is also in this story, for those who want to see it, a subtle reflection on the man's descendants. A deadly insult in the Kond hills is to call a man *mrivi'*—a victim for sacrifice[1]— and the circumstantial evidence of Tunde's arrival points to his having been a *mrivi*. But the main point of the story is the reflection it casts upon the status of the B3 sub-segment, and the insinuation that they are not true members of the lineage, but outsiders.

Neither of these stories is part of the explicit charter of village relationships. On most occasions the B1 segment descended from Goli and the B3 sub-segment descended from Tunde are indistinguishable from other segments and sub-segments. Their different origin cannot be used to challenge their title to land, or their status as owners of the earth. A marriage between one of these segments and the main body is, usually, just as incestuous as a marriage within the three founding segments.

From time to time the adoption of Goli and Tunde becomes more than a mere topic for malicious gossip. The B1 segment are unambiguously descended from a common stock with Rampara and Alari. They are in no way part of those lineages in their political aspect, but their tie of agnation is sufficiently recognized, and believed in, to prevent inter-marriage. Their position in

[1] Descriptions of the 'meriah' rite of human sacrifice are to be found in W. Macpherson, 1865, and J. Campbell, 1861.

Baderi, however, is not unequivocal: there remains an ambiguity which enables interested persons to make use of it for their own ends.

(Case 6)   (Time: *c.* 1950)

Panoka Kohoro came from Kampaderi in Ganjam, a village peopled by the distant agnates of the Baderi main lineage, and observing with them a rule of exogamy. Panoka worked in the house of Sarono Kohoro (B1) and he made pregnant the daughter of a neighbour, Tresu Kohoro, who is also of the B1 segment. The people of Baderi held a meeting, but, even before it met, Panoka and the girl fled back to Kampaderi. After a time the people of that village found out the status of the girl and once again Panoka and his wife fled. They wandered about, working in various villages. and after about a year they came back to Baderi.

There was some informal discussion about this in Baderi, but in the end people decided to do nothing. The grounds for this decision were that the girl belonged to the B1 segment, and that segment was not properly a part of the Baderi brotherhood, and therefore, strictly speaking, this was not an incestuous marriage, although it was not a desirable one.

I was not able to discover what made the Baderi people change their minds about the case during Panoka's absence. The original prosecution may have been engineered by someone who disliked Panoka: his misdemeanour may have coincided with the failure of the rains or with a blight on the crops, and the village may have been looking around for a scapegoat. But the point is that there is sufficient ambiguity in the structure to enable the Baderi people to change their minds. B1, at one and the same time, both are and are not members of the lineage, according as it suits people to make them so. The B1 segment and the sub-segment of B3 are presented as part of the Baderi genealogy, but in fact their assimilation is not complete.

Sisters' Sons

If B1 and the B3 sub-segment are counted full members of the main lineages as they were first presented to me, then the Baderi Konds are divided as in Table 2.

I have used the term 'sisters' sons' to refer to any household the

TABLE 2

LINEAGE AFFILIATION OF THE BADERI KONDS[1]

Main lineage	Sisters' sons	Other lineage	Total
264 or 79%	51 or 15%	19 or 6%	334

head of which traces his connection to the main lineage through a woman born in the lineage, or married into it. Thus the category includes men living uxorilocally with Baderi wives, the child of a Baderi girl born out of wedlock and never acknowledged to be any man's son, the child by a previous marriage of a woman who came to marry a Baderi man, and sisters' sons proper. I shall argue that just as the people of B1 and the B3 sub-segment have had to take on the attributes of agnatic kinship in Baderi, so also do persons resident in Baderi and connected to it through a woman become absorbed in the agnatic group and take on the rights and duties of agnates. Their status is ambiguous and moves from one extreme to the other. The fact that they are linked through a woman is brought to light when it suits someone to do so—especially when the collaterals of the woman are trying to prevent land from falling into the hands of a sister's son. On other occasions they are treated by their mother's brother and his collaterals exactly as if they were themselves *dada koku*—agnatic relatives—and not *seri ahpa loku* (lit: 'bride-seizing folk'). But at the same time there is a slow erosion of their status as affinal and uterine kinsmen, until a point is reached when it becomes rare for others to refer to them as anything but agnates. I cannot prove that there is a vanishing point in this progression. But there are no sisters' son lineages in Baderi deeper than four generations and this suggests that eventually complete absorption takes place.

A sister's son or a sister's husband is normally resident in another village in another clan territory in which he has the rights and duties of an agnate. All rites and ceremonies connected with marriage imply that the two lineages belong to different political units and different territories. This is clear in Case 7.

(Case 7)   (Time: contemporary)

When a girl is about to go in marriage she sings a lament in her own village. A Baderi girl would sing in this fashion: 'Dear fathers

[1] See p. 21, note 2.

descended of Nagusa! Respected fathers descended of Sepera! I am a poor daughter of Nagusa, I am a shiftless daughter of Sepera. To the land of Petura-Pujura how shall I go, how shall I bend my steps? What dowry are you giving, what wealth are you sending, you who went and came back having taken ten or twelve oxen? I do not know how to toil or work. Having eaten ten or twelve oxen in exchange for me, you will be shamed. Your honour will be gone. I am a poor child of Nagusa, I am a useless daughter of Sepera.'

When she arrives in her husband's village, which in the case of the Petura-Pujura people would be somewhere in Rupamendi, she laments again: 'Alas, respected fathers descended of Petura and Pujura, my brothers of Nagusa-Sepera have consumed a bride-wealth of ten or twelve oxen for a poor and useless girl of the Nagusa-Sepera who brings nothing to you. They have sent nothing with me. To-day when you behold the daughter of Nagusa-Sepera they will be shamed and dishonoured. How shall I bend my steps into the palaces of Petura-Pujura? I do not know the correct way to converse in the land of Petura-Pujura.'

In this text the girl says that she is leaving the territory of the Nagusa-Sepera people (the name of two Baderi ancestors) and going to the land of the Petura-Pujura. Her brother and his descendants are citizens of Baderi in the Balimendi clan: her husband has, and her own children will have, rights as citizens in the clan-territory of Rupamendi.

The two partners to the normal marriage are not just the husband and wife, but two lineages, or even the two communities to which those lineages belong. These lineages are of equal status. Women do not pass in one direction, as they do in certain parts of India. There is no distinction in status between the groom's people and the bride's people, or between the lineages of the mother's brother and the sister's son. The terms for cross-cousins are self-reciprocal, being *mrigi* for a man and *mrigali* for a woman. Behaviour between affines or uterine kinsmen varies, of course, with generation. There should be mutual restraint and respect between a man and his senior male in-laws, or the in-laws of his son. Behaviour between the mother's brother and the sister's son and between male cross-cousins is more familiar, but it is still correct for each partner to treat the other as a man of importance. All these relationships demand mutual respect. A man visiting his married daughter is received with extreme formality. A mother's brother must be formally and ceremonially consulted in important affairs which affect his sister, or her son, or daughter.

Further evidence of symmetry is provided by the frequent exchange of women. Sometimes this happens directly, and a man takes a wife who is sister of the man to whom his own sister has gone. More often a classificatory relationship is involved and a mother's brother arranges for a sister's daughter to marry a man of his own village or his own clan, or, conversely, finds a bride for his sister's son from these people.

Marriages tend to be arranged between those who are of approximately equal wealth. Occasionally there is a runaway match between a rich man and a handsome girl whose family is poor: more occasionally a poor man succeeds in marrying the daughter of a wealthy man. But these marriages are rare compared with those which are contracted between families of equal wealth. Marriage involves an exchange of property, as Case 7 (p. 28) shows. The man's house must pay bridewealth: the girl brings her dowry. The bridewealth is fixed by haggling. The girl's house aim to fix the price as high as they can. But they do not make it too high, because when the girl goes to her husband—about a year after the bridewealth is paid—she must take with her somewhat more than her family received. But this must be only a little more—hence the polite understatements which are conventional at the time of her arrival, to the effect that she has brought no dowry. If she brings a great deal more than her family received, then the groom's people are in disgrace, and it is with this prospect in mind that they do not risk trying to find a bride from a house very much richer than their own.

In short the normal relationships between a person and his affinal or uterine kin entails firstly that the parties should belong to different political communities and secondly that they should be of equal status and the members of the lineages concerned should treat one another with mutual respect.

Those who are living uxorilocally or avunculocally in Baderi, or who are descended from such men, are shown in Table 3. In addition, the genealogies revealed two uxorilocal marriages which were without issue: and there is one child of about 12 years of age who is being brought up in the house of his mother's brother (B4), and who will eventually, when he marries and has children, become the founder of a sister's son lineage. These households

contain 51 men, women, and children, out of a total Kond population of 334. The reasons for their presence in Baderi are given
briefly in Case 8.

(Case 8)   (Time: from *c.* 1880 to the present day)

(*a*) Borani is the son of a Baderi woman. He was born out of
wedlock. His mother later married and went to another village.
Borani remained, first in his maternal grandfather's house, and later
with his mother's brother. He lives jointly with this uncle, but the
estate remains entirely in the name of the latter, and Borani is not
a coparcener, but a dependent. His father is unknown.

(*b*) Libo's father's mother was a Baderi woman who went in
marriage to Budubari village. She was widowed there and returned
to her brother's house, bringing with her a son. The son remained
in the house of his maternal uncle, who arranged the boy's marriage.
Libo is the child of this marriage.

(*c*) Sime is the son of Sudra, whose mother was the sister of a
Baderi man called Brusa. Brusa's own son was called Sedoto. Sudra
and his brothers were born in the village of Bodosuga. My informant
said, 'Sedoto thought, "This is my own father's sister's son. He is
having a hard time in Bodosuga. I will bring him and his brothers to
Baderi." So he brought Sudra and his two brothers.' The brothers
died but Sudra grew to manhood and Sedoto paid the expenses of
bringing a bride for him. He also gave Sudra six irrigated fields and
four upland fields. In the present generation Sudra's son is Sime and
Sedoto's son is Ponga.

(*d*) Buduro and Moni are the grandsons of Krupa. Krupa was the
son of a Baderi woman who had gone in marriage to another village
and who had returned to Baderi after she was widowed.

(*e*) Nondo, Gongo, and Mundura are the great-grandsons and
grandson respectively of Dubuna, whose mother married Sindira
Kohoro (B1) of Baderi after she had been widowed in a previous
marriage in another village, where she had borne Dubuna. Dubuna
grew up in Baderi in the house of his stepfather.

(*f*) Tubutu belongs to Ambopara village. He married the sister
of Lesono Kohoro (B4). After a few years in Ambopara the couple
returned to Baderi and Tubutu lives there uxorilocally. Lesono is a
very poor man and the attraction of Baderi for Tubutu was his own
sister, who married a Baderi man and who is the mother of Gedalu
(B1), a rich man.

(*g*) Beda was a plough-servant from another village in the house
of Gedalu's father (B1). Gedalu's sister was made pregnant by a
classificatory brother of the B2 segment who lived in Dobenisai

(Case 2: p. 21). The offender fled to the Tea Gardens in Assam and the pregnant girl was married off to Beda. They said to Beda, 'What does it matter to you? It will be the child of a Kond. That is enough. There is no untouchable or person of another caste concerned in it.' Gedalu's mother (the father was dead and Gedalu still a minor) gave Beda some presents of money and oxen; and the offender's brother also gave him some presents. Beda and his wife live jointly with the rest of the family, but he is a dependent and not a co-parcener. From my own observations he is still treated very much as the plough-servant.

(*h*) Panoka. See Case 6: p. 27.

(*i*) Montona is a uterine descendant of Kinda Malik. Kinda came from Punuripara, a village one mile to the north of Baderi in Balimendi. He settled in Dudopara close to a friend, Sombaro Kohoro (BX), who gave him some fields. When Kinda died the fields were inherited by his son Basono. Neither Sombaro nor his sons Rupunga and Sanjo made any objections to the fields passing in this way.

Basono's sister had gone in marriage to another village where she bore a son, Montona. Her husband died and she returned to Dudo-para to live in the house of her brother Basono. Basono died without children, and Montona and his mother continued to work the land.

Rupunga and Sanjo objected to this arrangement. They said that Montona could not inherit land since he was a sister's son and not a member of their lineage, and the land should revert to them. They took the land by force. The widow went to the Government courts. The Magistrate decided that she had a right to live off the land, and the widow was able to get the fields registered in her own name. Montona now has undisputed title to the land.

In theory there exists for all these people a community, where, if they lived, they would belong to the main lineage and be counted as 'owners of the earth'. In practice this is not the case: one of them at least (Case 8*a*: p. 31) has no such community, for the identity of his father is not known. Others, although they might have been owners of the earth, did not hold any land in their father's community in proprietary right, and none of them in fact owns land outside Baderi. Apart from property rights, only the last four (Case 8*f*, *g*, *h*, and *i*: p. 31), who are all first-generation immigrants, maintain any kind of agnatic link with their father's kinsman. Even these links are tenuous, for in the case of Beda at least—I do not know about the other three—the rest of his family is like himself. His widowed mother lives with his brother who

TABLE 3

HOUSEHOLDS IN BADERI CONNECTED TO THE MAIN LINEAGE THROUGH A WOMAN

1 No.	2 Name	3 Generation	4 Patron	5 Hamlet	6 Income	7 Patron's income
1	Borani	1	B1	Pandrisai	—	58
2	Libo	2	B4	Dobenisai	22	40
3	Sime	2	B3	Baderi	66	523
4	Baduro and Moni	3	B4	Kendrisai	40	48
5	Nindru	2	B2	Majisai	8	32
6	Nondo				17	
7	Gongo	3	B1	Pandrisai	32	75
8	Mundura				22	
9	Tubutu	1	B4	Baderi	—	10
10	Beda	1	B3	Baderi	—	160
11	Panoka	1	B1	Kinisuga	16	40
12	Montona	1	BX*	Pandrisai	36	31

* The relationship of this lineage with the main lineage will be described in a later section.

Notes:

1. *Column 3.* Generation refers to the head of the household. Thus No. 1, Borani, is the first of his lineage to be in Baderi. No. 4 Buduro and Moni, are two brothers whose grandfather came to live in Baderi.

2. *Column 4.* There is no Kui word for the person whom I have called 'patron' or 'sponsor' and I have taken those who are genealogically closest to the woman who is the link between the outsider and the Baderi people.

3. *Column 6.* Income is reckoned in measures of paddy (see F. G. Bailey, 1957, pp. 279–84) produced annually by the fields which the persons own. It thus measures rather the amount of land owned than the actual income of the persons concerned.

4. *Column 7.* Where more than one person must be considered as patron, this figure is reckoned by averaging the income of all households in the genealogy from the point at which the outsider household is connected.

is working as a casual labourer in the Oriya village of Bisipara and who owns no land. In brief, the key to understanding the history and present status of men uxorilocally and avunculocally resident is to know that they are poor. They are either members of ex-patriate families, (like Beda), who are dispersed and have no ancestral territory or ancestral estates, or else, if they lived where their lineage was the main lineage, they were poor men. If they had not been poor, they would less readily have abandoned their 'aristocratic' status, and less willingly have enrolled as dependents in another community.

The attraction of the wife's community is usually that there such men have a better opportunity to make a living than in their own community. This is not always the occasion for the move: but even when the move is made for other reasons, property at home acts as a deterrent, while opportunities elsewhere are an incentive to making the move. Of the instances given in Case 8, all those movements which were voluntary movements by adult males had an economic incentive. Sime's father was given a small estate by his sponsor (Case 8*c*: p. 31) Panoka and Montona (Case 8*h* and *i*: p. 32) both own small plots of land which they have obtained from their wife's father and mother's brother respectively. Tubutu's wife's brother is almost as poor as Tubutu himself, but Tubutu can count for help on his sister who is married into one of the richer households of Baderi (Case 8*f*: p. 31). Finally Beda, although his marriage has secured him only a small amount of movable wealth and although he continues to be treated as a servant and has not been given fields or the chance to acquire fields for himself, has at least made his position in the house more secure as a son-in-law than it was as a plough-servant (Case 8*g*: p. 31).

The men in Case 8*f*, *g*, and *h* (p. 31) all came to Baderi as responsible adults, probably at the instance of their wives, and with the agreement of their wife's brother or father. In Case 8*c* (p. 31) the man concerned was brought as a youth by a maternal relative. The remaining cases are all the children of widows (except Case 8*a* (p. 31), who is illegitimate), who either returned to their father's house or brother's house (except for the woman who came from an earlier marriage bringing young children with her). These movements are motivated by hatreds and affections in a purely personal way, but property prompts or prevents the movement. A widow, whether or not she has children, has the right to live off her late husband's estate. She may not dispose of the land, but she may retain it and manage it until her death, or until she marries elsewhere. If this widow has had a son or sons, the land should descend to them, even if they are not brought up in their father's village. In practice there is often a struggle between the widow and the brothers of her dead husband for control of the estate. It is not easy for the widow, if she has no sons or if her children are still small, either to manage the property or to keep her hold upon it. She may give up the struggle and return to her father's house, from which she may marry again. She invariably brings young children with her to her father's house or her brother's house, and often they become the wards of the father or brother. Their agnates only try to bring them back if they themselves have no heirs, as when the children's paternal grandfather is alive and had no sons other than the dead father. Otherwise they are likely to remain, as in the instances I have given in Baderi, as dependents of their mother's brother and his descendants.[1]

Between men living uxorilocally and their wives' relatives, behaviour which is proper between affinals cannot be carried out. The elaborate etiquette required cannot exist between people who see one another every day, and who are likely to be living in adjoining houses, or around the same courtyard. The mutual equality, which the proper behaviour symbolizes, does not exist. A man living uxorilocally is likely to be poorer than his wife's brother, if not actually dependent upon him. Nor is he entitled to respect as a man of standing in another political community, since by living uxorilocally he has tacitly abandoned his rights in that community. He has become a dependent and is likely to be treated as one.

In the same way the pattern of behaviour between male cross-cousins becomes modified, when they live in the same village and possibly off the same estate. The essence of the relationship between cross-cousins, as distinct from paternal parallel cousins, is that they are never likely to be rivals for the same piece of property. It is true that a man has obligations towards his sister's son, especially when the latter gets married, but these obligations involve cash and movable property like cattle. These gifts may arouse the jealousy of a man's sons, or his sister's sons may feel that he is not giving with sufficient generosity and is being diverted from his obligations by his wife or his own sons. But these disputes cannot involve the land, so long as the sister's son remains in his natal village, as in the normal working of the system he should do. But when the sister's son comes to live in the same village as his mother's brother and that man's sons, it is no longer a question of occasional, if generous, gifts to a favoured nephew, but a constant and unremitting drain on the estate for his maintenance, and the fear that eventually, especially if the sponsor's

[1] I regret that I do not have enough examples to present this process numerically.

line dies out, he or his descendants will obtain as their own a part of the family estate which otherwise might have been shared among the collateral agnates (Case 8*i*: p. 32). In other words, the relationship between cross-cousins comes, in respect of property, to resemble the relationship between brothers.

But there are also differences. The relationship between such cross-cousins are not in fact symmetrical with regard to property. The sister's son has no right to a share in the property: what is given comes to him as a favour. He is kept as a dependent, almost a client, of the family. This explains the paradox in the behaviour of a mother's brother in accepting sister's sons into his own house —in particular Case 8*c* (p. 31), in which a man brought three male cross-cousins to share in his own property. Sedoto introduced the three youths in the hope that they would grow up to be his dependents and supporters in village affairs. Sedoto was—as is his son Ponga—an only child and a rich man, and the only household in the B3 sub-segment which originated from Tunde (Case 5: p. 25). The three youths would strengthen Sedoto's following in the village, both against other people in the village and against his own collaterals of the B3 segment, who were the true descendants of Bruska. Sedoto and his cross-cousins were not rivals for the same piece of property: rather the rivalry lay between Sedoto's collaterals in B3 segment and the immigrant cross-cousins. If Sedoto were to have died without heir, then his land would have gone to the B3 segment. From the point of view of these men the presence of Sudra and his descendants was bad, firstly because they might establish a claim to inherit the estate (as did Montona in Case 8*i*: p. 32), and secondly because they had already received part of the estate as a gift.

In this way a man who is resident either uxorilocally or avunculocally is the centre of several potential conflicts. His own sponsor, the man who brought him to the village, must try to emphasize the cleavage between his protégé and his protégé's agnatic kinsmen. If the protégé can still rely on the support of his agnatic kinsmen, he is able to manipulate his sponsor and gain a better position for himself in his sponsor's village. Secondly there is a potential conflict between the sponsor and his protégé. The latter's support depends upon the degree to which the sponsor can endow him with wealth and give him proper protection and a proper standing in the village. If he cannot do these things then the protégé may prefer to go elsewhere, or to attach himself to a more influential man in the village, or to try to win property and independence. If the sponsor is over-generous, he may defeat his own ends by making the protégé too independent. Thirdly the protégé is in conflict with the collateral agnates of his sponsor, and with the rest of the village, either because he is too much the personal henchman of his sponsor in the latter's struggles with other people in the village, or because he is freeing himself from his dependent position and acquiring land to which he has no ancestral right. A protégé is necessarily labile: either he can be forced to go elsewhere, which would serve the interests of his sponsor's rivals; or he can remain as a dependent, which is the position favoured by his sponsor; or he achieves independence, against the wishes of his sponsor, and against the wishes of others in so far as he remains in the village, but to their pleasure in that he ceases to be the henchman of his sponsor. On the whole such a person tends either to go elsewhere, or in the end achieves an independent position in the village and eventually comes to be reckoned an agnate.

People resident uxorilocally and avunculocally have to act in many situations as if they were agnates.

(Case 9)   (Time: 1954)

When the wife of Ponga Kohora (B3) died in 1954, Sime (Case 8c) behaved exactly as if he were a close agnate (*ejoni loku*). Like other persons in this category he was polluted for a longer period than the more distant agnates in the village. He contributed the same substantial amount which they contributed, and not the lesser amounts given by distant agnates in the village. He attended the ceremonies to which agnates come, and to which uterine and affinal kinsmen do not come. When the uterine and affinal kinsmen did come, Sime was ranged not with them but with the group of agnates. Sime's wife's people contributed as to a death in the lineage of their sister's husband, and not as if the death had been in the house of their sister's husband's mother's brother's lineage, to which they would probably not have contributed at all. Nor did Bodosuga people, who are Sime's own agnates, attend.

Sime's residence in Baderi makes it entirely reasonable that he should have behaved in this way. When a person dies everyone who is around lends a hand to bring wood for the pyre, and in this way automatically incurs pollution. Sime lives beside Ponga's

D

house, and it was natural that he should help with the work, just as did the close agnates who lived in adjacent houses. News of a death is sent quickly to affinal and uterine kinsmen, but they are not expected to attend 'officially' until a purification ceremony is held about a year later. The rites, in other words, take account of the fact that uterine and affinal kinsmen usually live in distant villages. When they are in the same village, and permanently so like Sime, they behave as if they were agnates. Sime was in fact described to me—I had not completed the genealogies at that time—as a classificatory brother of Ponga, and both he and Ponga at ritual crises behave towards one another as if they were in fact brothers and not cross-cousins.

There are other observances, however, in which the distinction is kept up. Sime's stepmother, Sudra's second wife, came from Balimendi. Such a marriage would have been incestuous for one of the Baderi group of agnates. Sime himself took a wife from Birabhui, also a village in Balimendi. Sime's sister eloped with Baloto Kohoro (B1) and another sister married Jongora Kohoro (B2), both of whom belong to the Baderi cluster. Both these marriages were frowned upon—an indication perhaps of Sime's lineage's progression towards agnation—but they were not branded as incestuous.

Sime is the cross-cousin and the protégé of Ponga, who is the richest man in Baderi and the village headman. Sime's continued status as a sister's son, as proclaimed by the number of marriages which he and his family have contracted within Baderi and within Balimendi, coincides with his continued dependence on Ponga. Ponga, having few agnates, welcomes dependents and can afford them. Table 3 shows that none of the patron lineages of persons avunculocally resident are strikingly wealthy, with the exception of the headman Ponga. No sisters' sons except Sime are the descendants of people deliberately invited by a wealthy man to be his clients. They are the children of widows who had nowhere else to go, and could expect some help from their patron, but not much. With the passage of years their link becomes weaker.

(Case 10. See Case 8*d*: p. 31)   (Time: contemporary)

Buduro and Moni are the grandsons of Krupa, whose mother was a Baderi woman of the B4 segment. B4 are not rich and have an unfortunate history as landowners (see Case 32: p. 103). One section of B4 is found in the hamlet of Kamopara, and the section which is geographically and genealogically nearest to the two brothers lives in Dobenisai. But Buduro and Moni live with neither of these sections and are vaguely attached as clients and dependents of Sudersun (B1), a wealthy and ambitious man who lives in Kendrisai.

Neither Krupa nor any of his descendants, male or female, have married within Baderi or Balimendi.

The only other client lineage which has been for three generations in Baderi are the brothers Gongo and Mundura, and their elder brother's son Nono. They have contracted no marriages within the three generations into Baderi or Balimendi, and, like Buduro and Moni, they are not in a position of intimate dependence on a Baderi patron, in the way that Sime has continued to be dependent upon Ponga.

There is no necessary connection between Sime's dependent status and the continued inter-marriages between his lineage and the Baderi and Balimendi people. The marriages—certainly in two cases and probably in the others—are the result of the fancies of the people concerned and were not arranged in order to symbolize Sime's continued status as an affinal and uterine kinsman. Sime's case is to be contrasted with the other two in that the two latter are further along the road towards incorporation in the main lineage. They have become landholders, in both cases by breaking the jungle, making new fields, and later buying land, and they have not contracted marriages within Balimendi or Baderi. The time will come when it will not simply be the case that they happen not to contract such marriages, but when both they and the people of Balimendi and Baderi feel that such an alliance would be wrong. Indeed that point has already been reached, and I was told that no marriage of this kind would be arranged, although a runaway match would be countenanced and would not lead to charges of incest.

The process by which the descendants of a woman become incorporated into the agnatic group is part of a general rule that those who live in the same territory must take on the obligations of agnatic kinship.[1] I have dealt so far only with the Baderi cluster

[1] In a typical north Indian system of kinship terminology (such as the Oriyas have) no distinction is made between brothers, cross-cousins, and parallel cousins, and the children of these people are addressed by the terms

and there is still another category of Konds within that cluster to be fitted into the system, and to be distinguished both from the main lineage and from the sister's sons. This is the lineage BX.

AMALGAMATION

The main Baderi lineage has not always been rooted on the same stretch of territory. At one time the territory of the Baderi lineage extended from the mouth of the Baderi valley southwards along the main valley of the Salki river as far as the present village of Rupamendi. Half way along this stretch is the village of Limasuga, which marked the division of land between two ancestral brothers in the Baderi lineage, Lamba and Ambi. Lamba owned the southern stretch. He yielded this to the Rupamendi people and went off to found the village of Lambavadi which lies in the south-eastern corner of the Kondmals, in a territory called Bengrikia (Map 2). Sometime after this the Rupamendi Konds invaded and conquered the territory of Ambi, bringing their boundary to the mountain which marks the southern edge of the Baderi valley.

When the Baderi Konds lived on the plain of the Salki river, the Baderi valley was owned mostly by a lineage called Malik. Some territory in the upper part of the valley around the present hamlets of Dudopara and Kinisuga was owned by a different lineage (BX), surnamed Kohoro like the Baderi Konds, but not related to them. As the Baderi Konds were pressed northwards by the Rupamendi people, they drove the Malik people into the upper end of the valley. Now almost the whole valley belongs to the Baderi people (both the main lineage and BX), and the Malik lineage has died out.

The Malik lineage is represented as the friend of the BX lineage. This relationship is 'tone', blood-brotherhood. BX has outlived the

---

used for the children of own brothers or sisters. But in Kui cross-cousins and their children are distinguished by terms of reference from own brothers and their descendants. In this way Oriya kinship terminology would facilitate the absorption into the agnatic group of people descended through a woman, while the Kui terminology would not.

In practice a Kond cross-cousin is often addressed not as 'cross-cousin' but as 'brother', even when he lives in another village. In my observation those who lived in Baderi were regularly addressed and referred to as if they were agnates. But it is to be noted that the terms for distinguishing them exist.

Malik lineage and is to-day represented in the valley by three families, the heads of which are descended from a common great-grandfather. These three men are the two brothers Rupunga and Sanjo, and their senior classificatory brother Sulobo.

At the present day no-one knows what part the BX lineage played in the struggle between the Malik lineage and the Baderi Konds. Since the BX were the blood-brothers of the Maliks it is to be presumed that they fought against the Baderi Konds, but I could find no legends about this, and there are no institutionalized survivals of hostility between BX and the main Baderi lineage. Indeed, since the Malik lineage survived until three or four generations ago, it seems likely that all three lineages, the Maliks, BX, and the Baderi lineage, had settled down to live together in peace. Just as the Baderi lineage could accommodate strangers into itself, so in a similar way the three groups which lived together in the valley settled down to become one political community. To-day BX and the Baderi Konds behave towards one another as if they were brothers. They do not marry one another, and sexual union between them is counted incestuous, pollutes the Earth, and demands, for the safety of the community, a ritual expiation. Towards outsiders they are all, indiscriminately, Baderi people. When the girls of the BX lineage go in marriage they lament by calling on the names of the Baderi ancestors, Nagusa and Sepera (Case 7: p. 28). BX people make contributions at marriage ceremonies and at the death rites in the houses of segments of the main lineage, in the same way as do distant agnates within that lineage, and the Baderi people contribute to their rites in the role of distant agnates. Finally, in the old days, when the Baderi people went to war with their neighbours, the BX fought on their side, as members of the same political community.

Nevertheless BX is recognized as of frankly different genealogical origin. The links between B4 and the others are not known, but believed to exist. B1 and the B3 sub-segment are descended from adopted sons, but on all except a few crucial occasions they are presented as true descendants of the founder. In these two cases, because B4 and B1 and the B3 sub-segment behave as brothers, they are represented on the same genealogy. But BX takes on the rights and obligations of agnatic brotherhood no less than any other segment in Baderi. Why, then, is there no tendency to include it within the main genealogy?

One reason, which I was given, is that on occasions BX functions for the main Baderi lineage—and sometimes for the whole of Balimendi—as the representative of society at large. If a Kond is outcasted and wishes to be re-admitted, his acceptance by Kond society at large is symbolized by the fact that a person who, to some degree, stands outside his own community, must administer the rite of re-admission.

(Case 11)   (Time: *c.* 1948)

A Kond of Birabhui in Balimendi, named Noboloko, is alleged to have made pregnant a woman of the Oriya DISTILLER caste. He was judged guilty by a council of his fellows in Balimendi and he fled to Mendipara in Ganjam, where he lived for two or three years. While he was away his father's younger brother cultivated their estate. When this uncle died Noboloko returned to look after the estate and applied for re-admission to caste. He paid the fine and sponsored the cost of the purificatory ceremony. At this ceremony his head was shaved and anointed by Sulobo Kohoro, the senior member of the BX lineage of Baderi.

(Case 12)   (Time: *c.* 1950)

Gora Kohoro of Manipara took a wife, while allegedly knowing that she had once been made pregnant by a PAN untouchable. The Balimendi Konds met and outcasted him. He sent the wife away and applied to be re-admitted and the ceremony of re-admission was performed by a Kond of Damopara village, also in Balimendi. The other Konds, led by the men of Baderi, protested that Sulobo Kohoro alone was qualified to re-admit Balimendi people by the shaving and anointing ceremony. The man who had presided over the re-admission ceremony performed by the Damopara Kond was fined Rs.25.

Sulobo's special qualification was explained in the following way. There are in the Kondmals a number of dispersed totemic clans. The totem of most of the Konds of Balimendi is said to be *Trasu*, a kind of tree. Sulobo has a different totem. The proper person to perform the re-instatement ceremony must be of a different totem.

This explanation is unsatisfactory in several ways. Most of those I questioned did not seem surprised that they might have a totem but few could say, or would say, what their totem was. This reticence was explained on the grounds that totemic names are an infallible sign of true origins, and might reveal a discreditable descent: as the *mohuri* (a brass oboe) is said to reveal descent from a PAN untouchable. But everyone cannot have a bar sinister, and some at least would be tempted to claim respectable totems. Again, there must be many others besides Sulobo who have a totemic affiliation different from the dominant *trasu* group. To name only two, this should be true of the B1 and the B3 immigrant sub-segment in Baderi, and it will be apparent later that there must be many other totems in Balimendi. Why Sulobo's different totem should be remembered, while that of B1 and the B3 sub-segment should be forgotten, remains a problem.

In an article written in 1904 Friend-Pereira, who had served as Magistrate in the Kondmals, describes a totemic system of the kind hinted at in the information I collected. He says that a common totem is a bar to marriage and that questions are asked about totemic affiliation when seeking to arrange a marriage. He also says that people respected their totem, did not kill it if an animal, or consume it if a vegetable. They also have attitudes of reverence and fear: '. . . a Khond of the Chita Krandi stock (chameleon according to Friend-Pereira, but probably *siti kradi*, a panther), on meeting his totem during a journey will turn back at once and tell his relations in an awed whisper: *mai penu mehte* (I have seen our God)'.[1] I saw no sign of this behaviour sixty years later, and indeed it is difficult to envisage this form of reverence to the brass oboe or towards the *trasu*, which is a not uncommon forest tree. Friend-Pereira also notes that people are reticent about their totem and often do not know it.

Apart from deficiencies of information the weakness of trying to tie Sulobo's special role into the system of totemic observances is that there seems to be no means of accounting in this way for Baderi's insistence that Sulobo *alone* was qualified to perform the ceremony of re-admission. There must have been many other lineages in Balimendi with a totem different from the *trasu*. Sulobo clearly enjoys—or is alleged by the Baderi people to enjoy—some kind of seniority in this situation.

Seniority was stated explicitly by my Baderi informants to be the issue in Case 12 (p. 42). They argued that Gora's re-instatement had been rushed through, without adequate consultation by the Manipara people, who had compounded their crime by making use of a man from Damopara to perform the shaving rite.

[1] J. E. Friend-Pereira, 1904, p. 54.

Damopara enjoys in the Balimendi clan a status similar to that held in Baderi village by the B1 segment, and on this occasion Baderi people did not hesitate to say that Damopara were not really agnates at all, but affinal kinsmen who had been favoured with agnatic status (Case 14: p. 49).

BX has, in a sense, been 'favoured' with agnatic status, but they are in a position different from that of the Damopara people, or from that of the B1 segment, or the lineages which are descended from sisters' sons in Baderi. BX has an undisputable claim to be owners of the earth in parts of the Baderi valley, and to have been in the valley longer than the main lineage itself. The immigrant segments (B1, the B3 sub-segment, and the sisters' sons) could not own the earth and become incorporated into the political community, unless they were also represented as descendants (albeit by a fiction) of the ancestors of the main lineage. Why then did not the main lineage itself become incorporated as a fictitious agnate in the BX lineage?

The Baderi lineage did not come as suppliants like Goli and Tunde (Cases 4 and 5: pp. 24 and 25): they took the land from BX. They had no political need to symbolize inferiority as adopted sons, since they were in fact superior in power. B1 and the B3 sub-segment became incorporated into the genealogy of the main lineage because they were politically subordinate to it and because they did not own the earth in Baderi valley. BX was saved from incorporation because it owned the earth. But the main lineage was not incorporated into BX, because it had conquered the BX lineage. This analysis may explain why my informants, who came from the main Baderi lineage, tried to account for Sulobo's prerogative by invoking the almost forgotten system of totemic clans. If they had not done so they would have had to draw attention to the high status of the BX lineage as owners of the earth in Baderi valley.

Within the localized lineage I have distinguished three types of relationship. The first, taking the available information at its face value, is true agnation: and this unites B2, B3, and B4. The second is a type of relationship by which outsiders are recruited into the main group. Of this there are two types: that which is marked by adoption and which gives complete rights of citizenship in the community and retains only a hint of an inferior status: and that in which a link through a woman is in the process of being converted into agnation. These forms of external recruitment I shall call incorporation. But the relationship between BX and the others is not so much incorporation as amalgamation. Amalgamation marks the union of two territories and two groups which are owners of the soil. Incorporation is a process by which a dependent assumes equality of status, and becomes an 'owner of the earth'. In both amalgamation and incorporation those recruited externally take on the rights and duties of a true agnate, and behave as if they and their ancestors had in fact been born full citizens of the community.

THE CONCEPT OF 'UNITY'

In dealings with outsiders, whether these are other Konds, Oriyas, officials, or myself, the members of the village feel that they ought to present an unbroken unity. They do not always do so. But the different statuses which I have described do not affect the degree to which a person is backed in his conflicts with outsiders by the other people of his village. If Buduro and Moni (Case 8*d*: p. 31) get into trouble with their in-laws, they have no more difficulty in gathering a party of fellow-villagers to accompany them to court or to a council, than do people who are thought truly to belong to the main lineage. In its external political relations the group of Konds is prepared to act as if it were in fact an homogeneous group. It is only in internal relationships—notably over title to land (Case 8*i*: p. 32)—that differences of origin may become relevant.

From one point of view the process I have been describing is recruitment: internally, when a son succeeds to the rights and obligations of his father: and externally when the status of an agnate is granted to a person who either was unrelated, or who was related in a different way. From another point of view the process of external recruitment is a safety-valve, a mechanism of elasticity, which helps to preserve the structure. When people become too numerous for their land and some of them must go elsewhere, or when there is faction fighting and the defeated party flee, they are able to join another group in a relationship which is of the same kind as that which they enjoyed in the group which they have left. Spatial mobility and conflict can occur without giving rise to structural change.

The unity and homogeneity of the Baderi cluster contains diversities. In the well-known epigram, they are all brothers, but some are more brothers than the rest. It is recognized that the people of Baderi village in fact have a heterogeneous origin, and the structure which I am describing can be envisaged as combating these tendencies to heterogeneity, and trying to mould everyone into the same pattern and join them by the same complex of institutions. But the result is always short of perfect uniformity, because it is to someone's advantage to keep alive the differences, or, against a shorter span of time, because the differences have not yet had time to be forgotten. The BX lineage and the main lineage do not want to be submerged in one another because they both are owners of the earth. From time to time the different origin of the B1 segment is brought out to justify an apparently anomalous situation or to gain a particular end of another kind. Finally, if we are right in assuming that some sisters' son lineages must have become perfectly absorbed into the main lineage or into the BX lineage, the system is still short of perfection in that new sisters' son lineages continually appear and the process of absorption goes on with different personnel.

The 'unity' of Baderi as I use the word 'unity' here, does not refer to something static: to, for instance, the feelings of the people, their loyalty to one another, their *esprit de corps*, which undoubtedly is strong. I am referring to a process by which conflicts are prevented from changing an established *system* of relationships, although they may break up particular groups. The 'unity' of Baderi is unification: a process by which heterogeneous elements are continually moving towards homogeneity. Unity as a state of affairs in which everyone would be welded into one perfect and homogeneous group, can never be realized. The end is never reached: unity consists in the movement towards that end.

CHAPTER III

THE CLAN

BADERI village is part of Balimendi *mutha* (Map 2). The *mutha*, like the village, is an administrative unit, in charge of an hereditary official, the Sirdar, and his assistants, the *paiks*. There are fifty *muthas* in the Kondmals: each has a name and demarcated boundaries. In Balimendi, besides four main clusters of Kond hamlets, there are also two large Oriya villages. Again, as with the village, the Administration has not imposed unity on the *mutha*: rather it has recognized an existing unity.

'Balimendi' has several references. Balimendi *mutha* is an administrative division. In this sense it includes not only Konds, but also PAN untouchables and Oriyas. Balimendi is also the name of a territory, the earth of which belongs to Balimendi clan. I have used 'clan' when referring to the people and 'clan-territory' when the reference is geographical. In the geographical sense Balimendi as a *mutha* coincides with Balimendi as a clan-territory, since the boundaries recognized by the Administration followed closely the existing boundaries between clan-territories. But from a social point of view the Balimendi clan does not coincide with Balimendi *mutha*. The Balimendi clan is a core of Konds within a larger group composed of Konds, Oriyas, and PANS, who are not united by bonds of clanship. With this larger unit I shall be concerned in later chapters. In this chapter I describe Kond clanship as a system in itself.

There exists among the Konds two kinds of clanship. The localized clan is a political unit. The dispersed clan is significant only in the kinship system. It is the localized clan which 'own the earth' in Balimendi. In this chapter I describe the process by which the unity of the localized clan is maintained. Essentially this is the same process as in the village and the lineage, but on a larger scale.

PUNURIPARA AND DAMOPARA

The Konds who own the earth in Balimendi are divided into

47

four village clusters, one of which is the Baderi cluster, already described. The others are Punuripara; Birabhui; and Damopara. The population of the clan-territory (excluding Oriyas, PANS, and a few Konds in a special category) numbers about 600, and these constitute the Balimendi clan.

The Baderi main lineage are putative agnates of the people of Birabhui. The 'proof' of this is that while a Baderi girl, going in marriage, laments that she is leaving the Nagusa-Sepera territory, the Birabhui girls use the names of Sepera-Sovera (Case 7: p. 28). Sepera is said to be the link between them, and this is taken as proof enough of common agnatic descent. Nagusa appears in the primordial stages of the Baderi genealogy, and neither Sepera nor Sovera appear at all. Enquiries were met with a vague answer that they must have been three brothers. The link between the Baderi main lineage and the Birabhui main lineage is putative and is similar to that within Baderi between B4 and, for instance, B2.

The people of Punuripara are linked into the clan in a different way.

(Case 13)   (Time: traditional)

'In olden days there lived on the site of Punuripara two brothers, called Paera and Dodu. They were a branch of the Malik lineage which formerly owned the earth in the eastern half of the Baderi valley. On the present site of Birpali [a hamlet of the Punuripara cluster] lived three brothers, but who they were and with whom they were connected is not known. About that time the Nagusa-Sepera people went on an expedition to the south-east to the site of the present Bengrikia clan, where their agnatic relatives are still living to-day. The three brothers from Birpali went with this expedition, and they stayed there to found the three clan-territories which are known as Tinpari, lying to the north of Bengrikia. Paera and Dodu also went, but after some time they returned. On their return they took over the rights in the earth of Birpali, where formerly the three brothers had lived.

'Paera and Dodu had no male children to succeed them. A sister of theirs had gone in marriage to the Jiura-Malika country [Besringia clan] and the two brothers invited a son of this sister to come to Punuripara and succeed them. The man came and when the Paera-Dodu group died out, they were succeeded by the Jiura-Malika people.

'The Jiura-Malika people who had settled in the Paera-Dodu country were not happy about their position, for as sister's sons they had no true rights in the soil. They called upon the people of Baderi and the Sepera-Sovera people to help them in their rites to the Earth and the Mountain and to be one with them. The Nagusa-Sepera people and the Sepera-Sovera people agreed to this, providing the pact was sealed by an oath, which took the following form. The Jiura-Malika people provided a sow: the others provided a boar and these two were set to copulate. While they were copulating they were hacked to pieces with battle-axes. From that day the Jiura-Malika people who live in the Punuripara village-cluster and the Nagusa-Sepera people and the other lineages of Balimendi have remained as brothers and they do not inter-marry.'

The text tells the story of two distinct changes in the Balimendi clan. The three anonymous brothers went off and founded their own clan-territories elsewhere. This left a void in Balimendi which was filled by the return of Paera and Dodu, who took over the vacant land, in addition presumably to the land they possessed already in Punuripara. The Paera-Dodu people could take over this land without further formality because they were already members of the Balimendi clan. The Paera-Dodu group was suc-ceeded by people related to them—and therefore to the rest of the community—as sister's sons. Their position was insecure because they were living on earth which was not their own, and because they had not acquired rights in the earth by becoming mem-bers of the Balimendi clan. They ran the risk of being attacked by the rest of Balimendi, just as Montona's right to land in Baderi was challenged by the BX lineage because Montona was a sister's son (Case 8*i*: p. 32). Between the Jiura-Malika group in Punuripara and their own agnates to the west runs the Salki river: between them and the rest of Balimendi there is no natural obstacle. Consequently they protected themselves by becoming members of the Balimendi clan, by no longer marrying with it, and by participating in its cult of the Earth and the Mountain. In the Balimendi clan their position is similar to that of the B1 seg-ment in Baderi village: they have been adopted.

The fourth village cluster has also been adopted into the com-munity, but the circumstances of its accession were different.

(Case 14)   (Time: traditional)

An informant wrote, 'If there had been a war for several genera-tions concerning land, then the weaker side would make blood-brotherhood with people of a different community. When they became blood-brothers they fought at one another's side. When the war was finished and won, they used to give land to their blood-brothers. Having given land, they have remained as blood-brothers to the present day. If they had made blood-brotherhood for the sake of war with people already related as in-laws, then afterwards they no longer married with those people, and they remained joined as brothers. Even though they are of a different origin, nevertheless, they do not inter-marry. This blood-brotherhood is called *kui kala prohpa tone*—"Kond war-making brotherhood".'

In the olden days there was a war between Balimendi and Gondrimendi, which lies to the north of Balimendi. Gondrimendi belongs to a powerful group of six clans, which are called the 'Six Lands', and it seems that the Balimendi people were getting the worst of the fight. A group came from the Damanikia clan, which lies ten miles away to the south in an area with which even to-day the people of Balimendi have little contact. This group became the blood-brothers of the Balimendi people, and together they won the war and took over a stretch of territory from the Gondrimendi people and added it to the northern boundary of Balimendi. This newly-won territory was shared between the Birabhui-Manipara cluster (Sepera-Sovera), which lies adjacent to it on the west, and the blood-brothers from Damanikia. The latter now inhabit the hamlets of Damopara, Nimbosai, and Bevasai, which together make up the Damopara cluster.

The Damopara cluster has remained a constituent part of Balimendi since that time. Damopara people count as agnates and they do not marry within Balimendi.

THE CLAN CULTS

Clan exogamy and the common ownership of clan land are linked with the cult of the Earth and the Mountain. The cult of the Mountain is dying out, but according to my informants it once was a communal activity by the clan. It is now the activity of a hamlet or sometimes of an individual. The cult formerly practised by the Balimendi clan involved the goddess Mungudi as a manifestation of the Mountain. Mungudi is a byword, even among the Oriyas of the Kondmals, for her vicious championship of Balimendi, and the men of Balimendi command a vague respect as her protégés. But Mungudi to-day is a private reserve of evil at the disposal of individual members of the Balimendi clan, rather than the community's tutelary deity. No joint public propitiation is carried out by the clan.

The positive cult of the Earth (*tana penu*) has declined in the same way. Individuals propitiate the Earth in their own fields at the time of planting the rice seedlings and at the time of the harvest, and the hamlet priests make offerings when the first seed is sown and when the flowers are first gathered from the *mahua* tree. The main propitiation of the Earth was done by the sacrifice of a human being, and the myths accounting for the ceremony are still a live tradition. But the rite has been suppressed for more than a hundred years. No-one knew who sponsored the ceremony. Accounts written by the soldiers of the East India Company, who suppressed the rite, indicate that the group concerned was the clan, but they are not explicit. Buffaloes are still sacrificed, but only rarely, and in this case it is not the clan which sponsors the rite, but an individual with the help of his village. However Case 13 (p. 48) seems to indicate that the Balimendi people as a group once carried on some kind of positive propitiation of the Earth.

In its negative aspects the cult is still alive, and still causes the whole clan to act as one corporate unit. If anyone who lives in the clan-territory defiles the Earth, the whole clan and those who live on its territory[1] are placed in ritual danger. Some of these are 'routine' defilements. A death pollutes the Earth, and all work on the soil is tabooed until a libation of liquor—and usually the blood of a chicken—has been poured. A suppurating sore, in which grubs appear, also pollutes the Earth, and the sufferer and his immediate household must sponsor a purification ceremony or leave the clan-territory. More serious and dramatic defilements follow in the breach of certain rules. If a woman handles a plough, the Earth is polluted.

(Case 15) (Time: 1955)

'This year a widow was watching her twelve-year-old son plough a field. "Fool!" she said, "that's not the way to plough. Here! Do it like this!" She took the plough away and drove it across the field.

'When the rains failed the men of the village seized this woman and put her in a yoke with a bullock. She was driven along, ploughing a furrow, and a sharp goad was stuck into her so that her blood dripped upon the Earth. Later she provided a goat for sacrifice.'

---

[1] See p. 79.

A serious defilement is caused by a breach of the rules of exogamy or prohibited marriage. I have given an example in Case 2 (p. 21). These offences do not always involve the clan, but may do so potentially. In Case 2 the initiative was taken by the kinsmen of the girl and the whole affair was concluded within the lineage and the village cluster. But if the kinsmen of the girl had not acted, then any other person in the Baderi cluster could have opened the proceedings by raising a party to go and kill the goats. Failing them, anyone within Balimendi clan could have taken action.

In its negative aspect the Earth cult is for the clan a boundary-maintaining mechanism. A breach of the proper relationships within the clan-territory—a disturbance of the moral order—involves potentially the whole clan and others resident upon its territory, but it does not involve anyone outside the clan-territory. Although the whole of the Kond hills—and indeed the whole of Orissa—was affected by the drought of 1955, no other localized clan could concern itself in the sins of Balimendi people. The community is defined by involvement or non-involvement in the defilement of the Earth. The Jiura-Malika people (Case 13: p. 48) enrolled as members of the Balimendi clan by placing themselves under the protection of Mungudi, and by agreeing to consider themselves defiled by breaches of the moral laws governing the relationships within the community.

DISPERSED CLANSHIP

The link which binds different village clusters into one clan is the same as that which exists within one village cluster. It is a complex of institutions: exogamy, land-holding, and the cult of the Earth and the Mountain. In one sense this is a segmentary descent system: the relationships which are typical of the largest groups are also found within constituent groups.[1] This is implied in the use of the word 'brother' to describe the link between the Baderi cluster and the Birabhui cluster. Agreeing that other things shall be equal, one may assume that the smallest unit—for instance a group of four brothers—can, with the passage of time, develop into the largest—four village clusters or four clans—by a process of segmentation. But this is only possible if this largest segment is isolated from other similar segments around it, and if the seg-

[1] See p. 62, note 1.

ments do not affect one another. The examples which I have given make it clear that the agnatic units were not in fact isolated, and that, at a rough estimate, three-quarters of the Balimendi Konds are not descended from the founding ancestors of Balimendi, and although they are the brothers of the Balimendi people, their 'true' agnatic relatives are in other clan-territories.

A formal outline of the relationships between localized clans in the eastern part of the Kondmals is easily presented. For any one clan, the rest are divided into two categories: those who are agnates (*dada-koku:* 'elder brothers and father's younger brothers') with whom one may not marry, and the uterine and affinal kinsmen (*seri ahpa loku:* 'bride-seizing-folk')'.[1]

Balimendi has agnatic connections with eight other clans. In Case 13 (p. 48) the expedition which is mentioned resulted in the founding of two clans, Betumendi and Tuniamendi (jointly called Bengrikia) in the south-east of the Kondmals, and of three other clans (jointly called Tinpari) to the north of Bengrikia (Map 2). The people of Balimendi consider these five clans to be their agnates and they do not marry them, nor did they, so traditions say, fight against them. On the contrary they were allies in battles against common enemies. Another segment of the Balimendi clan migrated to the north-eastern corner of the Kondmals where they form part of a group of three clans which are together called Rotabari. Balimendi people include everyone in Rotabari in the category of agnates, believing that at some time in the distant past they concluded with these people a pact of blood-brotherhood, possibly at the instigation of their kinsmen who were living there.

The ties within this larger group are attenuated links of localized clanship. The whole group is exogamous. They recognize a common title to land in that a migrant from one clan to another will be welcomed and given land on which to build a house, and allowed a free hand to make fields for himself in the waste.

(Case 16)   (Time: *c.* 1940)

Tokai Kohoro (B2), a poor man possessing one or two fields in

---

[1] Marriage with certain persons who fall into the category of *seri ahpa loku* is forbidden: marriage within three generations in the mother's lineage is not allowed: nor can a man marry a woman who is the widow of an agnate senior in generation or in age to himself.

E

Baderi went as a labourer to work in a road gang on that section of
the main road which passes along the southern border of Rotabari.
He eventually settled in the area, and the Rotabari people gave him
land on which to build a house. He acquired some fields. He came
back to Baderi seven years ago, sold the land which he had there,
went back to Rotabari, and has not been heard of since.

Panoko Kohoro (Case 6: p. 27) is in a similar position in
Baderi. He has been able to take over land there partly because he
is a distant agnate of the Baderi people. But the man of Rupamendi, a clan which is one of the traditional enemies of Balimendi, and with which they have many uterine and affinal
connections, could not gain admission to the Baderi community
(Case 1: p. 17).

The Earth cult does not operate within this larger group, nor,
with one exception, does the cult of the Mountain appear to have
extended beyond the boundaries of the localized clan. A sin which
pollutes the Earth in Baderi and puts the people of Balimendi in
ritual danger, does not affect Tinpari, Rotabari, or Bengrikia. I
was told that the Bengrikia people used to come to the annual
ritual for Mungudi in Baderi, but they do not do so to-day, and
there are no stories that the rite was ever attended by people from
the other clans which are agnatically linked.

At this stage the picture is clear. People are either agnates and
allies: or they are enemies, from amongst whom one finds brides
and to whom one sends sisters in marriage. At this level of analysis,
it would be possible to map the eastern Kondmals, for the benefit
of a Balimendi man, and colour the different clan-territories,
according as they were agnates or marriageable people. But it
would only be possible to do this if each localized clan was in fact
composed of people descended from one ancestor: if in fact each
clan had been recruited internally, by descent only. Neither of these
things is true, and there are in existence agnatic ties cutting across
the cleavage between communities which are related as bride-
seizing folk, and which are therefore enemies. The material which
I have already given should make it clear how this comes about.

(Case 17. Refer to Cases 13 and 14: pp. 48–49)

(Time: contemporary)

The Jiura-Malika people first joined Balimendi as sisters' sons, but
they later exchanged this tie for one of agnation. They came from

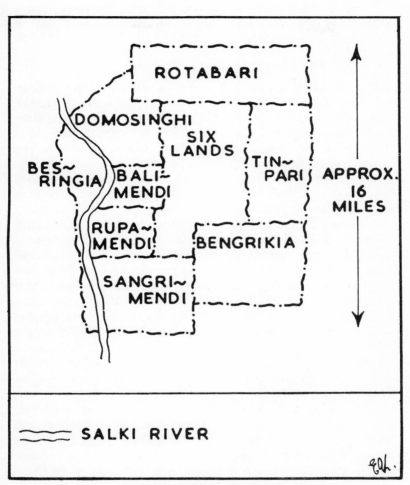

MAP 2.—EASTERN KONDMALS
(*Diagram: not to scale*)

the Besringia clan, where the main body of the Jiura-Malika people still live. The Jiura-Malika people of Balimendi (A), having taken on ties of agnation with the rest of Balimendi (B), cannot marry there: nor can they marry among the Jiura-Malika people of Besringia (C), from whom they believe they are in fact descended. But B and C continue to intermarry. The same is true, *mutatis mutandis*, of the Damopara cluster in Balimendi.

There are in this way two cross-cutting systems of clanship. The one is territorial, and the clans are named: Balimendi, Besringia, Gondrimendi, and so forth. The relationship within these clan-territories is recognized to some extent to be fictional, but politically it takes precedence over the other forms of clanship. The second type of clanship refers to categories of people rather than to groups: it is dispersed and not localized and it is based on what are believed to be true lines of descent: and these clans do not have names.

In a sense the group which is formed by Balimendi, Tinpari, Bengrikia, and a part of Rotabari is also a dispersed clan, in that it does not occupy a continuous piece of territory. But I have continued to call this form of clanship 'territorial' because the relationships between these clans are of the same type as those which obtain within a localized clan. They are political relationships. The dispersed form of clanship differs in that the segments which broke away did not found independent clan-territories for themselves, but became merged into other territorial clans. Politically what occurred was not segmentation, but fission. The political relationships which had existed between the three brothers who founded Tinpari and the main Balimendi lineages, continued after the two groups became geographically separated: that is segmentation. But the political relationships which had existed between the Jiura-Malika group which came to Balimendi and the group which remained in Besringia were severed (in spite of the fact that they lived in adjacent territories). This is fission, since the Jiura-Malika people in Balimendi have become the enemies of their former agnates in Besringia.

I have no doubt that in wars between Balimendi and Besringia, the Balimendi Jiura-Malika had a special role. But I have no evidence. There have been no wars for at least a hundred years, and I have no cases or traditions which show the Balimendi Jiura-Malika playing the role I would expect of them—that of mediators and peacemakers. I would expect the tie between the Balimendi Jiura-Malika and the Besringia Jiura-Malika to be especially significant, since Besringia and Balimendi are adjacent to one another.

Damopara and its parent clan Damanikia are different. Damanikia lies away in the hills to the south of Balimendi in an area with which the Balimendi people have scarcely any contacts. There are no traditions of warfare with the clans of that area, as there are between the clans of the eastern Kondmals, nor, even to-day, do the Balimendi people or anyone else of the eastern Kondmals make marriages with Damanikia or any other clan in that area. Indeed the Damanikia people can scarcely be classified, other than theoretically, as 'bride-seizing-folk'. They belong almost to a society different from that in which the Balimendi people live. The Damopara group in Balimendi would therefore lack the intercalary role which the Jiura-Malika people probably had.

In Baderi the adopted Bɪ segment has become almost totally submerged in the Baderi lineage, apart from the lingering exogamic ties with the people of Rampara and Alari. Why, then, in Balimendi have not the 'adopted' lineages of the Jiura-Malika and Damopara also become submerged and why have they not been written into a common genealogy? Why have the Jiura-Malika people survived as a discrete genealogical entity in Balimendi, when sisters' sons in Baderi appear to survive for no more than about four generations?

If the Jiura-Malika group did in fact play a special role as intermediaries in the political system, this may account for their survival as a discrete entity. But this clearly cannot be the only reason, for it does not apply to the Damopara group. The reason, I think, lies in territory and topography. The Bɪ segment live in the Baderi valley, and there are no natural obstacles within this valley. The Bɪ segment, it is true, is located mainly in Pandrisai hamlet, but their members are also found in Baderi itself, in Kinisuga, in Dudopara, and in Kendrisai (Table 5). Their fields are interspersed with the fields of the Baderi people, and there is no discrete stretch of territory in the Baderi valley which can be pointed out as the territory of the Bɪ segment and of no-one else. But this is not true of the Balimendi Jiura-Malika, or Damopara. These two lineages are located in discrete stretches of territory, separated from one another and from the other Balimendi lineages by streams and patches of waste and jungle, which, although they are in no sense difficult physical obstacles, are boundaries.

The system, therefore, would work in the following way. Where groups of different origin live mingled together within one valley, then, except when they were both owners of the earth (as in the case of BX), their genealogies tended to become fused. Where such groups lived in valleys separated topographically by waste and jungle, which does not offer a considerable physical boundary, they tended to form one agnatic territorial clan, but there would be no attempt to write the genealogies as one.

Thus, in a sense, the existence of the dispersed clan depended on the way in which the group which has split off becomes incorporated into its new territorial clan. A split could have three results: firstly there may have emerged a new territorial clan, in its own territory, and retaining attenuated political ties with the parent clan, an example being the formation of Bengrikia and Tinpari from segments (here the word is appropriate) which left Balimendi. Secondly, the group which moves away may become politically amalgamated with another territorial clan, but have retained its genealogical identity, and it may, if the move has been within one society of interacting territorial clans, have taken on a special intercalary political function. Thirdly the group—or more likely the person—which left its parent group may have become identified with the territorial clan which it joined, not only politically, but also genealogically.

Yet even in the third case the identification is not complete. The exogamic ban continues tenaciously, even when genealogical identification appears to be complete (Case 3: p. 24). The genealogical system is not conditioned entirely by territorial relations. If one can put it this way, there exists a 'genuine' system of agnatic descent, somewhat fragmentary but nevertheless different from the system of quasi-agnation in which territorial relationships are expressed. The latter is primarily a system of territorial relationships which has borrowed the idiom of agnatic kinship. But there is, apart from this, a kinship system of agnatic descent in the dispersed clans.

The system of dispersed clans is in evidence when a marriage is being arranged. Most marriages are with villages where there is already a connection by marriage, and where the dispersed affiliations of the different lineages are well known, or, if they are not known, are assumed to have been worked out on the occasion of the previous marriage. For instance, the Baderi people know that they can marry the people of Buduhari village, and when such a marriage is contemplated there is no search for a common agnatic descent. Where there is no such regular connection, then a search is made.

(Case 18)   (Time: 1955)

'We, Nasira, Manda, Ponga, Liringa, went together to Tikaballi village to arrange a marriage for Ponga. When they saw us the Tikaballi people asked us questions. We said, "The reason for our coming is that one of us wishes to take a bride." We stated our affiliations, "Nagusa-Sepera, Sepera-Sovera, Betu-Tunia, Raga-Bodo, etc.", and we asked theirs. They said, "We don't know our affiliations." We said, "If you don't know your affiliations, we will not make the marriage, for you cannot be true Konds like us." They had no answer. Then they reflected that there was an old man of theirs, a schoolmaster, who was teaching in Tentilagora. They sent for him and he came that night and said, "We are Pandru-Basti, Kaleti-Bopono, Sakidi-Munda, Totoki-Kutura, etc. Do you have affinal connections with these people or not?" We said, "Do you make affinal connections with Nagusa-Sepera or not?" Such marriages are proper and so the discussion ended.'

This was an unusual marriage in that Ponga, a widower with grown sons, had taken a fancy to a girl he had seen in the market, found a mutual friend, and gone along to Tikaballi and arranged to marry the girl. When he told this to his fellow-villagers, they were shocked and insisted that the affair should be arranged properly and formally. This visit was the result, and it was necessary because no-one within living memory had married into that village. The visitors were properly received with liquor, both parties were slightly drunk, and there was a fierce quarrel which came near to blows when the Baderi people insinuated that the others could not be true Konds—and therefore might be untouchables—if they could not name their lines of descent.

What I have been calling a dispersed clan has no single name, but is identified by listing pairs of ancestors who are presumed themselves to have a common ancestor, the totality making up the dispersed clan.[1]

[1] There is no Kui word for 'dispersed clan'. The general word for a group or category or class, *klambu*, will not stand by itself nor can it be made definitive

Marriages which are correct in terms of territorial clanship may not be suitable in terms of dispersed clanship and therefore are not permitted: and vice versa. Both systems exist so far as exogamy is concerned, and neither obliterates the other. But in political relationships the territorial clans cancel the bonds of dispersed clanship. No-one could be a citizen of two communities at the same time.

WARFARE

It was impossible to hold the rights of a citizen in two territorial clans at the same time, because these groups were organized for the defence of common property. The privilege of membership was the right to have one's land protected from outsiders, and the corresponding obligation was to defend the clan territory. A man could not fight on two sides at the same time.

Both Kond traditions and the reports written by soldiers during the Meriah wars make it clear that warfare was endemic in the Kond hills. It was not always concerned with land, and informants said that quarrels over women were a frequent cause of war. An eye-witness account of a Kond war has come down to us. The battle was carried on with much ceremony and champions were given

by any single adjective. In Case 19 the question about affiliations is asked by the phrase, 'With whom do you send?'

The localized clans have names, Balimendi, Besringia, and so forth, which accords with the fact of their corporate activity. There is no Kui term for the people of one localized clan and they must be referred to as 'the people of one territory (*dina*)' or, more ambiguously, as 'the people of one *mutha*'. *Dina* does not refer specifically to a clan territory and may be used for the territory of any group from a village up to a kingdom or even a nation: *mutha*, of course, is specific as to territory but not as to its population. It is not a Kui word in origin although it has been adopted into the language.

The Kui term for an agnatic descent group is *gossi*, but I have not heard this used to refer to a group larger than what I have called the Baderi segments (B1, B2, etc.). Above this level the terms for territory seem to supervene, and the next level, the main lineage for instance, would be called 'the people of one village'. 'Baderi people' are properly the people of the main lineage (and perhaps BX), and by extension the phrase usually includes those related through women and people of other castes living in Baderi. When my informants wished to refer to the main lineage alone, they used such a phrase as 'the real Baderi people'.

The meanings attached to *klambu* and *gossi* (*gochi*) by Risley (1891, Vol. I, p. 400) are wrong.

the chance to engage in single combat, and the women accompanied the men to spur them to greater efforts, and to weep when their husbands fell, or when their brothers fell on the enemy's side. The affair is made to sound like ceremonial violence, rather than a battle.[1]

But it is clear that a grimmer kind of war also was fought, and the prize was land. The Balimendi people fought the people of Gondrimendi for a stretch of level land on their northern boundary and with the help of the group from Damanikia they took it and have kept it up to the present day. To the north-west, the Domosinghi clan attacked Besringia and conquered a stretch of rice-land in the Salki plain, on the Besringia side of the river, and held it until the Administration restored it to Besringia. The prizes in these wars were not simply any kind of territory, but rather land which was suitable for growing rice, or which was already growing rice. Such land is limited in the Kondmals. The making of a rice-field out of virgin land is a long process, requiring considerable toil in levelling the land and channelling water. Levelling the field usually brings sub-soil to the surface, and it may be five or six years before constant flooding brings the right degree of fertility to the soil. Places in the Kondmals (where the steep hill-terracing which is found in Assam is unknown) suitable for development into rice fields are few. For both these reasons there was an incentive for those who became too many for their land and had to move elsewhere, or who moved elsewhere as a result of conflict, not to attempt to make new fields, but to try to take fields made by other persons. 'A head,' as one informant put it, 'falls more easily than a tree.'

Informants, both Kui and Oriya, dwell upon this insecurity. There are numerous stories of desperate fights, and most of them contain stories of trickery and treachery, and are not of the chivalrous nature described in the eye-witness account. People abandoned smaller settlements to join kinsmen in larger villages because they were frightened of attack. Men who left their own territory were attacked on sight. Women were not killed, but if they were young enough they would be seized as wives. Marriages were arranged by old women, since it was unsafe for anyone else to travel beyond their own territory. No doubt these stories are exaggerated, but the general impression of a society lacking the benefits of

[1] W. Macpherson, 1865, pp. 79-80.

large-scale law and order cannot be wrong. Kond wars impressed the earliest European visitors almost as much as the rite of human sacrifice.

The localized clan was a group organized for the defence of a common territory, and for aggression against others. Political loyalty could be only to the community in which a man lived, and his agnatic connections with other territories could not command his allegiance. These wars were also the reason why boundaries between clan-territories tended to fall along natural boundaries— wide rivers or belts of hill and jungle. The clans and the lineages within them were composed of men who co-operated for the defence of a common territory. This was the *raison d'être* of the system. But it is not a sufficient description. The cause for unity was the need to protect property. But the unity itself was not expressed solely in terms of this object—solely in political terms. It was also expressed in kinship, in the rights and duties involved in agnation: and it was expressed ritually in the Earth cult. In these three institutions—warfare, exogamy, and the cult of the Earth— the clan members acted together, and in this co-activity the unity of the clan was embodied.[1]

'Unity' refers to a process. There were conflicts within the clan: there were breaches of the rule of exogamy: there were changes in clan boundaries by conquest: there were migrations following on the growth of population in one quarter and its decline in another. From one point of view, and in actual relationships, the society was in a state of flux and disorder. But the element of continuity

[1] The political system of the Konds is segmentary in that it is composed of balanced segments, and that the links between these segments are mechanical rather than organic. The levels of segmentation would be: at the highest, the allied clans (which I have sometimes loosely called a 'federation'): then, linked clans territorially adjacent, like the Tinpari group (see p. 48) or the Bengrikia group (see p. 53): then clans: then villages: then hamlets.

The relationship which characterizes segments at all levels is expressed in terms of agnatic kinship, and for this reason I have called the localized groups 'clans'. But the political system is *not* based on a segmentary lineage system. Territorial relationships cannot be expressed through a genealogy at all levels of the system. At the level of the hamlet lineage ties cross-cut territorial ties. The inhabitants of a village can be placed on one genealogy (with the reservations already made about the fictitious nature of this genealogy), but there is no attempt to relate the villages of one clan to a common genealogy, and differences of descent are recognized and accepted. 'True' genealogies, if they were known, would define rather the 'dispersed clan' than the territorial clan.

was a constant movement towards the same kind of relationships that had previously existed. By the rules of the system brothers ought not to fight brothers. In fact they did, and a section of the brotherhood was forced to move elsewhere, as did the people of Damanikia. But in its new situation the Damanikia group took on ties of agnatic brotherhood which were politically of exactly the same type as those which they had in the parent Damanikia group, and the ties of agnation which they retained with the Damanikia people no longer commanded their allegiance. The conflicts which arose in the structure caused it to be fluid but unchanging.

Conjectural History

As I have become more deeply involved in the dynamic aspects of the system of territorial clanship, it has become the more difficult to describe it as if it were a model, and to remember that in fact we are holding 'other things equal'. The 'other things' are the presence of Oriyas, the caste system, the Administration, and the representative democracy. These are discussed in Part III of the book. In the meantime the question remains whether or not the structure of territorial clans was in fact 'fluid but unchanging', and did in fact survive for several hundred years. What, in other words, is the political reality which the clan structure is supposed to describe?

The structure of territorial clans, as I have presented it, is in fact a point somewhere near the end of a long history of political development. It has not continued to exist in that same form for countless years: it can be shown (if that is not too strong a word to use in this reconstruction of the past) to have been a development in response to technical changes, and probably in response to political pressure from outside the system. There was a time, however, when the clan political structure was the 'main' political structure of the region.[1] We do not know enough about the working of this structure to be able to present it convincingly, especially in its dynamic elements. I therefore confine myself to this brief discussion of the antecedents of the territorial clan structure, and I present its history, somewhat diffidently, as conjectural history.

The Konds believe that they were once axe-cultivators and knew

[1] See p. 173.

nothing of irrigated rice. This, they say, is the reason why to-day the Konds supplement the cultivation of wet rice with axe-fields, while the Oriyas never make an axe-field. The traditions are full: first they cultivated with digging sticks, as they sometimes do to-day: later they got hoes. The plough, they say, was introduced by an Oriya whose name was Dolobehera, and first it had a wooden point. Later they learnt to fit it with an iron share. Tribes else-where in the hills are axe-cultivators, some, like the Konds in the eastern Kondmals, practising it as a secondary occupation, a few, like the Kuttia Konds, living mainly from axe-fields. In many parts of the Kondmals an axe-field is the only means of getting a crop from the land, for the hills are too steep to grow wet rice.

Axe-cultivation for subsistence permits and demands spatial mobility in several ways. An axe-field is a short-term investment. In the Kondmals the ground is exhausted within three years and it is then necessary to make a new field. To maintain a community indefinitely an area of fallow very much larger than the area under cultivation is required, and the community must move around in this area. Secondly axe-cultivation allows only a slight concen-tration of population. It is difficult to expand the area under cultivation without running the risk of upsetting the cycle of forest regeneration. The balance between population and land is a delicate one and once disturbed it is readjusted not by expansion of existing fields so much as by the fission of the community, since a section of it goes elsewhere. I never found a single knowing Kond who asserted that so far as he knew his ancestors had always lived on the one site. A typical informant said: 'First we dwelt in Kimedi: from there we went to live around the Atisalo mountain near Sarungodo: then we went to Motingia *mutha* in Kimedi: then we went to Solaguda in Kimedi: then we went to Jeheno-gando in Petingia: then we came to Doberi. Our brothers are found in Jarugando and Bindani in Jehelingia and we do not marry in those places.' Kimedi was the name of a small kingdom about forty miles away to the south-east of the village in which the informant lived. In another village, five miles away from the first, an informant said: 'Our home was in Sagoro in Boad: then we went to Budenipara: then we went to Beserabando near Sorukui: from there we came to Malikpara. From Malikpara our brothers have gone out to Ukusuganda, Bobtingia, Mundru-maska, Udanpara, Prekori, Bhalruga, Mandruga, and other

places.' Sagoro in Boad, from which this group believes it originated, is about twenty miles to the north of the village, and about
sixty miles from the place in which their neighbours originated.
A short investment in land facilitates migration of this kind, to a
much greater extent than does rice-cultivation.

It is a Kond tradition that in the time of axe-cultivation they
lived in small groups and the land was much less densely populated
than it is to-day. Arguing on this, different informants several
times produced this story: 'There cannot have been many people
in the hills then. When you came to a new place then you lit a fire
and as far as the fire burned the land was yours. That is why to-day
the boundaries run along stream beds and ravines. You could not
do that if the land was densely populated.' The fire to which they
refer is not that made in an axe-field after cutting the jungle. It is
one which is still lit to-day in the hot season when the ground is
carpeted with dead leaves and it does spread in a slow line up and
around a mountain until it is stopped by the bed of a stream. Nor
could my informants conceive that the groups in those days, besides being small—'the sons and grandsons of one man'—could be
anything but patrilineal. It is, of course, conceivable that they
were bilateral groups, or organized in some other way, but we
have no means of settling that question. The structure was composed of small groups and the stories of migration show that it was
not static. The system was sufficiently flexible to allow a changing
population to be adjusted to the capacity of the land.

Later the Konds learnt to cultivate wet rice. Both they and the
Oriyas say that the new technique was introduced by, or at least
learnt from, the Oriyas of the Mahanadi valley. Konds to-day
continue to make axe-fields, but in most parts of the Kondmals
either cash crops or subsidiary crops are grown in these. The staple
now is rice grown in irrigated fields. The cultivation of wet rice
makes fission and migration more serious and costly. Wet rice is
grown in a permanent field in which there is a considerable investment. This investment will give a return, other things being equal,
in perpetuity. Labour has to be expended on levelling the ground,
on building the retaining banks, and on bringing water to the
field. Once this main task is done there is some annual maintenance
on the banks, but, compared to the initial labour, this is slight. A
wet rice field is a capital investment vastly more durable than an
axe-field. It seldom requires a fallow period: and, within limits, it

is capable of expansion to meet a growing need for food without running into the danger of destroying natural resources. It represents considerably greater control over nature than does the axe-field. Besides the investment in rice fields, it becomes worth while for the cultivator to invest in a more permanent house, since he will not have to abandon it after a short time.

Rice-cultivation in wet fields also allows a much greater concentration of population. A larger group than the descendants of one grandfather can live together, if there is some reason to make them do so. Whether the Kondmals, given the relatively large area of mountain and small area of valley land suitable for wet rice fields, can support a bigger population under paddy-cultivation than under axe-cultivation is a question that does not concern us. The point rather is that rice-cultivation draws people down from the remoter hills into the valleys and concentrates them in larger groups. Although there is no straight connection between numbers and the complexity of social organization, we would expect the development of social relations of a more complex type in these larger wet rice-growing communities than in the smaller communities of axe-cultivators.

Rice cultivation tended in the Kondmals to bring about a concentration of population. This fact, combined with the relatively heavy investment in a wet rice field, strengthened and extended political alliances. There is now something worth fighting for. The local group must develop sufficient coherence to fight to protect itself and its property. We would expect the development of institutions capable of uniting in co-ordinated action a group larger than five or six elementary families. We would also expect that the structure would harden out and become less fluid.

This does not mean that the structure becomes completely rigid. Although the ease of movement and the frequency of movement may have diminished, the importance of moving increased. Nor need we suppose that wars of conquest and fighting for land only occur when there is an overall shortage of land: 'It is easier to cut off a head than to cut down a tree." It is easier to kill off the owners and take the fields, than to construct new fields out of virgin land. It requires only a local imbalance to start the process off. This argument, of course, does not exclude the possibility that there was also much greater pressure of population on rice land, than there had ever been on land suitable for axe-cultivation. One possibility is that the population grew: another possibility is that while there is sufficient mountain land available for a given population, there is not enough valley land for the same population, even though it did not increase. There is no means of allotting priority to any one of these three processes, since we do not have the facts.

The structure was, so to speak, hardening out into larger and larger groups, and at the point at which I describe that area, the eastern Kondmals had become two camps. The process by which hamlets amalgamated into villages, and villages into clan-territories had continued almost to its conclusion in which the eastern Kondmals consisted of two opposed political federations. This process of growth and development underlies the 'timeless' structure of localized clans which I have presented.

There are many questions remaining which I cannot answer. I have presented fission as the result of quarrels and the differential growth of population. But the process must have been more complicated than this. In a following chapter I describe in detail the causes of fission at the present day in a village, but it is impossible to do the same for a clan, since the process has been stopped for more than a century. Again we would like to know much more about the frequency of warfare, the mechanisms of reconciliation, the size of the units involved, whether or not whole 'federations' were ever involved, or whether these were rather 'non-aggression pacts' than pacts for mutual defence. All these questions cannot be answered. Again, among the vast array of gods and godlings presented by Macpherson[1] there must have been some which acted as ritual foci for the clan, but I have been able to get at no more than the fringe of this system.

We also lack knowledge of the internal authority-structure of the clans. The older writers speak easily of 'elders' and councils, and they stress the democratic air of these assemblies.[2] But I would conjecture that with the growing severity of the conflict between clans (not to speak of Oriya pressure from outside) and the hardening out of the political groups, there must have been a corresponding hardening out in the authority system, reminiscent of that discussed by Lowie among the Plains Indians.[3] Even if there were

[1] S. C. Macpherson, 1852.
[2] W. Macpherson, 1865, pp. 74–8.
[3] R. H. Lowie, 1927, pp. 94–111.

no institutionalized authoritarian chiefs, one would expect the appearance of charismatic leaders in response to the need for cohesion and organization. There are hints of this in the literature. Some names stand out, usually as leaders of the Kond resistance to the East India Company's armies.[1] But we have insufficient information to notice more than the bare fact of the existence of such people.

All these factors could work for or against the continuance of the system of territorial clans as political units. I have not been able to take them all into account, but I have concentrated mainly upon the process of fission and amalgamation, and I have considered it as the structure's response to disturbances set up by the differential growth of population.

I have presented the clans as a political structure in its maturity. The growth of these clans and the hardening out of the political structure has had to be taken for granted. In the following chapter I lift this structure out of the perspective of structural time, and consider what happened to it a century ago, when the Administration first arrived in the Kondmals.[2]

[1] Some are Oriya names, like Dora Bisoi and Sam Bisoi (W. Macpherson, 1865, p. 47 *et passim*). Others are Kond names like 'Mahadeb Khonro and Nowbhun Khonro, who held all the Boad Khond forests and hills' (*Calcutta Rev.*, 1846, Vol. VI, p. 84).

[2] I have not attempted, in this monograph, to make a comparative study. There are, however, many points of comparison between the Kond material presented here, and, among others, the Mundas (S. C. Roy, 1912, especially pp. 402–21), the Juang (V. Elwin, 1948, p. 24), the Hill Bhuiyas (S. C. Roy, 1935, p. 80), and the Maria Gonds (W. V. Grigson, 1949, pp. 233–48).

2*a*. Pandrisai.

2*b*. Building a House

CHAPTER IV

THE DECAY OF THE LOCALIZED CLAN

AT the extreme south-eastern end of the Baderi valley, in a glen which runs southwards before losing itself in the mountains which divide Balimendi from Rupamendi, lies the hamlet of Bandibari (Map 1). Bandibari is within Baderi valley: the fields which its people own cluster about the hamlet, but some are mingled with Baderi fields. There is no regular pathway over the mountain to Rupamendi, and the Bandibari people travel down the Baderi valley to reach the road. The earth they cultivate is Baderi earth. None of the children in the hamlet go to school, but if they did, they would go to the Lower Primary School in Baderi. There is no marked physical boundary between them and the Baderi people, any more than between, for instance, Dobenisai or Kendrisai and the other hamlets of Baderi cluster. Geographically Bandibari is more a part of the Baderi valley than is Dobenisai, the fields of which drain ultimately to Punuripara and not into Baderi. The Administration treats Bandibari as if it were part of Baderi: if a Bandibari man has to be summoned, it is the Baderi watchman who must go.

But Bandibari is not considered by the Konds to be part of Baderi. Bandibari belongs to Rupamendi. Bandibari people marry into Baderi, and when the Bandibari girls go in marriage they lament with the names of Petura-Pujura, the Rupamendi ancestors, not Nagusa-Sepera. They are not part of the Baderi lineage. Geographically Bandibari is closer to Baderi than is Punuripara, but its people have not amalgamated with the Balimendi clan. The people of Punuripara who came from a clan hostile to Baderi changed their allegiances in order to secure their land (Case 13: p, 48). Bandibari people have not done so, and they hold their land in security, although they have not identified themselves with the Balimendi clan, and in spite of the fact that they are separated by considerable geographical obstacles from their own agnatic kinsmen in Rupamendi.

Bandibari is about five generations old, and at first sight this comparatively brief time of settlement might explain why its people have not been incorporated or amalgamated. The people of Punuripara have lived in their village for a much longer time, so long that it is not possible to use even the vague method of dating their coming by genealogies. But there is no evidence that the amalgamation of the Jiura-Malika group or the Damopara group (Cases 13 and 14: pp. 48 and 49) required a long time. In both cases a single rite marked their accession. This was not a process of slow assimilation, as with the sisters' sons who live in Baderi. There is no sign of any developing agnation between the Bandibari people and the people of Baderi. They are treated firmly as *seri ahpa loku* ('bride-seizing folk').

Allowing twenty years to a generation, the Bandibari people have lived on their present site for about a century. Just a hundred years ago, in the middle of the nineteenth century, a regular Administration was established in the Kondmals. There had been garrisons in the country for twenty years before that. So far as the absence of accurate means of dating permits us to say this, Bandibari was established after the Administration had pacified the Kond hills, at a time when fighting between clans had been ended, and when security was derived from the Administration and not from allegiance to a territorial clan.

'JOMBA TANA' AND 'KODA TANA'

The Meriah Wars, which lasted intermittently for twenty years, were not expensive even by the standards of colonial campaigning in the nineteenth century. Very few regular troops were involved, and what fighting took place was mostly done by irregulars called 'Sebundies'. Nevertheless the economies which the officers engaged in these wars were compelled to observe, show that the East India Company thought that the cost was high. There could be very little return in taxes, direct or indirect, from so wild and sparsely-populated an area as the Kond hills, and the campaign was justified, in many sanctimonious phrases, on moral grounds: a rite so abhorrent as human sacrifice could not be permitted on the frontiers of the Company's territory.

When the country was pacified, administration was handed over to civilians. India has always been governed with the minimum of expenditure in money and personnel, and the Kondmals, being unremunerative, were governed with maximum economy. The district was put in charge of a Tahsildar, Dinobandu Patnaik, who had been a corporal in the irregular cavalry, and had served in the Police. I do not know what his establishment was at that time, but as late as 1888, when there was a European Tahsildar, the staff, apart from the police, consisted of two clerks and a sweeper and the Magistrate himself, for an area of 800 square miles. Taking into account the character, training, and resources of the first Tahsildar, who ruled for 25 years, the district had to be governed through existing institutions. There were neither personnel nor resources to create a new system. Local groups were recognized and were written, more or less as they stood, into the framework of administration.

The new administrative *muthas* were the old clan territories. Here and there the boundaries between *muthas* were made to correspond more exactly with geographical boundaries. The territory which Domosinghi had won from Besringia on the Besringia side of the Salki river was restored to Besringia (Map 2).[1] But even this, not surprisingly, was done unsystematically. The boundary between Balimendi and Besringia crosses and recrosses the Salki river along the line of ancient conquests. There was one major change in the eastern Kondmals. (I am not familiar with the western Kondmals and cannot say whether or not there has been re-organization in that area.) A tidy-minded Administrator, whose identity I have not been able to discover, made a new *mutha* out of the Oriya village of Bolscoopa and its environs, in order to bring the total number of muthas from 49 to a round 50. But, by and large, boundaries were left as the Administration found them, and clans were left intact on their own territories.

The suppression of warfare, and the codification of boundaries between *muthas*, modified the traditional system by which population was adjusted to land. It was no longer possible for Balimendi and Gondrimendi to settle the ownership of a disputed tract by fighting for it. A clan could not expand its territory by conquest. But fixed boundaries did not stabilize the social system. Quarrels and the differential growth and decline of population still made necessary colonization or migration. Migrants could no longer set out as armed marauders in search of a community weak enough to fall before them, or in need of assistance in a battle

[1] See p. 61.

with another clan. The movement had to take place by peaceful means. Migrants now gained land by purchasing it. There is some evidence that this had gone on before. But the presence of the Administration made it impossible to obtain land which was already claimed by someone else, except by buying it, or by various illegal manipulations.

In every clan-territory to-day there is a category of people who live on bought earth, which, significantly, is readily referred to in the Kui language as *koda tana*, and distinguished from *jomba tana*, which means 'earth settled upon'. 'Bought earth' does not refer to fields, which also are bought and sold. Rights in the earth are not registered in the Record of Rights, since that is concerned exclusively with cultivated land. *Koda tana* refers not only to cultivated sites, but also to house sites and to the surrounding forest.

(Case 19)   (Time: c. 1930)

'The following have written this certificate of the sale of earth, Sanu Kohoro, Udu Kohoro . . . etc. . . . Kui men, village Sujapaju, *mutha* Besringia, *thana* (police-station) Phulbani, country Kondmals, district Angul.

'Through poverty we are selling to Rosei Kohoro of Bobtingia of our *mutha* the earth at Atimesa. The earth which belonged to our ancestors from the large cottonwood tree to the east, westwards to the large *mardo* tree, to the right as far as the big *sal* tree, to the left as far as the *arju* tree we have drawn the boundary, and we the undersigned with the knowledge of our brothers are selling this earth for 20 *khondi* of paddy and Rs.100. The earth belongs to no-one else of our brothers or any persons other than ourselves. If any of our brothers should make trouble then the Government are not to hear their case. We proclaim that it is our earth. If there is trouble then Rosei can make a case against us or our brothers for the return of all the money we had for the earth. Rosei can raise what crop he likes from the earth for as many days as the moon continues in existence.

'If our descendants make trouble with the descendants of Rosei Kohoro, then they may dry up and vanish as does salt when it is dropped into liquor.

'For this purpose Rosei Kohoro is given this document so that he can make a case against our descendants, using our name.'

Rosei Kohoro would then be living on bought earth. This text was written in Oriya about 1930, when the sale took place, and when the Kondmals were still part of Angul District. It refers to a transfer of land within the *mutha*, between people who are not themselves members of the Besringia clan. It is quoted for two purposes here: firstly to show that such sales were of whole tracts of land and not of particular fields: and secondly to show that the right to such land is expected to be validated ultimately in the courts of the Government.

Those who live on 'bought earth' are not members of the localized clan. The proportion of territorial clan members to persons living on bought earth varies from one *mutha* to another, and in order to show this I will compare Balimendi with its neighbour Besringia. Balimendi has a high degree of agnatic homogeneity (using 'agnatic' here to include all those people who are incorporated or amalgamated into the localized clan). There are four Kond village clusters and these comprise in all seventeen hamlets. The people of all these hamlets, whether they are counted as 'true' agnates, or are the descendants of men who came originally from elsewhere, are considered to be owners of the earth. Damopara and Punuripara fall within this category. In addition to the seventeen there are four other hamlets. Three are very small, consisting of two or three houses each, sited on the border between Balimendi and Rupamendi on the Salki river plain, where there is no very clear geographical boundary. They are in Balimendi because the Administration happened to draw the boundary at that point. The inhabitants of these villages are Rupamendi people. Baderi claims to own the earth of these hamlets, but the people of the hamlets say that the boundary was incorrectly drawn and the earth really belongs to Rupamendi. The dispute is verbal, although it could have important ritual implications, as I will make clear later. In fact there is no record of any incident which would make crucial the ownership of the earth of these three hamlets. They pay their taxes to the Balimendi Sirdar, but they are not part of the Balimendi clan and they marry Balimendi people. The fourth hamlet is Bandibari, already described, sited on bought earth at the head of the Baderi valley. All but these four hamlets belong to the Balimendi clan.

In the neighbouring *mutha*, Besringia, the territorial clan forms a much smaller part of the total Kond population. The Besringia clan, so far as I could unravel it, is composed of four lineages, each of which originated in a different area of the Kond hills and all of which were later amalgamated into one localized exogamous clan. But this clan occupies only about half the territory of the *mutha*, and forms about half the Kond population. The remainder consists of many different communities who live on bought earth, who have settled in Besringia within the last hundred years, and who are not incorporated or amalgamated by agnatic ties to the founding clan. Besringia is named after Besera, one of the eponymous ancestors of the Besera-Masera lineage, which is acknowledged as the senior lineage in the Besringia clan. But this is now more an academic point than a practical issue, since there is only one old-established house of this lineage in Besringia itself. Besera-Masera people are also found in Maseragando and a cluster of related villages in Jarupangia *mutha* to the west of Besringia. A segment from this village has recently returned to settle at the north-western end of Besringia. Apart from Besera-Masera, the large lineages of the Besringia localized clan are Suna-Mottra, Boboto-Binjari, and Jiura-Malika. These lineages came from different places. Jiura-Malika came from the neighbourhood of Sagodo village in the former Boad State. Boboto-Binjari came from the south-east, and while the descendants of Mottra are found in various villages in Besringia, the descendants of Suna are in Sunapanga in Ganjam. Jiura-Malika are said to have been the protégés of the Besera-Masera group and an old man of that lineage claimed that his ancestors had brought them and settled them on the land. Suna-Mottra and Boboto-Binjari claim that they were the first settlers on the land they occupy. All these four lineages, Jiura-Malika, Suna-Mottra, Boboto-Binjari, and Besera-Masera unite to form one exogamous clan. Beyond the story that Besera-Masera people brought the Jiura-Malika lineage, I heard nothing similar to the stories of the incorporation of Damopara and Punuripara in the Balimendi clan, and it may well be that these were three independent lineages, each settled on land which they held as the first occupiers, and all later amalgamated into one clan.

One of the largest of the immigrant villages in Besringia is Arapaju, which contains 61 houses and 274 people. The village was settled either five or six generations back from the present elders, which would put the event a little before the coming of the Administration. I discussed this with the informant who told me the story about the Arapaju people which I give below (Case 20:

p. 75). When I objected that genealogies might not be a sound method of dating, he replied, 'How can they have been here in olden times, when they are to-day marrying with all the other villages in Besringia?' The argument which I am advancing is also one which occurs to the people themselves: the Arapaju people marry with all the other people in Besringia; therefore they cannot have lived in Besringia when the Konds were making war on one another.

The people of Arapaju originate from Pobingia in the south of the Kondmals. Pobingia people are found in several villages in the area of the Salki river valley around Baderi and Bisipara.

(Case 20)   (Time: *c.* 1860)

'In Pobingia there were once two brothers. The fields were being much damaged by monkeys and other animals and birds from the jungle. One brother put medicine in his field, and from that day whatever ate in the field died on the spot—wild animals, cattle, everything. Seeing this other people became much afraid and they fled from the village, some to Srasananda and some to Kornora and some further north. A little later the sorcerer himself was driven from the village and he came to Besringia, where he settled for a time in the village of Sikopara, the people of which were themselves recent immigrants from Sangrimendi. But they too drove him out and he went to the Boboto-Binjari people (one of the lineages of the Besringia clan) and bought land from them and founded the village of Arapaju.'

Arapaju people marry into all the villages of Besringia, with the exception of a hamlet of Ramadi village, which is itself populated by their own people.

The three villages of Sikopara, Sujapaju, and Diparsai all have as their lineage name Dasula-Divula. This lineage came originally from Daspalla State (Map 3), which lies to the east of the Kondmals, and they are settled in numerous villages in Sangrimendi *mutha*. From one of these villages a segment migrated to Sikopara in Besringia and bought land, probably from the Suna-Mottra group, one of the founding lineages of Besringia. From Sikopara other segments migrated to Diparsai and Sujapaju. The people of these villages do not marry with one another, nor into the parent Sangrimendi, but they marry everywhere in Besringia.

Trosepodro is a village in Besringia of the Kotoro-Damudu line. They came from Katringia *mutha* which lies to the north-west of Besringia. They are said to have been brought and settled there by the people of Duduki, which is of the Suna-Mottra line. They marry everywhere in Besringia, including Duduki.

Doberi is a village in the extreme north-west of Besringia. I do not know the name of their line, but they came from Katringia, where their agnatic kinsmen dwell to-day. They marry everywhere in Besringia except in a number of hamlets in their immediate neighbourhood. This seems at first sight to contradict the hypothesis that the bonds of agnation were forged in conditions of insecurity and have not developed since the area has been pacified. Doberi does not marry into Jurapanga, which is peopled by a segment of the Besera-Masera line, which came from Maseragando ten years ago. Nor do they marry into Bilabari, a hamlet of people who came from the far south near the village of Sankerakhol in Ganjam; nor into Duduki, a Suna-Mottra group; nor into Jarugando which is inhabited by people from far away to the south-west; nor, finally, in Nakuripanga or Ukusuganda, both of the Suna-Mottra group. A man of Doberi explained it to me in the following way.

(Case 21)   (Time: contemporary)
   'Formerly the old ones [i.e. our ancestors] made marriages everywhere in Besringia. But we do not do so now with nearby villages. We have come to help with one another's funerals and so we do not intermarry. We are become like one lineage. The villages around Doberi are very small. The proper people to undertake the labour of the first three days after a death are the agnates of the dead man. This is a lot of work, especially bringing wood to burn the corpse. So the people of these villages call on their neighbours to help them. They act as if they were agnates and so they do not marry. Of course, now and then someone steals a girl from one of these villages, but I would not count that as a proper marriage connection. A proper connection is made when there are five brothers [i.e. a *panchayat*] sitting down together and making the arrangements, and then they would not permit a marriage with these villages.'

A large and self-contained village like Arapaju would not need to call upon its neighbours as Doberi does, and, unlike Doberi, which lies with many other small hamlets on an elevated plateau, Arapaju is situated in a secluded valley. The peculiar kind of agnation which has grown up in Doberi and its neighbourhood is the result of special circumstances and I do not think that it invalidates the general hypothesis, which I discussed at length in the last chapter, that agnation has widened out of the need for security. The exogamic tie between Doberi and its neighbours is different from that which holds within the clan or between the founding lineages of Besringia, since it is not backed by supernatural sanctions. If a man from Doberi steals a girl from Nakuripanga, this is not a desirable marriage, but it does not involve Besringia *mutha*, or even the two villages concerned, in ritual danger. Such a union is a bad marriage: but it is not a sin.

In Balimendi the original territorial clan is still in occupation of almost the whole of the clan territory: in Besringia it is not. The reason for this is ultimately geographical. Balimendi, a *mutha* smaller in area than Besringia (Map 2), lies mainly in and off the valley of the Salki river, along a main line of communication. It was colonized and—speaking approximately—virtually all the available land must have been taken up by the time the Administration came to the area. Besringia, on the other hand, once one gets away from its south-eastern tip which lies in the Salki valley and which is monopolized by the Oriya village of Bisipara, is a wild and mountainous tract of country, with small valleys and great areas of jungle. It is less desirable land than that of Balimendi and it was colonized later. When land could no longer be taken by force, and had to be bought, any migration of size was directed to marginal land, which was still uncolonized. In Besringia there was much of this land, and therefore that *mutha* has received many more immigrants in the past hundred years than has Balimendi. In other words Balimendi has continued to be recruited largely internally, by the natural growth of the Balimendi clan, and without external recruitment. But the population of Besringia has grown mainly by external recruitment. The result is that, from the point of view of the founding clan, Besringia is much more heterogeneous than Balimendi. Those who have been recruited externally since the coming of the Administration, have not been absorbed into the clan. To-day the Balimendi community behaves much more as a unity than does Besringia. Indeed, from the Kond point of view, the latter is scarcely a community at all.[1]

[1] See pp. 209–216.

IMMIGRANTS AND THE FOUNDING CLAN

Relationships within the localized clan were expressed in three institutions: warfare, exogamy, and the cult of the Earth. The unity of the clan was a process by which those who lived on its territory were brought to fight at one another's side, not to marry one another's sisters, and to consider themselves in ritual danger if the Earth of their clan was polluted by an incestuous marriage or in other ways. The first of these institutions, warfare, clearly cannot operate after the pacification of the area, and it ceases to be a link between the lineages and segments of the founding clan.[1] *A fortiori* it cannot be a link between the founding clan and the immigrants who bought land from it, or found themselves for other reasons resident upon its territory.

The immigrant lineages could marry into the founding clan, although they lived upon its territory. Indeed this is the first criterion which my informants used to distinguish immigrant from founding lineages. Baderi people marry into Bandibari: Arapaju people marry everywhere in Besringia. In special circumstances, where the villages are small and close together, a form of exogamy emerges, and the idiom of agnatic brotherhood is used to describe it, but it is less rigorous than that which obtains within the founding clan. A breach of its rules of exogamy is rather a breach of good manners than an act of incest (Case 21: p. 76). Exogamy, then, is not an institution organizing relationships between the founding clan and the immigrant lineages.

Between the founding clan and the immigrant lineages there is no rule of exogamy, but in other respects they have a common dependence for their ritual welfare on the Earth. Everyone who lives within the boundaries of the *mutha*, whether on bought earth or on earth ancestrally colonized, is polluted when the Earth is defiled. I have no cases, either directly observed or obtained from informants, to prove this assertion with reference to the founding clan and the immigrant lineages. There are, of course, innumerable examples to show that sexual relations between the founders and the immigrants do not lead to a prosecution for incest. But I know of no case of incest *within* an immigrant Kond lineage being followed by corporate action against the offenders by both the founders and the immigrants acting as one community. In-

[1] But see p. 254.

formants told me that this would happen, and the more cautious informants said this should happen. But it did not in fact happen while I was there. However, there is no reason to doubt that incest or any other breach of the Earth taboos within an immigrant lineage does pollute the entire community in the *mutha*. There are three reasons for thinking so. The first is that my informants thought so. The second reason accounts for the absence of cases. The hamlet or lineage itself takes action almost before the *mutha* knows about the offence. It is in fact rare for action to be left to the *mutha* because the hamlet or the village is dilatory, even within the founding clan. The case of incest in Baderi was dealt with by Baderi itself, with the tacit approval of, but without the intervention of, the rest of Balimendi (Case 2: p. 21). Incest, or some other sin against the purity of the Earth, in Bandibari is dealt with by the people of Bandibari, and is not left to the people of Baderi, still less of Balimendi. The third reason is the most compelling. It is that action is taken against immigrant Oriyas, even though they profess not to believe in the cult of the Earth. If this can be done in the case of infidel Oriyas, how much more likely is it to be done in the case of the immigrant Kond lineages, who believe in the Earth? Had the people of Balimendi known of an unsettled case of Earth pollution in Bandibari or one of the other immigrant communities during the drought of 1955, I have no doubt that they would have taken action against the offender, just as they did in the following case.

(Case 22)   (Time: *c* 1950–5)
    'A man of the Oriya POTTER caste of Gomapara village in Balimendi five or six years ago [this text was written in 1955] impregnated his father's younger brother's widow. The couple fled. Four or five years ago a Kond of Manipara hamlet impregnated a girl who was his classificatory younger sister, and they too fled. This year, both the women having died, the POTTER and the Kond returned to Gomapara and Manipara respectively. Our *mutha* Malik [the senior Kond] had summoned the people of Baderi, Damopara, Manipara and the other villages to discuss the sin in Gomapara in the year that it happened, but since the couple had fled, nothing was done about it, although we discussed cutting the goats and throwing down the pots [i.e. performing the rite of expiation].

    'This year their spouses having died, the offenders returned. Our *mutha* Malik called the men of the *mutha* together last Thursday. Hearing of the assembly the two offenders went into hiding and could not be found. So nothing was done. We assembled again on Friday morning and the village headman of Gomapara [an Oriya of WARRIOR caste] and the headman of Manipara [a Kond] brought the offenders along. A discussion was held in the Gomapara school-house. The Gomapara POTTERS said, "In our caste we do not throw down the pot nor do we cut goats." We Kui people replied, "In the Kond lands if the pot is not thrown down and the goats are not cut, then we get no rain and no crops. Even though you refuse, we shall do it on our own responsibility and you can go and make a case before the Government that the men of Balimendi have slaughtered your goats. We shall most certainly do it to-day." Thus we spoke. They asked for it to be done the following day, and so went along there on Saturday.

'On Saturday morning all the men of the *mutha* assembled and bathed the Malik, who had fasted. Then they filled a new pot with water, and taking it on high before the house of the offender in Gomapara, the Malik threw it down. We all saluted *tana Penu* [the Earth]. Then we went to the herd of goats of Gomapara, and looking for the biggest we chased it and cut it down as it ran, while the PANS played their drums and pipes. The goat happened to belong to a POTTER of Gomapara. The POTTERS then gave us Rs.1 to pour a libation of liquor.

'Then we went to Manipara. But when the father of the offender saw us coming he started to run away. His son had not been seen since the meeting on Thursday. The people of the *mutha* persuaded the father to come back. The Malik filled a new pot with water and going into the forecourt of the offender's father's house, he saluted the Sky above and the Earth below, and lifted the pot of water above his head and threw it down. The father then gave us Rs.1 to pour a libation of liquor. When the libation had been poured we went to the Manipara herd of goats and picked out a big one and cut it down as it ran. It belonged to the headman of Manipara.

'The goats were then taken to one place and butchered. Four shares were allotted according to the four village clusters. These were again divided for each hamlet.'

My informants stated clearly that sins against the Earth's purity within an immigrant lineage were sins against the purity of the Earth of the whole clan-territory. But this is a statement of theory and it does not mean that such offences are always in practice followed by the prosecution of the offenders and the purification of the Earth. Such offences tend to be winked at, unless they are committed brazenly, or unless it is in someone's interest to make trouble for the offenders or their relatives. Offences are often brought to notice only when natural disasters indicate that the Earth has been polluted. These crises result in the clearing of an accumulation of offences from previous years. In a *mutha* such as Balimendi it is more likely that offenders will be prosecuted. Balimendi is much more a corporate group than is Besringia. In Besringia corporate action in such a situation by the entire *mutha* is usually taken at the initiative of the Oriya Sirdar, and not by the Konds themselves, and this action usually has reference to Oriya values rather than to Kond values. But in Balimendi the Konds are still capable of united action in defence of their own values, not only without reference to the Oriya Sirdar, but even in opposition to him (Case 38: p. 197). As one would expect, the institutions in which the old territorial clans were active survive to-day in Balimendi to a greater extent than they do in Besringia.

RELATIONSHIPS WITHIN THE FOUNDING CLAN

The founding clans continue to exist—being recruited internally—within a larger community. The clans no longer have important political functions. They can no longer make war. The positive parts of clan cults have declined, and the negative part of the Earth cult, although as strong as ever, applies not now to the clan but to everyone who lives on clan territory. But in the kinship system the localized clan still continues to function as an exogamous group.

The cult of the Mountain which formerly activated the whole clan has now become a village cult. The positive part of the Earth cult is carried on by the hamlet or by the individual. I have conjectured that in the past the clan's act of positive worship was the rite of human sacrifice, the successor of which to-day is the buffalo sacrifice. At the present day this rite is sponsored by a hamlet and an individual, and although it draws people from a wide area of the countryside, it is not a cult which in any way defines the clan: and it is very rarely performed. The negative parts of the Earth cult, on the other hand, survive intact, both as a means of defining relationships within the founding clan, and relationships between the founding clan and the immigrant lineages.

Within the founding clan the rule of exogamy survives, but occasional challenges are made.

(Case 23)   (Time: *c.* 1945)

A girl of Daminga was made pregnant by a man from Dakpal. These two rank as brother and sister, so that this was an act of incest. The men of Daminga went and axed some goats from the Dakpal herd. The people of Dakpal then went to the Magistrate and complained that some drunken men from Daminga had butchered their goats. The men of Daminga were imprisoned, until a deputation, organized by the elders of Daminga and supported by an influential Oriya contractor, explained the motive for their action. The men of Daminga were then released.

I doubt whether the Dakpal people were denying their common dependence on the Earth with Daminga, so much as denying that their man was responsible for the girl's pregnancy. I was not able to find out how the case was subsequently settled. Another case which happened in the early 1930's was a definite and conscious attempt to evade the obligations of territorial clanship.

This case needs some explanation. The events happened in one of the *muthas* of the Six Lands.[1] The founding clans of these *muthas* are of a heterogeneous origin as are the clans of Balimendi and Besringia. Almost everyone in Besringia and Balimendi is surnamed Kohoro, and the few who do not bear that name are called Malik. But in the Six Lands Kohoro and Malik share the field with several other lineage names: Jani, Jhankero, Behera, Maji, Dehuri, Podhan, and others. Despite the difference of surname all were considered to belong to the one clan.

(Case 24)   (Time: *c.* 1940)

The daughter of a house surnamed Behera was made pregnant by a man of the same village cluster, whose surname was Maji. The Behera men held a council and then went along to attack the herd of goats of the hamlet where the Maji man lived. But the Maji people, having got word of what was coming, locked up all their goats and met the other party with the bland assertion, 'You are a Behera house. We are a Maji house. Therefore we cannot be brothers. There is no need to attack our goats. We will certainly take the girl for our bride.' The Behera people, baffled, finally went to the Government courts and tried to lay the case before the Magi-

---

[1] See p. 49.

strate. But when the Magistrate grasped its implications, he referred it back to be decided by the Konds themselves. Because the case had come before the Magistrate and he had instructed certain leading Konds to concern themselves with it, it was heard not only by the hamlets concerned, but in the presence of a large body of elders and advisers, from outside the Six Lands as well as from within it. The meeting had no hesitation in upholding the traditional patterns of exogamy, and the offending Maji houses had to provide goats for slaughter, to recompense the Behera people for their trouble in going to court, and to undertake the proper ceremonies of purification.

There was no doubt in the minds of those who told me about the case—nor it seems in the minds of the Kond council which decided it—that the Maji people were in the wrong, and knew that they were in the wrong. The case does not indicate a trend away from exogamy in the founding clans. It was an exception that tested the rule, and found that the rule was still backed by strong sanctions. The rule is, of course, evaded from time to time, and I have given an example in which the ambiguous status of the B1 segment in Baderi was used for this purpose (Case 6: p. 27). But, as an institution in which the unity of the founding clan is emphasized, exogamy shows no sign of a decline parallel to that which has taken place in the positive clan cults.

The founding clan has continued in existence by the process of internal recruitment and is still activated in exogamy and in the associated negative aspects of the Earth cult. These activities have not been affected by the presence of the immigrant lineages. On the other hand the corporate activity of the founding clan in the positive parts of the Earth cult has vanished, probably because that cult was initially suppressed by the Administration, and later because its substitute, the buffalo sacrifice, is both expensive and is frowned upon by the Hindus. The cult of the Mountain has also declined. These were institutions which linked the different villages in the clan, and there is now not the same need for this linkage, because the clan is no longer a group which is united for warfare. The founding clans, even with their known heterogeneous origins, have survived as kinship groups within the modern *mutha*. But they are no longer political communities in opposition to other localized clans.

DISPERSED CLANSHIP

The system of alliances and enmities between clans was frozen, so to speak, by the pacification of the area, and the corresponding system of agnatic relationships between the clans in different areas continues to this day. The people of the Balimendi clan still do not marry into the Tinpari clan, nor into the Bengrikia clan, nor with their blood-brothers of Rotabari. But they do marry with the immigrant lineages of those areas, and they say that such people do not really belong to Bengrikia or Rotabari, as the case may be, but are really Rupamendi people or Besringia people who have migrated there.

Although the 'alliances' which this form of agnation reflects can no longer be alliance in war, territorial clanship does survive to-day in relation to land. Those who migrate and go to the territory of a clan which had agnatic ties with their own clan are welcomed, and given the right to make fields in the waste, and may even be given cultivated fields by a friend, without objection by the community; and they will certainly, provided they are not well-known mischief-makers, be given a site on which to build a house (Case 16: p. 53).

The wider system of dispersed non-political clanship is changed and augmented as migration continues to-day. The Baderi people still refrain from marrying in certain villages in Ganjam—for instance in Mandipaderi, from where the B3 sub-segment came—in which they believe their distant agnates live. Nor do they marry into villages which have been colonized by segments which have broken away since the time of pacification from their own territorial clan, even though these segments come from lineages in that clan which originated elsewhere. For instance no member of the Balimendi clan, of any of the four clusters, will marry into a village which is peopled by the Jiura-Malika segment which comes from Balimendi, although they will marry into villages, which come from the Besringia Jiura-Malika group. In the old days, in the time when it was still possible to make war, a migration might result either in the dispersed form of agnation, where the migrant segment became a part of another already existing political community (as in the case of the Jiura-Malika people who came to Balimendi), or it might result in the political type of clanship, where the migrant segment colonized its own independent clan-territory. At the present day migration beyond the boundaries of the *mutha* must result in non-political agnation. Every one of these migrations, since the time of the pacification of the area, has diminished the total number of people who are united to others in the old system of territorial agnation. In former days their movement meant only a transfer of members from one territorial agnatic group to another or the creation of a new localized clan. Now they pass, so to speak, out of this system of political relationships altogether. These migrations represent, to use another metaphor, a running down of the stocks of the old type of territorial clanship, which is now maintained only by internal recruitment.

When I described the system of dispersed non-political agnation and the relationship between the clans,[1] I was in fact describing the total society. For Balimendi this consisted of the valley of the Salki river and the country to the east of it. People who lived beyond that area to the north and south and west occasionally appeared as migrants to intervene in the social system of the eastern Kondmals (as did the people of Damopara), but there were no regular and continued institutionalized relationships be-yond the boundaries of that area. Within that area, so far as Balimendi was concerned, everyone could be placed according to the clan-territories in which they lived, as either agnates and therefore allies, or as in-laws and potential enemies. For Balimendi the people of Katringia or Pobingia or Bakolomendi or Keringia in the western Kondmals belonged to another society. It is true that there were occasional remembered ties—as that with Mendi-paderi in Ganjam—and it is true that migrations do not seem to have respected cultural boundaries, but nevertheless contacts with these areas were sufficiently infrequent to make unnecessary any institutionalizing of relationships, of the kind that took place with-in the eastern Kondmals and the Salki valley. Except as migrants the people of the more distant clans do not appear in the Kond myths, or in the Kond traditions of warfare. The boundary was in fact a cultural boundary and remains one still to-day. The people who live to the west call the Konds of the eastern Kond-mals the '*sasi Kuinga*' or 'foreign Konds'. There are differences in dialect and small differences in custom which reflect this cleavage. The people of the east call the rest '*aria Kuinga*', the exact meaning

[1] See p. 53.

G

of which I do not know, but which was invariably translated into the Oriya '*osikhito*', which means 'uneducated', and in this context clearly meant 'jungly'.

The cultural differences between the country to the east of the Salki valley and the tract to the west clearly reflect the greater influence of Oriya culture on the east. Nevertheless the country to the east is not merely the area in which Oriya culture has penetrated most strongly. It was also a society—a group within which there was greater interaction than there was between any part of it and the world outside. Balimendi lies close to the western edge of this cultural area and it is much more Kui in its culture than are areas farther east. Kui is still the language of the home, whereas to the east Oriya is spoken in the home, and many of the brides who come to Baderi have to set about learning to speak the Kui language, and continue in old age to speak Kui with some aspirated consonants which are typical of Oriya and not of Kui. People who come from farther east will refer to Baderi as a jungly place. Nevertheless all the traditions of Balimendi point to its belonging to the eastern cultural sector and not to the west, and to its having been part of the society of the east and not of the west.

One would expect, with the pacification of the area and the growth of trade and the improvement in communications, that these social cleavages might have been crossed to such an extent that they would become blurred. In fact this has not happened. The sisters of the Baderi men do not marry any further afield than they did in the time when the area was not pacified, nor do the men of Baderi go further afield in search of brides. There are exceptions: but these are sufficiently exceptional to arouse comment. In the Baderi genealogies I recorded 235 marriages in which I was told where a wife had come from or the village to which a sister went. Of these 23 per cent connected Baderi with the eastern part of the Kondmals and 57 per cent were in *muthas* adjoining the Salki valley. Only 12 per cent were to the mountainous country in the west and 8 per cent were to distant villages outside the Kondmals, in Ganjam or Boad. 80 per cent of all recent Baderi marriages were within the region in which Baderi had political alliances and political enmities in the time of warfare.

The new economy has not promoted greater spatial mobility within the Kondmals. The people are still peasants, and the Konds in particular are still tied to the land, either as owners or as labourers, and they do not go far afield in search of work.[1]

Nevertheless the change that is taking place in the group that was formerly the Kond political community is the result of migration and spatial mobility. But this change is not the result of any large-scale immigration of Konds from outside the society. The boundaries limiting interaction *between Konds* (disregarding for the moment the most recent developments which have resulted from the Adibasi movements[2]) have remained the same. The personnel, if I can put it that way, has not changed. The movement which has given rise to change is internal and does not spring from the arrival of strangers. (It does of course spring from the arrival of the Oriyas and the Administrators, whose role in the changing society I will discuss in more detail later.[3]) The change I am discussing here is within a society. The immigrant lineages of the last hundred years are no more strangers than were the immigrant lineages in the old days of warfare: the change lies not in the personnel or the numbers of people involved, but in their mode of incorporation, and in the fact that this incorporation was no longer in the traditional pattern.

CHANGE AND CONSERVATION

In setting out to describe change I have in fact been more concerned with conservation. Warfare came to an end one hundred years ago: the *raison d'être* of the system of incorporation and amalgamation of stranger lineages into the territorial clan vanished one hundred years ago. But the territorial clans are still clearly discernible, and I had no difficulty in identifying the members of the founding clans in each *mutha* which I surveyed.

From one point of view the change can be described in terms of institutions. The territorial clans were identified by the three forms of institutional activity: warfare, agnatic kinship, and a common dependence on the Earth.[4] Warfare has gone com-

[1] See pp. 186–192.
[2] Migration to the Tea Gardens of Assam is an exception (see p. 102). But I am here talking of movement within the Kond Hills.
[3] See Chapter VII.
[4] Day-to-day economic activities are carried out by the household, with extra labour hired or recruited through inter-caste links, which are described in Chapter VI. These activities do not involve wider lineage or clan relationships.

pletely. The common dependence on the Earth is not now the exclusive badge of the territorial clan but of the modern *mutha*, which is a territorial group, but not a clan. The territorial clan scarcely survives as a political unit. But this is essentially a description in terms of structure—of groups and the activities which relate them to one another. For various reasons it is unsatisfactory.

There are two ways to describe these changes. One way is to identify the two ends of the process and to take, so to speak, a still picture of the structure of the society before the process of change and after the change. The structure from which the analysis begins is one of agnatic clans, localized on particular stretches of territory, membership of the clan being a condition of the right to live on that territory and exploit its earth. At the other end of the scale is a society in which agnatic affiliations have nothing to do with the membership of territorial groups, and in which the right to land is validated by the Government and by the status of Indian citizenship. But there is a degree of extremity about this kind of description, a certainty of radical change, which is not borne out by our material. This kind of statement is a delimitation —a preliminary mapping-out of social change. But by itself it is an inadequate description of change.[1]

The 'unity' of the clan is not merely the relationships between its parts. It is a process by which uniformity was imposed on relationships which were initially heterogeneous; a process by which political loyalties were diverted from one group to another; in concrete terms, a process by which outsiders were incorporated into the territorial clans. The change consists not in the disappearance of one type of structure and its replacement by another, but in the ending of the process of incorporation. Conflicts within the clan may now pitch people into a different political system. But as a structure of relationships the territorial clans survive, and can continue to survive indefinitely by the process of internal recruitment. The founding clans *may* vanish: but there is no reason to conclude that they *must* vanish. I have identified the point at which the political structure of localized clans stopped growing: the point at which strains in the system cannot be adjusted within it and lead to structural change. But the ending of growth is not the same as extinction.

[1] Techniques for describing change are discussed again at pp. 251 ff. and 262.

CHAPTER V

CONTINUITY IN THE VILLAGE

IN this chapter I discuss the way in which the agnatic structure of Baderi village, described in Chapter II, is affected by migration and an unequal distribution of wealth at the present day. The total society has ceased to be an arena in which territorial clans compete for the control of land: and the territorial clans have ceased to be political units. Membership of them alone no longer gives command over resources. But the village is still an arena in which individuals compete with one another for land, and membership of the agnatic group in the village is still an important qualification for land. In the struggle for land within the village external relationships are important, and these are of a novel kind, since they are with the agents of commerce and with Government officials. In spite of this the village remains both a political community and a political arena, in the way that the clans have not. It remains difficult for outsiders to compete for land within the village unless they first enrol as members of the lineage which owns the earth of the village, and furthermore the village acts as a corporate political unit, not against other villages, but against individuals who attempt to make use of the rights guaranteed to them by the Administration (Case 1: p. 17).

UNEQUAL WEALTH

Some migrations are caused by local shortages of land. But this statement, although it is not false, does not indicate the complexity of the process. Shortage cannot adequately be described only by the ratio of people to land.

By the standards even of India the Kondmals are poor. For the land under cultivation there are too many people: few can save and fewer invest. Out of 75 Kond households in Baderi there are 71 which own some land: the average income per household from their own land is 66 units of paddy a year. This is gross income and the expenses of cultivation and the maintenance of implements are not deducted from it. The average needs in these same house-holds *for food alone* is 69 units of paddy. No allowance is here made for clothing or other expenses, and even in the category of food allowance is made only for the two main rice meals of the day, and nothing is allowed for the snacks which most people take in the morning, and for the rice which is used to entertain both in-formally and (more expensively) at ceremonies. Consequently the real deficit is bigger than the average of 3 units a year. Against this there are other sources of income from which this deficit may be made up, the principal one of which for a Kond is turmeric grown for a cash market.

The absolute shortage of land in the village could be represented directly by giving the ratio of population to cultivated area. But no figures are available for the cultivated area. Even if they were, this ratio would be unsatisfactory without qualification. Shortage must be measured against a given technique of exploitation, and against the capital available for opening further land. There is land in the Baderi valley which, with extensive use of capital to level, to provide fertilizers, to sink wells, and to build dams or tanks for the storage of water, might be brought under cultivation. But no capital is available. The shortage is not simply of land, but rather of land which could be brought under cultivation by existing techniques and with the capital that is aavilable. Alternatively there is a shortage of capital, which, with new techniques, might bring under cultivation land which is now beyond the margin.

This absolute shortage is not the cause of migration, so much as shortages caused by unequal distribution. There are rich and poor in the village and potential migrants are among the poor. The distribution of land is shown in Table 4. Among the eleven people in the top category, all but two enjoy an income of between 100 and 160 units[1] of paddy from their estates. One has 358 units: and another 523.[2]

---

[1] For the method of calculating these figures see F. G. Bailey, 1957, 277–84.

[2] These figures are enough to show the unequal distribution of property in the village, but they are not in themselves adequate measures of the prosperity of the households concerned, particularly in the middle of the Table. Those who have land bringing them in less than 40 units of paddy every year are badly off, for that figure is just enough to provide food for two adults. Those in the topmost category, conversely, are likely to be well off, but in the middle range those who have large families are likely to be poor, and those who have small families or none at all, are well off. However, my purpose is not to

TABLE 4

DISTRIBUTION OF LAND AMONG KONDS IN BADERI VILLAGE

(annual income from land owned, measured in units of paddy)

Categories	100 plus	80–100	60–80	40–60	20–40	10–20	–10	Total
Households	11	5	12	13	16	10	4	71
	15·5%	7%	17%	18%	22·5%	14%	6%	100%
Income	2,144	438	822	652	457	134	21	4,668
	46·5%	19·5%	17%	14%	9·5%	3%	·5%	100%

The accidents of inheritance are in some cases responsible for wealth and poverty. A single line of heirs tends to keep an estate intact. A rich man is likely to be succeeded by poor men, if the estate has to be divided among several heirs. The converse of this is inheritance from collaterals. The biggest estate in the village— that of the headman Ponga—was built up in this way. Ponga's grandfather inherited not only from his father, but also from his father's classificatory brothers, one of whom, Sahebo, had been very rich. Both Ponga and his father were only sons. Nikara is another example.

(Case 25)   (Time: contemporary)

Nikara Kohoro is one of the richest men in the B4 segment and the richest man in Dobenisai hamlet. He has inherited the estate of his father's younger brother, Seme, who is now in the last stages of senility. His own younger brother Petura died, and Nikara has inherited his father's estate intact.

The estate of a man who has no sons does not always go to his heirs in collateral lines. Konds, no less than Hindus, dread to die without an heir. Without sons and grandsons an ancestor does not get proper and preferential offerings, and in time he is forgotten. Nor do men like the estate which they have maintained or built up during their lifetime to pass to their brothers, real or classi- ficatory, when very often the estate has been built up and kept intact through a series of disputes with these same brothers. The sons of these brothers, it is true, will make offerings to their uncle as an ancestor, but only after they have made the offerings to their own father. There are also practical questions. A man needs a son to support him and protect him in his old age. For these reasons

---

measure prosperity as such, but only to show that there is a great disparity in property-holding in the village.

men often adopt a son, who will be heir to the exclusion of collaterals in the lineage. Such an heir rarely comes from outside the lineage and I found no recent cases like those of Goli and Tunde (Cases 4 and 5: pp. 24 and 25). A favourite person to adopt is a real or classificatory brother's son, if that brother has more than one son. This son is often the one who would have succeeded if no adoption had taken place, but the arrangement ensures the survival of the social personality of the dead man—the fact that the son was an adopted son is forgotten as time passes—and it provides someone to look after the owner in his old age.

(Case 26)   (Time: 1955)

'On June 16th, 1955, Nasira Kohoro adopted Nojira, the son of Pudunga of the same lineage as himself [they have a common great grandfather], in the presence of the following persons: the Sirdar of Balimendi *mutha*, Goneswaro Bisoi; the village headman of Baderi, Ponga Lohoro; Liringa Kohoro; Kaboli Kohoro; Gunara Kohoro; Mongola Kohoro; Tuka Kohoro; Kari Kohoro; Binuro Kohoro; Beda Kohoro; Pudunga Kohoro; Manda Kohoro; Kosto Podhan; Nasira Kohoro; Jongora Kohoro; and from Bendisai village Sordaro Kohoro and two other persons.

'Nasira said, "I have no son and therefore in the future I might find life very hard. Therefore I decided that I will adopt a son. When I am an old man, he will look after me and my wife. That is why I have called you to this meeting."

'The meeting said, "If it is the wish of you two to make him a son, then we have nothing else to raise."

'The Sirdar of Balimendi then asked Pudunga, "Pudunga, is it your wish to give your son Nojira to be adopted by Nasira?"

'Pudunga replied, "I will give my son to him on condition that he should no longer cause trouble, and that he should not lose his temper with my boy. If he does lose his temper and the boy comes crying to us, then I will make trouble."

'Nasira agreed to this. Pudunga would not have spoken like this but beforehand Nasira had taken Pudunga's elder son Padri to adopt him. Nasira had beaten the boy who had returned to his own parents. Pudunga added, "The boy is very affectionate towards him, and he must take full responsibility for him and I will take none. But if there is trouble and the boy comes crying to my house, then I will not send him back again."

'Then everyone agreed that a document should be written by Pudunga and given to Nasira saying that he gave him his son for adoption, and a similar one written by Nasira saying, "From to-day

I have taken the son of Pudunga Kohoro, Nojira, to be my son. When I die he will be the owner of my land."

'This is done so that in the future no-one can make trouble.

'So that everyone in the village might know, Nasira gave the village one unit of rice, one goat, and three bottles of liquor. This was accepted and a feast was held with much rejoicing. According to their Kond custom in the place where they had met they poured a libation to the Earth, the ancestors, and the deity of the Sky, and then they drank the rest of the liquor.

'The Sirdar refused to sign the paper because he was waiting for his 'betel money' [i.e. a gratuity]. Then Liringa and the rest said to him, "Whether you sign or not we all know that to-day Nasira has adopted Nojira. It is nothing to do with the Sirdar."

'Before listing all his fields and naming Nojira as heir to them Nasira said that he was giving two fields, which he identified by name, to his daughter Ruduna. Even if she went elsewhere in marriage she could still enjoy the produce of these fields so long as she lived. When she died Nojira would have the fields. Nojira agreed to this.'

Nasira's motives are made clear in the text. If Nojira had not been adopted then all Nasira's land would have gone to Pudunga had he been alive, or would have been divided between his two sons. In the long run the result would have been much the same for the distribution of wealth in the village. But if there had been no adoption, and if Pudunga had but one son, then two estates would have fallen into the hands of one man—as it did in the case of Ponga.

I have dealt cursorily with inheritance since it is in no important respect different from the same process described in Bisipara.[1] But there are other ways in which fortunes are made or in which estates are broken up and their owners reduced to poverty. Bad management or misfortune can bring land into the market in Baderi as in Bisipara.[2] Such land usually goes to the rich. Those who have the resources and the skill to engage in financing, acquire large estates.

(Case 27)   (Time: contemporary)

Rupunga and Sanjo (BX) are to-day poor men. In their early manhood they were better off but they fell into difficulties and

---

[1] F. G. Bailey, 1957, 85–90.
[2] *Ibid.*, Chapter 4.

borrowed money and grain from Dibi Kohoro (B1). In time they became virtually his clients and whenever they needed money to tide them over to the next harvest, or to finance a ceremony, they got it from Dibi. From time to time Dibi made up the reckoning and took over a field belonging to Rupunga and Sanjo. He acquired the major part of the land around the hamlet of Dudopara, where Rupunga and Sanjo lived, and he built a house for his second wife near this land, so that she might manage it. Rupunga and Sanjo and their several sons work on this land, either as plough-servants or as casual labourers. Dibi died many years ago, but the widow still survives, living from this part of Dibi's estate. Rupunga and Sanjo have very little land of their own now. They need each year 225 units of paddy for food alone: the land they own brings in 63 units.

There are some differences between the pattern of contingent expenditure of the Konds and the Oriyas. The purificatory rite after a death is performed by a Kond at his own convenience, sometimes after two or three years when he has had time to get together the money required for the feasting. An Oriya must perform the equivalent rites within twelve days of the death. While the brideprice among the Konds is on the whole much higher than among the Oriyas, nevertheless the girl's father does not try to extract more than he can return in the dowry. To be the father of many daughters is not a calamity for a Kond as it is for an Oriya. Thirdly the practice of 'stealing' a girl as wife is more common among the Konds, and Kond youth-dormitories, where unmarried boys and girls may flirt with one another, makes 'stealing' much easier than among the Oriyas, who maintain a rigid sex-division between young unmarried people. An Oriya can get a wife for nothing, but even the poorest rarely do so. Konds do so frequently.

Inheritance and management contribute to the rise and fall of estates, but there is also a third process which causes a differential distribution of wealth in Baderi. The politest name for it is 'legal brigandage'. I found some evidence of this in Bisipara, but not much: a great deal of this brigandage had gone on in Baderi. The difference may lie only in the information I collected, but it is also likely that land-grabbing was inhibited by the relative sophistication of the people of Bisipara. The most spectacular 'brigand' in Baderi since the turn of the century was Dibi Kohoro, whose name is known throughout the eastern Kondmals, both among Konds and Oriyas.

'Even from his boyhood days Dibi Kohoro, the son of Manura Kohoro, was a wicked person. He got married when he was about twenty and from this wife he had no issue. At that time he was the strong man of Baderi. As a result of being a powerful man he was able to get a large amount of land registered in his own name. But the Government was helping him. The Saheb [Magistrate] at that time was "The dried-up one" and Dibi got on very well with him. The Saheb took his word on everything. Thus Dibi paid no attention to anyone else. If he went to Phulbani or even to the courthouse then the *babu* [clerk] or even the Saheb himself would have a chair put for him. In this way he got to think of himself as a great fellow. But when it came to reading and writing he was a fool [i.e. he was illiterate or barely literate]. But he thought to himself, "I have got everything except a son." And he was sad. "God's will!", he said, "I'll take another wife." So he brought a wife from Donisugi, a village in Khejuripara. The marriage went on and after three or four years there was still no issue from this wife, and so he decided to get divine favour by adopting an attitude of indifference to worldly wealth and by doing virtuous deeds. With this in mind he began to build a tank. After he had begun the second wife gave birth to a son. The building and sanctifying of the tank was done at great cost.

'It was the Kond custom to give as bride-wealth cattle and buffaloes and large brass pots and so forth. But as the years went by the price of cattle increased and a number of educated Adibasis canvassed a policy that money should be given in place of cattle and buffaloes. Dibi sided with this party, and said that although there was much more money about, the price of cattle had risen very much. The other side said that they should stick to ancient custom and give cattle and buffaloes, and important men on this side enlisted the support of the Government. At this Dibi said, "If poor Adibasis can give cows and buffaloes for a brideprice, then, if the need arises, and an Adibasi is filing a suit, let him give the court fees in the form of cattle and buffaloes. If the Government accepts them, then we agree to go on giving cattle and buffaloes for bride-wealth."

'When he had become a wealthy man Dibi thought he would have a word with the Saheb and become the Sirdar of Balimendi. He secretly prepared a petition. Goneswaro Bisoi's brother Kasia Bisoi, who was then the Sirdar, heard about this and he too wrote a petition. He also went about saying, "What sort of Sirdar would this ignorant Kond make?" Dibi heard about this and was very angry and made a petition even to Cuttack [the capital of the Province in those days]. On hearing this Kasia Bisoi himself went to Cuttack, and Dibi's petition got no further. The Government told him that he could not become Sirdar. So he said to himself, "Well I can't be the Sirdar. I'll be the village headman." Hearing this Kasia Bisoi called together all the important men of Baderi and of Balimendi *mutha* and said, "Look! If Dibi becomes village headman he will make a lot of trouble for you. So I've called you together to discuss it." Everyone said, "Well, we won't give him the job." They wrote a petition to the Government. Several petitions were sent in, but in the end it came to nothing. So Dibi was disappointed.'

I have given this text at length because parts of it will serve later. It gives the current mythology about Dibi: his strength, his lack of scruples, the astute use he made of his personal friendship with the Administrators, his ambitions, and his championing of the Kond cause.

Dibi's father, Manura, was a man of moderate means. The enormous fortune, much of which was spent in building the tank, and of which enough is left to make Dibi's surviving widows two of the richest landholders in Baderi, was amassed by Dibi himself. He died about 1930, and I am unable to substantiate the account which follows with quantitative detail. I do not know how big was the estate which Dibi inherited from his father, nor could I put together the estate as it was before Dibi started to run it down. The account has to be fragmentary and relies on anecdotes, which concern his more spectacular—and discreditable—transactions.

(Case 29)   (Time: *c.* 1900)

Many years ago two Baderi men had a dispute about the ownership of a stretch of land which lies across the Salki river from Bisipara. One of these men was Dibi (B1) and the other was Sedoto (B3), the father of the present village headman, Ponga. The case went to court and in the absence of a proper Settlement and Record of Rights the court called for the testimony of the Baderi elders. The most telling evidence was given by Gugu (B2), and his testimony decided the case against Dibi.

After this Dibi made life very difficult for Gugu and his son Druba. They were waylaid and beaten up from time to time, and in the end Dibi took over some of Gugu's best fields. Druba and the old man abandoned their fields around Baderi and moved across the Salki river and founded the hamlet of Majisai, where Druba's son

Silu, now an old man, heads the hamlet. These events must have taken place about the turn of the century.

Dibi and his heirs have kept the land in Baderi and their title to it is undisputed since it was later registered in Dibi's name.

(Case 30)   (Time: *c.* 1910)

Jaya and Mongola are two brothers who live in Baderi and are now about fifty years of age. When their father died they were still small children. Dibi approached the widow and offered to cultivate her land as a share-cropper. This arrangement continued until the boys were of an age to take over the land themselves. Then Dibi refused to hand back the fields. With the help of other men in the village the boys took the case to court, but Dibi had anticipated them and had registered the fields in his own name. They never got the land back.

After this the leading men of the village sat down together and made a rule that the same man should not be allowed to cultivate a field as a share-cropper for more than one season. This rule is still observed to-day in Baderi.

Jaya and Mongola have been to work in the Tea Gardens of Assam. They are still very poor men and own between them land bringing in only 24 units of paddy each year, while their needs are for 90 units. Jaya's son works as a plough-servant in the house of another Baderi Kond. They have between them one yoke of oxen, which they use for cultivating turmeric, and which they hire out, with themselves as ploughmen, when the work on their own land is completed.

(Case 31)   (Time: *c.* 1926)

The fields in Kendrisai (Case 32: p. 103) were built and owned by several different people from Baderi, but the only person who went to live there was Sudersun, who was urged to do so by his classificatory brother, Dibi. Both belonged to the B1 segment. Sudersun began to encroach on the fields of the others. Time and again the village council had to consider complaints against Sudersun, that he had diverted water from other fields, planted them before the owners had a chance, stolen crops, and developed fields on the margins of other people's fields, where the latter had themselves intended to expand. Nothing the village council could do seemed to restrain Sudersun, and he has almost the whole of his life been ostracized by the village. But no-one else, other than the family of Buduro and Moni, who were poor men and in any case clients of Sudersun, would go and live in Kendrisai and attempt to restrain him.

Finally Dibi said that he would use his influence with the Government to get title to the fields in Kendrisai registered. That would put an end to the constant dissensions, since there would be a clear title to be produced before the Government courts.

When, some time later, someone attempted to bring a case against Sudersun, it was discovered that Dibi had arranged to have all the fields in Kendrisai registered in Sudersun's name.

I have records of other transactions of this kind by Dibi and there must be other less spectacular coups which I failed to record. Dibi acquired many fields in more regular ways by purchase. Other things being equal, a rich man can get richer, and the difficulty lies in acquiring the first capital sum. The more flagrant violations of justice probably belong to Dibi's earlier years. So far as I can work out the dates, the persecution of Gugu and Druba and probably the seizure of the fields from Jaya and Mongola must have taken place in Dibi's early manhood. Later he had sufficient capital to purchase fields, and to engage in a more subtle form of 'land-grabbing'.

ALTERNATIVE SOURCES OF INCOME

The main source from which the village makes up its deficiencies in subsistence farming is turmeric, a root which is exported to the plains of India, partly for culinary use, but mainly for dyes. Not inappropriately the root has the colour of gold.

In Bisipara almost everyone trades for turmeric. Capital is provided by the merchant-shopkeepers, and there are virtually no restrictions upon or qualifications required of a trader. Trading takes place during the hot months, when there is no cultivation, and no resources in time and labour are drawn off from subsistence farming.

Growing turmeric, as distinct from trading in it, is not free to everyone. A minimum capital is required, and this cannot be got as an advance from middlemen and traders. Secondly, in order to grow turmeric, some resources have to be diverted from rice-growing. Turmeric fields are made on patches of fairly level ground on the mountainside. In some parts of the Kondmals the fields are made in very steep places and are cultivated with a hoe, but no-one in Baderi will grow turmeric where they cannot use oxen to plough the land, and those who have no oxen do not grow turmeric.

3a. Turmeric in the yard of a house.

3b. Turmeric field in the jungle

Considerable labour is involved in turmeric, and in the initial stages the work clashes with the rice-harvest. In an example which I recorded the cultivator began in October 1952. He selected a site, and cut down the trees and brushwood. This took eight days. He let the brush lie for a few weeks and then set fire to it. The conscientious cultivator spreads the piles of ash evenly over the field, but my informant said that there was not enough ash to make this worth while. In November he ploughed the field for three successive days. He and his wife and their young daughter spent a week in picking stones off the field and piling them at its lower edge, along with the larger stumps which had been axed out of the ground before ploughing. In May 1953 the field was again ploughed and tubers from turmeric roots were planted. When the planting was finished branches were cut from the surrounding jungle and spread over the field to shelter it from the hot sun. A fence was built to stop cattle from eating the young shoots and from damaging the plants when they were grown higher. This complete operation took eight days and the family was helped by the informant's wife's brother who was visiting them at the time. The field should have been weeded in August 1953, but my informant was too busy with his rice fields. The field was then left until the hot weather (February to May) of 1955, when the roots were dug out at leisure. The family spent about two months, off and on, at the task. After this they broke off parts from the better roots to be used as tubers the following year and stored these in a specially built bin. The remainder of the crop was boiled, scrubbed, and dried in the sun. It took my informant a week to gather enough wood to make fires to boil the roots and a further three or four days to boil them and scrub them clean. At the time I took down this information 106 pots had been boiled, and it was hoped that the field would yield altogether about 140 pots, which, at the rate current at the time, would bring in about Rs.180. Most cultivators start a new field every year, and so at any one time have three fields at one or another stage of growth.

In spite of the labour involved almost everyone who has oxen grows turmeric. Out of 25 sales of which I have record in 1955, the growers received an average of Rs.220 each, with the lowest figure at Rs.30 and the highest at Rs.400. The income from turmeric, therefore, must be counted as a main factor in keeping landed estates intact and enabling the farmers to balance their budgets, although in many cases they are short of irrigated rice-land.

There are virtually no ways of making a living available to the Kond peasants in Baderi outside the agricultural economy. The substantial peasants lend paddy and rice at interest, just as men of similar status do in Bisipara, and there are some who lend money.

There are no crafts which a Kond can take up, for these are all in the hands of the appropriate castes. Most men know some carpentry, but there is no-one who makes a substantial income out of it, as do several men in Bisipara. There are in Baderi no ritual specialists with a profitable clientele. There are no shops and no non-agricultural employers of labour, as there are in Bisipara. Only one Kond, in the whole of the Baderi cluster, owns a cart, and that was acquired in 1954. There are no traders of any kind among the Konds of Baderi, and very few among Konds elsewhere. In Bisipara old women peddle salt and spices around Kond villages: other women trade for paddy to be made into parched rice or to be husked and sold as rice: the men trade for turmeric and the flowers of the *mahua* tree, for eventual sale to the distilleries, and for oilseeds and lentils which the Konds grow. Other men work as agents in the weekly markets. But no Kond, in Baderi at least however poor, will try his hand at trade. The Baderi Konds will not even carry their turmeric to the merchant's shop in Bisipara: but they will sell it to a Bisipara middleman and then act as his porter. They consider trading to be at once beneath their dignity and beyond their capability. Trade, they say, is better done by the Oriya, and any Kond who tried to break into the market would soon find himself outwitted.

Most of those in Baderi who have not enough land work as agricultural labourers. Six are regularly employed as *holya* (plough-servants) and they are fed and clothed for nine months of the year. The great majority, men, women, and even children, are *mulya* (casual labourers) who are paid little more than is required to feed them for the day on which they are employed. The need for this labour rises to a peak during the planting season, and there is another and smaller peak during the paddy harvest. The conditions of employment, and the seasonal demands, are the same in Baderi as in Bisipara,[1] with the exception that men find work in the turmeric fields.

[1] F. G. Bailey, 1957, 117-24.

Planting Turmeric.

4*b*. Spreading leaves on a Turmeric field.

MIGRATION

An obvious recourse for a man whose estate is too small is to break new land. This cannot be done by the destitute, for new land requires capital. No-one who is without a team of oxen can break new land or cultivate it. Even if he has oxen he also needs a surplus from other sources to maintain himself and his family when the new field is being made. New land is broken not by those who are in desperate need, but rather by those who have capital to invest, by the rich and not the poor. Even if a poor man has capital, there are other difficulties. Land which is available for breaking to-day in the Baderi valley is marginal. It is in the remoter valleys, Dobenisai or Kendrisai, and to cultivate without also living there is difficult. Time is spent in travelling: the plough-cattle are tired by the daily journey: and the land must be watched to see that no-one drains off the water or steals the ripening crops, and that herd boys do not let cattle stray into the field. It is instructive to remember the way in which the Baderi community dealt with the man from Rupamendi (Case 1: p. 17).

Breaking new land by a poor man, except on the smallest scale, usually involves migration. The migrant may move within his own village, just as Sudersun went to Kendrisai (Case 31: p. 97), or as Druba went to Majisai (Case 29: p. 96). The migrant has to face the difficulties of maintaining himself while the land is not yet in full production. If he has enough land to do this, he is usually compelled to dispose of it once he has settled in the new location. Druba (Case 29: p. 96) could not maintain his hold upon the lands in Baderi.[1] The migrant may go to another village in his own clan-territory or to a *mutha* in which the founding clan is agnatically related to his own. The difficulties of procuring the necessary capital remain, and the difficulties of distance, if the migrant attempts at the same time to cultivate fields in his old village, become insuperable. He has either to sell those fields or to share-

---

[1] This does not mean, of course, that the land around each hamlet is culti-vated only by those who live there. It applies rather to the hamlets on the extremity—Majisai, Dobenisai, and Kendrisai. Land in the central belt around Baderi, Kamopara, Atisai, Pandrisai, and to a lesser extent Dudopara and Kinisuga is owned by people from all those hamlets, and there are no clear lines of demarcation among the fields according to the hamlet in which their owners reside.

H

crop them, and most people, in the end at least, prefer to sell them (Case 16: p. 53). The migrant who moves within his own village, or to another village in the *mutha*, or to a *mutha* where he has agnatic ties, has rights in the waste. He has a right to a house-site, and to cultivate in the waste, providing he does not injure another man's existing rights by, for instance, diverting the flow of water, or taking a site which someone else had already marked out for himself. If the migrant goes to a *mutha* where he has no agnatic ties, he is faced with a further difficulty in finding capital to buy his rights in the earth from those who own them (Case 19: p. 72).

These three courses are open to a man who has the resources and the determination to remain or to become a landowner. But not every migrant is able to do this, and some are forced to find other means of making a living. Some attach themselves as dependents to affinal or uterine relatives.[1] Some go to another village as agricultural labourers. Beda, who in the end became an affinal relative of the Baderi people, first came to Baderi as a plough-servant (Case 8g: p. 31). The larger Oriya villages, like Bisipara, offer a better opening both for those who go by themselves as plough-servants, and for those who go with their families and become either plough-servants or casual labourers.

It need hardly be said that Konds who are forced to leave their own village because they cannot make a living there, are not the sort who are qualified for jobs in the Administration or in commerce. These positions fall to the more educated Oriyas or Oriya PANS, who, even without formal educational qualification, possess the necessary sophistication. This does not mean, of course, that there are no Konds employed as messengers or peons. There are a few, but the Konds in general are less able to find employment with the Administration than are the Oriya-speaking peoples.

Some of those who fail to gain a living in the village, and a few people who have got into trouble go to the Tea Gardens in Assam. Once the migrant has enrolled and is accepted, his fares to Assam are paid, and he is escorted by a regular staff of agents from the moment he leaves the depot in Phulbani until he reaches the place where he is to be employed. The Tea Gardens preferred to recruit whole families, because an important part of the work is done by women, and because married labour is more stable. In view of informants who had been to Assam, there were many advantages:

[1] See pp. 27–40.

the rate of pay, even discounting such incidental benefits as housing and medical attention, was higher than the daily wage paid to a casual labourer in the Kondmals. The contract could be for three years or could be renewed indefinitely and some families settled in Assam. If the labour migrant returns, the same organization brings him back as far as the depot where he was enrolled, and there he is paid the bonus which he has earned. These bonuses could be quite substantial, and the small amount of land which Jaya and Mongola (Case 30: p. 97) now own, has been purchased with money which they made out of one trip to Assam.

Assam is often a phase through which the landless pass, trying one alternative after another. Tubutu Kohoro, who settled in his wife's village of Baderi under the patronage of his wife's brother and his own sister who is married into Baderi (Case 8*f*: p. 31), went to Assam on a three year contract. He returned and spent a year in his own village, and then came to Baderi. Of three Kond families which are settled on the outskirts of Bisipara, and which maintain themselves by casual labour, two have been to Assam. In a hamlet near Bisipara lives one of the only two Kond traders whom I met over a period of three years: he had been to Assam and with his bonus he bought a stock of trade goods which he uses at markets and fairs. From Baderi I have records of eight Kond families which migrated to Assam at one time or another for reasons of poverty. Three other persons went because it was the easiest way out of a difficult situation. (All three men had made pregnant either a classificatory sister, or a woman in one of the other forbidden categories (Case 2: p. 21).

Not all migrations in the Kondmals are the direct result of economic factors. But even when the occasion is not economic, poverty is usually a condition of the move: the ownership of a large estate both protects a man from pressures which might make him move and gives him a good reason for not moving. None of those who went to Assam because they had polluted the Earth were rich.

(Case 32)   (Time: *c.* 1870–1900)

The land around Kendrisai first belonged to the Maliks (see page 40). They gave it to their friends and allies BX. From the BX lineage the land passed into the control of B4 and about four generations ago, from the present grandparental generation, B4 are alleged to have sold the land to B3. There was a dispute about whether or not the land had been sold and the case was settled by an oath (*sarara*). It soon became apparent to the Konds that B3 had been in the right. One after another the people of B4 segment were afflicted with disaster: their cattle died: their crops were blighted: their women died in childbirth: their children died. It was apparent that the oath was working, and that the B4 segment would die out.

In fear of this they fled. One man went to Bengrikia and settled in the village of Lambavadi where the distant agnates of the Baderi people lived (Case 13: p. 48). Another went to Bisipara and worked as a labourer. A third went about from village to village, a different one each season, working sometimes as a plough-servant and some-times as a casual labourer. The fourth brother stayed where he was and he died without children, and was succeeded by his sister's son, who had lived with him (Case 8*d*: p. 31).

After a generation the B4 people slowly returned to Baderi. The man who had been to Lambavadi and the man who had been a labourer in Bisipara settled in Kamopara. The third man's family went to Dobenisai. By the present day several of them have become the owners of modest estates (Case 25: p. 91).

In this case the main motive for migration was not economic. Had it not been for the oath, the B4 people could have continued to make a living in Baderi. The same is true of the Pobingia sor-cerer and his victims who fled to other *muthas* (Case 20: p. 75)

The founding of Majisai (Case 29: p. 96) shows a mixture of economic and other factors involved in migration. The quarrel began over the ownership of land. Dibi, having lost his case, did not choose to attack the man who had defeated him, because this man was rich and powerful. He attacked the man who had given evidence against him, and who was poor and unable to protect himself. This man was beaten up and Dibi took his land. The victim abandoned his land in Baderi and went across the Salki river where both his person and his land were safer from Dibi's revenge.

There are various ways in which those who do not have enough land can maintain themselves and still remain in the same com-munity. But it is among the category of small landowners, or among those who have no land at all, that potential migrants are found. The occasion for the move is usually a conflict, which may have nothing to do with economic factors, but often has. Even then the ownership of property provides a powerful motive for not migrating, and makes for stability. Migrations and the process of fission and fusion in the Kondmals must be seen against a background of changes in the ownership of property.

THE EFFECTS OF MIGRATION

Migration can be considered within an equilibrium system and does not necessarily lead to social change. Those migrants who are related to the lineage through women take on the role of agnates, and in time become agnates. Otherwise they cannot acquire rights or power in the community. The number of these immigrants is small relative to the size of the whole group. The known accumulation over four generations amounted to no more than 15 per cent of the total Kond population in Baderi. The greater part of the heads of households among these had been born in Baderi and were advanced along the road towards integration.[1] The very small category of plough-servants is transient and their presence does not affect the structure of the village. There is no minority in Baderi clamouring against the monopoly of land by the main lineage. There are no strains and conflicts apparent, which might indicate that the structure is changing.

There is more ground for thinking that the founding of new settlements in the Baderi valley by segments of the main lineage might be a sign of structural change. The migrants who are dependent upon Baderi patrons do not form a corporate group in their own right, and they are a category of persons who do not act together and have no common aims. But the people in the newer settlements are corporate groups, and it might seem at first sight that these internal migrations, particularly when they are the result of conflict and violence (Case 29: p. 96), might threaten the unity of the village and the existing structure.

The people who live in the different hamlets describe themselves as Baderi people: they sit on the Baderi village council: when there is a death or a funeral in one of these hamlets, it involves people from all hamlets (with an exception to be noted below). The council which sat to witness the adoption of Nojira

---

[1] This figure, of course, does not represent the total immigration into the village over the last four generations. There are at least two cases known to me of men who had been attached to the agnatic core in this way and had died without leaving descendants behind them. There are likely to have been others, too, who either died, or who did not settle permanently in Baderi, but moved elsewhere.

(Case 26: p. 92) included people from Dobenisai and other hamlets, although both Nasira and Pudunga belonged to Baderi hamlet. The people who helped at the wedding in Sukara Kohoro's house (Case 35: p. 128) came not only from Kamopara, where Sukara lives, but also from Atisai and Pandrisai and Baderi and Dobenisai. Finally the meeting which met to consider what to do about the rebellious PANS (Case 35) included people from all the hamlets. On the other hand relationships within hamlets are not exactly the same as relationships which pass between hamlets. Each hamlet has its own priest and priest's assistant. The cattle and goats of the hamlets are herded separately. The men spend more of their time with one another than with people from other hamlets. But in spite of these differences the agnatic structure, as it is expressed in the cult of the Earth and in rights to land, is not impaired. The founding of new settlements is segmentation and a continuance of the existing *type* of relationship.

All hamlets, however, are not in the same position. Between Pandrisai and the rest of the group, particularly Baderi, there are hostility and exclusiveness which indicate fission rather than segmentation. Pandrisai men are not invited to marriage ceremonies or asked to assist in funerals in the other hamlets. If a Pandrisai man attends a ceremony in another hamlet it is because he is a particular friend of the sponsor of the ceremony, and he comes in this capacity, rather than as a member of the agnatic group. Rites and ceremonies in Pandrisai tend to be boycotted by the people of the other hamlets. I was told that this hostility goes back to an incident when the men of Baderi gave evidence in the Government courts against several men from Pandrisai who had been receivers of stolen goods.[1] The cleavage has developed in a series of disputes of greater or lesser importance. In the dispute with the PANS (Case 35: p. 128) it was the Pandrisai people who set the example of disregarding the decision of the village council. Pandrisai, too, is becoming a ritual centre for the propitiation of Pitobali, in whose honour they hold an annual festival which draws people from over the whole of the eastern Kondmals. This cult is an activity of Pandrisai alone of the Baderi hamlets. The organization of the festival and the perquisites arising from it belong exclusively to the people of Pandrisai. In this respect Pandrisai has achieved an identity before the world outside, separ-

[1] See p. 146.

ate from and not submerged in the identity of the Baderi cluster.
There is a similar cult—to Visnu in this case—in the hamlet of
Majisai, but it is not so well known as the Pitobali cult and does
not identify Majisai as a separate community, although, of course,
with better management, it might do so. Nevertheless both
Pandrisai and Majisai are in other respects counted as part of the
Baderi community. Men from both these hamlets attended the
important meeting about the PANS (Case 35: p. 128).

The tendencies towards fission which these migrations within
the village might bring about are counteracted in two ways.
Firstly no hamlet has exclusive rights to any particular patch of
waste (the turmeric field discussed at page 99 belonged to a
Baderi man and was adjacent to Pandrisai hamlet) and the irrigated
fields of the men who live in one hamlet tend to be interspersed
with the fields of men of other hamlets: secondly the hamlets
themselves are not all occupied exclusively by one segment.
Table 5 gives the residence of Konds of the main lineage.

TABLE 5

RESIDENCE OF SEGMENTS OF THE BADERI LINEAGE

(persons in main lineage segment)

Hamlet	B1	B2	B3	B4	Total
Baderi	25	17	28	10	80
Atisai	18	10	—	—	28
Kamopara . . .	—	—	—	10	10
Pandrisai . . .	71	—	—	—	71
Majisai	—	29	—	—	29
Dobenisai . . .	—	13	—	23	36
Dudopara . . .	4	—	—	—	4
Kendrisai . . .	4	—	—	—	4
Kinisuga . . .	2	—	—	—	2
Total	124	69	28	43	264

Of these segments only B3 is found in one hamlet only. Only
Pandrisai and Majisai have a large population of one segment only.
The fission involved in geographical separation is counteracted by
ties of descent and genealogical separation is balanced by ties of
residence. Spatial fission leads not to social fission, but to segmentation. Neither the immigration of individuals nor the movements

of groups within the village territory are evidence of structural change. They are rather to be counted part of the fluidity and flexibility, on which the strength and continuance of the agnatic structure of the village depend.

THE EFFECTS OF UNEQUAL WEALTH

Migration is one of the results of unequal wealth. I now ask what are the other effects of unequal wealth, both upon the agnatic structure of the community, and upon it in other respects.

It might seem that the presence of a small number of very rich people would make for a class division within the village. The dependents of the richer peasants are not only uterine and affinal dependents and the menial servants who have come from other villages, but also the many people in their own village who live either exclusively as dependents or who supplement an income from inadequate land by hiring themselves out for labour. Are any of these people second-class citizens in the community?

Dependents related through women and the menials are second-class citizens in that they have either no right to land, or a right which is doubtful and can be contested: they derive their membership of the community through their patron. They sit on the village councils, but they do not play a conspicuous part in the management of the village. In affairs of 'state' they are treated as of no importance. But they are not a separate class. There is no institutionalized way of symbolizing inferior status, as in the caste system, nor are they in less formal ways persons of 'lower class'. Their poverty earns them disrespect, but their manners are no different from those of their patrons. One of them, Beda (Case 8g: p. 31) married into his employer's household. Secondly they are not a class, but a category. They have no corporate sense, and they do not act together in opposition to the rich.

The same is true of the poor or landless Konds who have full agnatic rights in the community. There is no symbolization of their economic inferiority. They are not a group ranged against their employers. In the councils of the village they behave as equals and in some cases native wit or a ready tongue more than counterbalances their relative poverty. Wealth is unstable and for this reason does not give rise to economic classes with corporate aims and interests. Mobility up and down the economic scale is so rapid that it inhibits the development of groups with corporate interests, either among the rich or among the poor. The ambitious man does not fight to organize the poor and make the rich share out their wealth: he directs his energies to becoming rich.[1]

The instability of wealth has another effect, already partly described.[2] Fields are continually being bought and sold, as men are going up or down the economic scale. The buying and selling is not restricted within one hamlet, and the landowner is likely to possess fields in several parts of the Baderi valley, and not only fields which are adjacent to the hamlet in which he lives. This scattering of estates works against fission in the village cluster.

The concentration of wealth in a few hands is, paradoxically, a form of community saving. The poor are forced to accept a low standard of living and resources which they might otherwise have consumed are freed for investment. The wealth is not always invested in projects which are of benefit to the community. It is used to buy jewellery for the wives and daughters of rich men or to provide rich living. But in Baderi there has been some public investment. Dibi made many new fields and directly or indirectly caused two new hamlets to be founded and new fields to be broken around them. At Dibi's instigation and with Dibi's backing Sudersun emigrated to Kendrisai (Case 31: p. 97). Dibi was responsible, in an indirect way, for the founding of Majisai (Case 29: p. 96). The colonization of the Baderi valley is in part the result of the entrepreneurial activities of Dibi and people like him.

Dibi also made more spectacular investments. In his old age, with the intention of earning spiritual merit for himself in the way of the Hindus, he spent a fortune excavating a tank in Baderi. He was following an honoured Indian tradition and he was not especially concerned with the welfare of his fellow-villagers. Had he been, he would have sited the tank near the head of the valley so that the waters might be used for irrigation in the dry season. But the tank is beside the road, where the Baderi valley comes out on the plain of the Salki river, and its only use is for bathing, to the convenience of travellers and of the villagers, who would otherwise have to walk half a mile to the river. Even this benefit is restricted, since the tank is convenient only for those who live in the hamlets of Baderi (where Dibi himself lived), Kamopara, and

[1] F. G. Bailey, 1957, p. 166.
[2] See p. 107.

Atisai. People in other hamlets make use of springs and shallow wells. Dibi's largesse stimulated a rival, the father of Ponga (B3), to erect a small brick enclosure near the village well in Baderi, so that the women of Baderi might bathe there with modesty and not under the eyes of the village youth or of the ribald men who pass along the road on their way to market.

THE VILLAGE AS A POLITICAL COMMUNITY

I have up to this point evaded the main issue. Agreed that the system still survives, but does it still have the same functions? I have been calling the village a *political* community. To what extent, then, is a right to land still achieved by the status of an agnate in the village?

For rights in the waste, clan membership is necessary. I am, of course, talking about Kond relationships and a Kond system. The Forest Department is not inhibited by Kond rights from declaring tracts of forest reserved, or from selling the rights of exploitation to outsiders, who are not even Konds. But within the Kond system only clan and lineage members have an absolute right to make fields in the waste and to use it in other ways. Resident affinal and uterine kin, and persons of other caste who live in the village are also given the privilege of using the waste, but members of other Kond communities, unless they are agnatically related, are not given this right. The ambitions of the Rupamendi man (Case 1: p. 17) were thwarted by the Baderi people who refused to give him a house site. Here is another case, this time involving a Baderi trespasser.

(Case 33)   (Time: c. 1945)

My informant cut down a large tree in order to use it in building a house. This tree was growing close to the crest of the mountain which divides Baderi territory from Rupamendi *mutha*, and here the border runs not along the crest but below it on the Baderi side of the mountain. This border is not mapped or marked by the Administration, but my Baderi informant himself admitted that he knew all the time that the tree belonged to Rupamendi people.

They brought a case against him in court, when he had refused to pay compensation. The Magistrate ruled for the Baderi man, on the grounds that all borders of this kind must be reckoned according to drainage, and since the land drained into Baderi territory, it must belong to Baderi.

My informant quoted this case with enjoyment, relishing both his own duplicity, and the way in which he had been able to exploit the ignorance of the Magistrate.

The Magistrate thus made a clear pronouncement that rights in the waste were governed by residence, and, by implication in Kond eyes, by membership of an agnatic group.

At first sight membership of the community and agnatic status within it also govern rights in cultivated land. Rupunga and Sanjo tried to disinherit Montona on the grounds that he was a sister's son (Case 8*i*: p. 32). Pressure is put upon widows if they try to dispose of their late husband's lands to persons who do not have agnatic rights in the community. The rule that land should pass to heirs related through males is quite clearly stated, and even when fields were reserved for a favourite daughter (Case 26: p. 92), it was stipulated that when she died they should revert to the agnatic heir. Baderi put up a united resistance to the man from Rupamendi, who in the Government courts would have had a clear and undisputable title to the land (Case 1: p. 17).

But this last case makes clear the limitations on the power of the community to make membership of the agnatic lineage a condition of holding land. The right of the Rupamendi man to cultivate the field, in which he had bought the proprietary right, would have been upheld in any court. If he had been more determined, he could at least have prevented any Baderi man from cultivating the field, even if he had been unable to raise a crop himself. In an outright conflict, the right which is dependent on membership of the community must fall before the right which is validated by the Administration through its courts. It so happens that the methods of cultivation, and the comparative poverty of even the richest cultivators, make it difficult to work an estate which is dispersed over several villages. (There are estates of this kind in some Kond villages, usually owned and managed by Oriyas, but there are none in Baderi.) Residence elsewhere is not a legal bar to holding land in a Kond village. *In this respect* (legally but not always in fact), the Kond village has ceased to be an exclusive political group: it no longer has the last word in the distribution of land, and membership of the group is no longer a condition of owning land within it.

In internal relationships (that is, in the village as a political arena) command over land is not validated solely in the system of agnatic

relationships. If the community is to get its will, it has to make use
of outside relationships, not always with the results intended.

(Case 34)   (Time: *c.* 1890–1950)

In all Dibi had at least six wives. Some of these were divorced or
ran away and one died in childbirth with the child she bore. After
Dibi had devoted himself to a life of charity one of the wives bore
him a son, called Narongo. This son grew to manhood, but died a
few years before Dibi himself. When Dibi died his property was
held by two widows, who are still alive and who are known in
Baderi by the villages from which they came, Donisugi and Giruti.
Dibi had two houses, one in Baderi hamlet and the other in Dudopara, and each house was maintained by a number of fields. Giruti
has the house in Dudupara and the fields attached to it: Donisugi
has the Baderi house and its fields.

Dibi has no lineal descendants and the property should eventually
revert to the two persons nearest to him in the lineage. These are
Baloto and Sudersun:

```
 ┌─Nonga─ ─ ─Dada─ ─ ─ ─ ─ ─ ─Baloto
 │                                        (Persons in italics
 ├─Manura─ ─ ─Dibi ─ ─ ─ ─ ─ ─Narongo        are alive.)
 │
 └─Kolya ─ ─ ─Sudersun─ ─ ─ ─Mokola
```

When Dibi died his major good work—the tank—was unfinished.
The two widows completed the work and paid for the expensive
ceremony of consecration. The widows have a right to maintenance
from the estate as long as they continue to live in Baderi and remain
unmarried, but they may not, under ordinary Kond custom, dispose
of the estate. In fact this rule is interpreted liberally and there would
be no objection if land were sold to other Konds in Baderi for a
good reason. The widows did sell some fields when they were
completing the tank. The village would only take action and would
only support the collateral heirs Sudersun and Baloto in restraining
the widows, if they proposed to sell the land to outsiders, or if they
tried to hand it over to their own kinsmen from Donisugi or Giruti.
After their death the land will be parcelled out between the two
collateral heirs. So long as they live they can continue to hold it,
and both of them cultivate the land with the help of plough-servants
and casual labourers.

One year Sudersun took some fields. He ploughed them and
planted them in spite of the protests of the widows. When he
continued to disregard them the widows started a case against him

in the courts. The men of Baderi, no doubt remembering what had happened to the fields in Kendrisai (Case 31: p. 97), turned up in force to give evidence in favour of the widows. The case went in their favour. All of Dibi's property, which had still appeared in the Record of Rights under his name, was then registered in the names of the two widows.

I suggest that this was dangerous. My informants agreed that it might have been, since the widows, having the land in their own names, might eventually be able to leave it to their own agnates. No-one thought this likely to happen, not only because the widows were upright and well-disposed towards the village, but also because it was well known that the land had belonged to Dibi.

It was suggested to Baloto about this time that he might get himself adopted as a son by the widows acting in the name of the dead Dibi. Half the land would in any case fall to him, and if he were already the adopted heir, there would be no more encroachments by Sudersun. The widows, apparently, were willing to make the arrangement just for this purpose, and the village would have been glad to see Sudersun excluded. But Baloto himself refused: he said that Dibi was fated to die without a son, and if he were adopted as Dibi's son, he too might die. The people do not anticipate trouble when the widows die, because they are sure that Sudersun will already be dead. Sudersun's son Mokola is a decent man who will take his share without making the trouble that his father would undoubtedly make.

After they had won their case the widows made a present to the village of the crop that Sudersun had sown in the fields. This was used to start a grain loan fund, which has grown from year to year under the management of the village council.

Sudersun lay low for a year or two and then again he took some fields and planted a crop in them. Fifteen fields were involved and they all belonged to the Donisugi widow. She went again to Phulbani, but instead of starting a case she approached the Magistrate and said that she was too old to go to all this trouble, and she would like to hand the fields over to the Government. The Magistrate said that the Revenue Department could not accept fields, but the Department of Tribal and Rural Welfare were looking for a site to start an Ashram School. If she would give a suitable building site for the school the Government would erect it, and it could be endowed with the fifteen disputed fields, and any other fields she or other people in the village cared to give. The widow agreed to this and provided a site beside the main road. When the site was inspected it was found to be too small and several other people were impressed into giving part of the land which adjoined the waste which the widow handed over. They did so, much against their will, and the school was built. It now owns the fields and lets them out to share-croppers, apart from one large irrigated field which has fallen into such dilapidation that no share-cropper will take on the work of bringing it again under cultivation.

The village does not like Sudersun and he has been virtually ostracized since his misdemeanours at Kendrisai (Case 31: p. 97). But the village has no effective sanctions with which to restrain Sudersun, other than appealing to the Government courts. Such appeals do not always have the results intended. Power within the village community is achieved not only in the relationships which exist inside that community, but also by manipulating relation-ships with the Administration.

CHANGE AND CONTINUITY

In its outward appearance the village must have changed considerably during the last hundred years. The tank which Dibi built has been in existence for less than thirty years. The Ashram School is hardly more than ten years old. The appearance and siting of the village houses have changed. A hundred years ago, so my informants said, the hamlet was ringed about by a six-foot fence of thick planks driven upright in the ground, to protect the village both from raiders and from wild animals. The jungle was thicker and came down close to the edge of the hamlet. Much less of the village land had been brought under cultivation.

These changes are to be attributed to a growth in population and to the greater security in which people have lived in the last hundred years. The ending of warfare, the cutting back of the jungle, the slow elimination of the more dangerous animals, pre-ventive medicine, the control of epidemic diseases, and the control of famine, have all combined to lower the death rate and permit an increase of population.[1] Pacification, the control of famine, and preventive medicine are the work of the Administration. The Administration has also brought about less tangible changes.

[1] It is not possible to substantiate this statement with figures since one hundred years ago no counts were taken, and I was unable to get population figures for the village even a decade ago. I base the assertion that there has been an increase in population on my knowledge of what has happened else-where in India under similar conditions in areas for which figures are available.

There have been changes in the economy, particularly towards diversification: there are many more ways of earning a living outside agriculture than there were a hundred years ago. Most important of all, the burden of securing life and property has been lifted from the village and the clan: it is now the business of the Administration. Men still travel through the jungle armed with axes, but this is no longer because they fear other men when they are outside the boundaries of their own community.

But in the village there is also much unchanged. The village is still a Kond village: there has been no inundation of alien settlers. The men of the village still make their living from the land, and they are still peasants tied to the land. They do not invest capital outside the village, and very few of them make a living by leaving the village and working elsewhere. The village continues to be recruited internally, by descent, and all but a few in Baderi are living where their grandfathers lived and tilling the land which their grandfathers tilled. The village continues to be a group of people related to one another by agnatic descent (or its fictions), and even when strangers come into the village, these are mostly Konds and, if they remain, can eventually be absorbed as agnates.

Even the struggle for land within the agnatic group is not new. There has always been competition between the different households. There have always been quarrels, and fission and migration. There have always been bullies like Dibi, and even the techniques which bullies use are not entirely new. The prize has always—during the period I am surveying—been rice-land. But there is one difference: property is protected by the Administration. Formerly the ambitious man relied to a greater extent on obtaining within the village a following, which would back him against his rivals: such a following is still desirable, but it is no longer necessary (Cases 31: p. 97 and 34: p. 112). There is now an additional resource in the hands of the ambitious man: the relationship which he can establish with the Administrators. He can use this relationship to achieve his ends within the village. Even this is probably not entirely novel, for before the coming of the Administration there were other powerful personalities whose backing would enable a man to overcome his rivals within his own village. But in so far as there is now a single and ubiquitous authority, relationships of this kind take on increasing importance in the struggle for land within the village.

The clan lost its political functions. Formerly fission had not changed the type of political relationships: later it resulted in some people taking on a new type of political relationship. Fission takes place in the village just as in the *mutha*. Those who go to Assam, or who go to work in Oriya villages, or who go as migrant labourers from one village to another, have, so to speak, passed out of the system of agnation and land, and entered a new system of political relationships. Such command as they have over resources is not achieved by membership of an agnatic group within a village. But they are not landowners. For a Kond to own land it is still to a large degree necessary to be a member of a group of agnates in a village. There are exceptions: some Oriyas own land in Kond villages: occasionally Konds own land in villages which are not their own. But these are very few. By and large the village and the lineage have preserved their integrity as a political community. The village has not, like the localized clan, become a kinship group within a larger political community, within which right to land is not connected with agnatic kinship. We cannot identify a 'before' and 'after' in the case of the village: nor can we identify a process by which one type of relationship is taking the place of another. The ending of external recruitment is the process in which the clan loses its political identity. But in the case of the village external recruitment is still only achieved by the recruit eventually taking on the obligations of agnatic kinship.

The changes—or rather the absence of change—in the village are seen more clearly against the background of what happened during the same period in Bisipara. There, at the beginning of the period power lay in the hands of the WARRIOR caste alone. They owned the land and they monopolized force. They formed about one fifth of the population of the village, and persons of other caste achieved their share in the resources of the village by being dependent on the dominant WARRIORS. During the past hundred years the WARRIORS have largely lost this power. Land is now distributed among other castes, and the people of lower caste are no longer dependent on WARRIORS for making a living. The other castes now tend to act as corporate political groups in their own right, and in opposition to the WARRIORS, and this change in the distribution of power has led to many conflicts in the village. At the same time Bisipara is involved much more deeply in the wider economy, and has been affected to a much greater degree than

Baderi by immigrants, who have not been absorbed into the traditional system of WARRIOR dominance.

But this has not happened in Baderi. Baderi was, and continues to be, a Kond village. Power and property have always been, and still are in the hands of Konds. Individuals have always risen to and fallen from wealth and power. The difference now is that the ambitious man has a new weapon—his relationship with the Administration.

I have carried my analysis from the simple to the more complex. I first described, as a static structure, relations within the main Kond lineage of Baderi village: ties of kinship and ritual coincided with and re-inforced political ties. I then made a dynamic analysis of the clan. Taking for granted, for the time being, the factors which set the structure in motion, I considered the ways in which the structure coped with these disturbances, and how various kinds of relationships were converted into a type of agnation. In the third stage of the analysis I began to consider outside forces which affected the Kond political structure. The structure always has been affected by such outside forces as the fertility of the land, the rise and fall of population, and so forth. Without considering these one could not explain what makes the structure dynamic. But there are also outside forces of a different kind. These are not demo-graphic or natural factors, but the coming of 'rival' political systems—that of the Oriyas and that of the Administration. The Kond clans, as a political system, have been changed: the Admini-stration, so to speak, has put them out of business as political units. In the village this has not happened: the village continues as a political arena and a political community: but in the working of this political system the Administration has become an important 'outside' factor.

In the following chapter I continue to describe Baderi village, but at a level of greater complexity. Political activity takes place not only between the Konds of the village, but also between them and the PANS and other dependent castes. I shall describe the Kond-PAN political structure, both in its static and in its dynamic aspects. I shall also show that political activity takes place not only in the Kond system and in the Kond-PAN system, but also across these systems and between them and the 'modern' system.

I

PART TWO

KONDS, PANS, AND ORIYAS

CHAPTER VI

THE KONDS AND THEIR DEPENDENTS

BESIDES Konds there live in Baderi four other castes:[1] Kond PANS, Kond SMITHS, Kond HERDSMEN, and Oriya HERDSMEN. Their numbers in the population are given in Table 1. Throughout the Kond hills PANS, SMITHS, HERDSMEN, and POTTERS are distinguished in the relevant contexts by the adjective 'Kond' or 'Oriya'. The Kond SMITHS and Kond HERDSMEN and Kond POTTERS are castes distinct from their Oriya counterparts, and the two communities, despite a similarity of name and usually of occupation, neither intermarry nor interdine. The Kond groups are inferior. Most clean Oriya castes accept water from an Oriya HERDSMAN, but none take it from a Kond HERDSMAN. The latter will accept not only water but also cooked food from an Oriya HERDSMAN, but this is not reciprocated. I met no Oriya SMITH families, but informants said that they are ranked above the Kond SMITHS, and, if an occasion were to arise, the latter would accept food from the former. The origin myths of these castes indicate inferiority. They are said to be the descendants of an Oriya man of the caste concerned and a Kond woman, both of whom lost caste by this union.

PANS are untouchables. The gulf between Kond and Oriya PANS does not seem to be so great as in the clean castes. They may dine with one another, although they do not often do so. An Oriya PAN girl of Bisipara married a Kond PAN of Baderi and this union was recognized as a proper marriage. The children of the marriage were acknowledged by their relatives on both sides. Nevertheless, although the difference is not expressed in ritual, Oriya PANS consider themselves much superior to Kond PANS, and although they recognize the latter as their 'brothers', they nevertheless regard them as stupid and uncouth.

In Bisipara there is a large group of Kond POTTERS, who are culturally almost completely Oriya. They supply a priest who performs village rituals in the Kond idiom—principally the cult of

---

[1] For the way in which I use the term 'caste' see F. G. Bailey, 1957, p. xv.

the Mountain and the Earth; but in all other respects they are Oriyas. They speak Oriya: they live in Oriya-type houses: they are admitted into Hindu temples as a clean caste (as are the Konds and all the clean hybrid castes) and they practise Hindu rites. But the Bisipara Kond POTTERS are exceptional. For the most part the adjective 'Kond' attached to the name of one of these castes, indicates that its members live in Kond villages, speak the Kui language, and follow the Kond rather than the Oriya ritual idiom.

Hybrid castes which live in Kond villages are ritually, politically, and economically subordinated to the Kond landowners. Konds will not accept food or water from their hands, whereas the specialist castes will accept these things from a Kond. They are forced to build their houses either in a separate location (in the case of untouchables) or else at the ends and not in the middle of a Kond street (in the case of SMITHS or HERDSMEN). At a feast they sit apart from the Konds and are served after them. They are not landowners. For their living they are dependent on the Konds, typically in *jejemani* service.[1]

In this chapter I describe the system through which PANS and other dependent castes achieve command over economic resources; and I ask how this system is maintained in spite of differential growth in population, and how far it has changed in the last hundred years.

HERDSMEN AND SMITHS

The numbers of HERDSMEN and their distribution between the hamlets of the Baderi cluster are given in Table 1. The Oriya HERDSMEN who live in Baderi, Pandrisai, and Kendrisai are one lineage, and are said to be descended from a common great-grandfather, whose name is not known, of the present generation of middle-age. An unrelated lineage lives in Majisai. All these households are employed by their respective hamlets as cowherds. They also make a living from the sale in Oriya villages of milk which Konds never drink. Some trade in salt and spices, and all work as casual labourers in agriculture. The household in

---

[1] For a description of the *jejemani* relationship in the Kond Hills see F. G. Bailey, 1957, p. 97. Briefly, the *jejemani* servant receives an annual grain payment, and in addition daily or *ad hoc* payments at less than the rate paid by customers who do not make the annual payment of grain.

Kendrisai has land which brings in 14 units of paddy a year (less than is required to provide food for one person), and one of the households in Pandrisai has land worth 17 units of paddy a year. The annual needs for food alone of these two households are 54 and 72 units respectively. No other Oriya HERDSMAN owns land in the Baderi cluster.

The Kond HERDSMEN are two separate lineages. One of these consists of two households in Baderi: the other also has two households, one in Dobenisai and one in Dudopara. All these families find employment as cowherds, the two in Baderi taking the cattle of one street, while the Oriya HERDSMEN take the cattle of the other street. They sell milk and work as casual labourers in the fields. One of the households in Baderi has land which brings in 2 units of paddy each year. Neither caste of HERDSMEN can be called landowners. Their living is derived partly from herding and partly from agricultural labour. Their upbringing and traditions fit them for herding, and both they and the people of other castes consider herding to be their proper—in both senses of that word—task.

Just as the landowners may grow too many for their land, so also the number of HERDSMEN may exceed the demands of the community in which they live. In other communities there may be a shortage of HERDSMEN. The genealogies of HERDSMEN—and SMITHS—show migrations in every generation which far exceed in number migrations in the landowning castes. I failed to write a genealogy of the Oriya HERDSMAN who lived in Majisai. The genealogy of the other lineage of Oriya HERDSMEN reveals a wide dispersion. My informant's grandfather first came to Baderi. The elder brother of this grandfather lived in Robingia *mutha* in the western-central Kondmals, and his descendants have dispersed to other villages, all of which my informant did not know. My informant's elder brother was born in Baderi but has since gone to work in Phiringia village. The younger brother of the grandfather also came to Baderi and settled in Pandrisai. Then, for reasons unknown, the family moved to a village called Subornokhol in Ganjam. After some years they came back to Pandrisai to take the place of a Kond HERDSMAN who had moved to Baderi. One of the descendants of the youngest grandfather has gone to be the herdsman in Kendrisai, where Sudersun has given him a small plot of rice-land. The Kond HERDSMAN lineage which lives in Baderi has a similar history of migration. The grandfather of my informant lived in Komari village, where he and his elder brother looked after the herd. They were unable to make an adequate living and the younger brother came to Pandrisai, and from there to Baderi. Of the grandsons, the informant lives in Baderi hamlet; the children of his eldest brother live in Pandrisai; the next eldest brother lives in Kumberiguda village; the next has gone to Koladi village. The other lineage of Kond HERDSMEN is found in Dudopara and Dobenisai. The father of my informant in that lineage came from Manipara village and settled in Dudopara. The informant's elder brother, who now is dead, went to Dobenisai where the work is now done by his widow and her three young sons.

There are several alternatives open to a HERDSMAN family which grows too large to be supported as herdsmen by the village in which it lives. In the instances I have given they migrated elsewhere. Speaking roughly, there seems to be a shortage of herdsmen in the Kond hills. Two factors contribute to this. There are occupational hazards in herding greater than in any other type of work in the Kondmals. The good herdsman takes his cattle or goats up into the jungles, where good grazing is found well away from the cultivated areas. This exposes him to the dangers of the jungle. Tigers and leopards are attracted by the herds, and although very few of these are habitual man-eaters, the herdsman may be killed because he excites the tiger's suspicions or, in a few cases, because he tries to defend the herd. One of the Kond HERDSMEN from Dudopara was killed about three years ago. Both the father and the maternal uncle of the Bisipara HERDSMAN were taken by tigers, and the Bisipara HERDSMAN is a reluctant herdsman who stays in the valleys and is in constant trouble because his herds get into the crops. The second factor which makes the demand for HERDSMEN exceed the supply is that the smaller the herd under his control, the better the herdsman can look after it, and the more willing he is to take it higher into the jungles where richer grazing is found. Every hamlet prefers to have its own HERDSMAN, and a large hamlet like Baderi divides its herd into two parts and employs two HERDSMEN. In Bisipara there are two cattle HERDSMEN and a third looks after the goats. Finally, perhaps because of the occupational risks and perhaps for other reasons, the castes of HERDSMEN, both Kond and Oriya, have remained small in number.

All the HERDSMEN in Baderi make at least a part of their living in their traditional work, but they all support themselves as well by casual labour in agriculture. In a few cases in other villages HERDSMEN live completely from this latter source, but there are none in this category in the Baderi cluster. The opportunities in the diversified economy which are open to landless Konds are also open to HERDSMEN, and one of the lineages in Baderi contains a household which went to Assam. In the eastern Kondmals there are two villages of HERDSMEN—in both cases Oriya HERDSMEN—who are landowners, having been settled on land granted them by the Administration in return for service as *paiks* (militiamen).[1] It may be that these settlements contribute to the shortage of HERDSMEN who are willing to follow their traditional calling.

Seasonal variations in demand for their services do not affect herdsmen as badly as agricultural labourers. Cattle are herded for about nine months in the year, from the second half of June when the first rice seed is sown until the last of the lentil crops are reaped in late February. The work is spread relatively evenly throughout the year and does not come in two periods of crisis—planting and harvest—as for the agricultural labourer. Some HERDSMEN find work looking after buffaloes in the hot season. At that time cattle are turned loose. Cows and oxen return to their stalls in the evening, but buffaloes wander off into the jungle and become wild. They are then exposed to wild animals (although a herd of buffaloes will defend itself against a tiger), they wander far afield, they become difficult and dangerous to catch, or they fall a prey to thieves. For these reasons well-to-do men, who own several buffaloes, band together and employ a HERDSMAN throughout the hot season to pasture buffaloes and bring them home at night.

Like the HERDSMEN, the SMITHS have few difficulties from seasonal variations in demand. Demand rises during the cultivating season, when ploughshares and other iron tools are most in use. But work continues throughout the year for, like cultivators everywhere, the Kond peasant employs the leisure of the hot months in repairing and renewing his implements. Axes are needed the whole year round, and if the SMITH can acquire a stock of iron, the slack months can be spent in making goods for a future market. The SMITHS are few in the population and

[1] See p. 201.

demand for them exceeds the supply, although the SMITH's clientele is drawn from a wide area, covering many villages, while the clientele of a HERDSMAN is confined to the hamlet in which he lives. The genealogy of the SMITH family in Baderi and Pandrisai reveals a pattern of migration similar to that of the HERDSMEN. This, together with the fact that in three years during which I visited many villages, I never found a household of SMITH caste which was not employed in its traditional work, seems to indicate that their numbers have not yet grown to a point where they cannot all be employed.

Neither the HERDSMEN nor the SMITHS have been much affected by the coming of the Administration and the arrival of a commercial economy (with the exception of the founding of the HERDSMAN villages which I mentioned above), nor have they been affected by changes in the political system of their Kond masters. Change has tended rather to preserve the traditional *jejemani* relationship between Kond and HERDSMAN or SMITH than to destroy it, and the relationship is not marked by the conflicts which are found in the Kond-PAN or Oriya-PAN relationships. The dispersal of Kond villages and the founding of new hamlets have provided new work to meet any growth in the HERDSMAN population that may have occurred. The thinning of the jungle and the campaigns which the Administration from time to time organizes to exterminate the more dangerous vermin, must have made their work safer than it was in former days. The veterinary services, meagre though they are, must tend to raise the cattle population and so contribute work for the HERDSMEN. The SMITHS do not seem to have been hit by competition from factory-made goods, which are better and cheaper than those locally produced. Any loss which this might have caused is made up by the greater number of iron implements which cultivators now possess and the need to service them. Konds do not throw away worn implements. Axes, ploughshares, and hoes are used year in and year out, and sharpened down until the stump is welded to another piece of iron to make a new implement. This work is done by the SMITHS, and, indeed, there are not enough SMITHS to do all the work. Both in the Industrial School in Phulbani and in an Ashram School at Boida village there are facilities for training blacksmiths, but the output of trained men is as yet too small to affect those who learn their craft in the traditional way. The outlook for

SMITHS is good in that there will be more iron implements, both on the farms and elsewhere, and SMITHS will be employed to service them. Even now they derive a small income from repairs to bicycles and umbrella frames and the iron tyres of cart-wheels.

An indication of the absence of change is that in Kond villages those who belong to specialist castes are almost all employed in their traditional occupation. They make ends meet, when a family grows too large, or in times of seasonal difficulty, by working as agricultural labourers. But they have not become landowners. It is difficult for them to do so, for while the Konds do not object to the giving of a small plot of land—and it often is given as an incentive to come to the village—they would not look with favour on a person of specialist caste who showed signs of becoming a substantial landowner. The fields which Sudersun has given to the Oriya HERDSMAN in Kendrisai are still registered in Sudersun's name, and Sudersun would not hesitate to resume the land and give it to another HERDSMAN, if the present owner did not work efficiently. It would be difficult for a specialist to work anything larger than the smallest estate, because his own work keeps him occupied throughout the cultivating season. In short, ready migration and an overall shortage of SMITHS and HERDSMEN have allowed the traditional system of relationships between them and their Kond masters to continue unchanged.

THE BADERI PANS

There are 81 PAN untouchables in the Baderi cluster, comprising in all fourteen households, making 17 per cent of the total population. There is one household each in Atisai and Majisai: six households in Kamopara: and six in Baderi hamlet. The household in Majisai and the household in Atisai belong to one lineage. The grandfather of my informant lived in Baderi first, and then migrated to Darikeju village, where his sons and grandsons were born. The two grandsons returned to Baderi village, one to Atisai and the other to Majisai. Of the remaining twelve households which live in Baderi and Kamopara, ten are of one lineage and two households are one lineage attached to the large lineage by links through women.

For their rice meals alone these houses need 1,224 units of paddy a year. Their total holding of land provides 159 units. Their average need is 87 units per household: average income is 11 units. As a group, therefore, the PANS need to earn over 1,065 units of paddy each year, and the average deficit in each household is 76 units. Three households are without any land at all: one has land worth 52 units: one has 27: two have 18: and the rest have less than 10. The PANS, with 17 per cent of the total population, hold less than 3 per cent of the cultivated land.

I shall describe the role of the PANS in the village, and the changes in that role, by analysing a dispute which took place in 1955 between the PANS and their Kond masters.

(Case 35)   (Time: 1955)
'On 22.3.55 there was a feast in Kamopara. The reason for the feast was that Sukara Kohoro's eldest son Komolo had brought a bride from Jambopara on 21.3.55. Invited to the feast were Konds and PANS who had come to escort the girl. On 22nd, a Tuesday, the feast was held in Sukara's house. When the cooking was finished the Baderi people called their in-laws to eat. When they were coming to eat the Baderi PANS, Dulu Digal, Balu Digal, Telungu Digal and Bira Digal, sat down with the visitors to share the feast. While the men of Baderi were serving their visitors with rice and dal and vegetables they noticed that the Baderi PANS were sitting with the visitors. Seeing this they got angry. Liringa and several other men went over to them and said: "When we have first served our visitors we will eat whatever is left. Why are you sitting down here with our visitors? You get up quick and go away. We won't allow you to sit with our visitors." The Konds gave the PANS a good telling-off. The PANS got very angry and fled away to their own street.

'They called all the PANS there together and had a meeting, and then they all came along to pick a quarrel with the Konds. They said, "The Konds invited us and so we came. Then, in front of the visitors, why did you make a show of us and drive us away?" The Konds too got very angry and they went on quarrelling for a long time. The Konds were about to set on them and beat them up when the PANS took fright and fled into their street.

'That same night the Baderi PANS went in their anger and slashed the leather on the side-drums and iron-drums of the visitors. When the visiting PANS saw what had happened they told the Konds, and the Konds summoned a meeting and ordered the Baderi PANS to attend. When told of the reason for the meeting the PANS were furious and only thought of fighting. The PANS slapped Liringa twice, and they slapped Ginda from Pandrisai hamlet once. The PANS didn't listen to what was being said, but they just left the meeting. So the Konds arranged that on the 24th they would hold a meeting in the schoolhouse to discuss the affair.

'On 24.3.55 the Konds of Baderi, Pandrisai, Majisai, Atisai, Kamopara, Dudopara, Dobenisai, and Kendrisai, all of them, assembled under a mango tree near the school and held the meeting. The gist of what was said was this: "We brought the PANS here and set them up. Since the Government started calling them Harijans, they now no longer obey us. If we say anything to them, then they just come out for a fight. A day ago they hit someone. To-morrow they will surely hit us again. There is no doubt about this." This was in everyone's mind. At the meeting they made these decisions. "From to-day no-one will give fire or tobacco to the PANS. They will not be called to funerals or feasts. If anyone has made a loan to a PAN, then he will press to have it back. If anyone has given them a *mahua* tree, then he must take it back. In the same way those who have given gardens or fields to PANS, as their clients (*proja*), must take them back. Anyone who breaks these regulations will pay a fine of Rs.25 to the meeting." They all agreed to this. Then this was added: "If the PANS want to rejoin us, then a full meeting must be called." All this was written down and everyone signed it. The paper was handed over to Silu Kohoro of Majisai and they told him to keep the paper safe, for it might be of use to them.

'After this the meeting broke up.'

This text was written by Damodoro Bisoi, an Oriya of WARRIOR caste from Bisipara, who is employed as a schoolmaster in Baderi. He attended the meeting on March 24, 1955, he wrote out the declaration, and he wrote in their names against the marks of the illiterate. I discussed the case with him, with Liringa, and with Ponga (the village headman), but I did not make satisfactory contact with the Baderi PANS and hear their point of view.

The incident at the wedding seemed at first inexplicable except on the assumption that everyone was drunk. When a Kond bride comes to her husband's house she is accompanied by four categories of people. Her main escort consists of the women of her village. Three or four men from the groom's village guide the party (a ceremonial role since everyone knows the way between villages and no marriage reaches that stage without an interchange of several visits). From the bride's village come about half a dozen men, not her close kinsmen, but men hired by her father to carry the bridewealth which she takes to her husband's house. The party is accompanied by the band of the bride's village, consisting of five or six men, all PANS.

The visitors are feasted by the groom's father. They do not all sit down together, but in separate castes, each group sitting in a straight line, and facing so as not to be looking at anyone else who is eating. Then men are served before the women, and the Konds before the PANS, the hosts passing along the lines and ladling out rice and curry onto the leaf-plates and leaf-cups, which are placed before each person. The guests are joined by one or two people of the host's village. These are not the host himself and his immediate family, but people who have special ties of friendship or kinship with the visitors or who have played an important part in arranging the marriage. It is expected that the Baderi band of musicians, who perform with the visiting band when the bride arrives in the village, will also share in the feast: and other PANS, who have not played in the band but who are close friends of the visiting PANS, or who are connected by some special tie to the groom's father, may be invited to the feast.

All PANS are beggars. They symbolize their dependent status by begging from the Konds. They are not beggars by profession, living solely from this source, nor do they beg indiscriminately and continually, but only on certain occasions. At harvest-time they are licensed to wheedle a handful of paddy out of the owner of each field. At every festival they visit each house and ask for food. They are skilled and importunate beggars, and they do not ask as a favour so much as by a right which is theirs as the dependents of the Konds. They are doing a favour by giving the Konds an opportunity to demonstrate superior status and wealth. The Konds at Komolo's wedding knew beforehand who would be invited to eat, but they attended the feast ostensibly to give assistance and to entertain the visitors. The PANS made no bones about it and sat down in a line with the PAN visitors, without waiting to be asked.

Sukara Kohoro was unfortunate in living in Kamopara. The hamlet consists of the houses of himself and his classificatory brother, and, fifty yards away but still part of Kamopara, six PAN houses. The feast was on the PAN doorstep and they turned up in force. Not only the four men named in the text, who as elders and musicians would probably have been accepted as legitimate guests, but also a host of younger men who had been standing around looking on, presented themselves to be fed. One man after another joined the line until the Konds felt they had to call a halt.

This could have been done tactfully, as I have seen it done on other occasions, by appealing overtly to the status of senior PANS and implicitly to their cupidity. It would not do to say bluntly that there was not enough food to go round, for this would brand the host as mean or poor. Rather an appeal is made to the senior PAN to keep his young men in order, and to see that they behave like juniors waiting until the end and not sitting down beside him as if they were themselves elders. This gambit might have been successful, but Liringa did not use it. He may have been too heated to think about it, or he may have thought that it would not work. He rounded on all the PANS. He did not strengthen himself by splitting elders from juniors, but castigated all indiscriminately, treating the older men who undoubtedly had a customary right to attend the feast as if they were juniors, thus welding all PANS into a solid opposition. The senior PANS had a real grievance: they had been invited by the Konds (perhaps by Sukara), or they may have been presuming upon their customary right as dependents and musicians. Then Liringa abused them in front of the visitors and drove them away.

They made a vain attempt to return and have the matter out on the spot, but were driven away by Liringa's vituperation and by the threat of violence. That night they damaged the visitors' drums. I do not know why they did this and my informants would only say that they must have been drunk. It is, however, possible that they had tried to persuade the visiting PANS to show solidarity either by walking out of the feast, or by making some kind of demonstration against the Konds—such as by refusing to play when the visitors left the village. The Baderi PANS may have been angry at the visitors' refusal to do so. By tradition a PAN has no loyalty to other PANS, and his loyalty is due rather to his own master and to the dominant caste in his own village. In the traditional system the castes were not ranged in opposition to one another: rather the dependent castes are divided among themselves by their loyalties to masters of higher caste. Political cleavages ran not between castes, but between villages, or between factions within villages. This is now changing and the lines of cleavage are beginning to pass between castes. There is a tendency, in other words, for the castes rather than the residential groups to become corporate political units. The Baderi PANS may have appealed to the Jambopara PANS to help in the struggle against the Konds in Baderi, and may have been angered by an old-fashioned assertion that what went on between the Baderi PANS and their masters was no business of the Jambopara PANS.

Liringa took the initiative in driving the PANS away from the feast, and he took it again the following day when the PANS were called to account for damaging the visitors' drums. His prominence earned him a blow in the face and he took the initiative for the third time in organizing the meeting near the schoolhouse. The second meeting differed fundamentally from the first. It was intended by Liringa and those who supported him that the first meeting should be a judicial assembly. The Baderi PANS would be summoned before the meeting: evidence would be given against them by the Jambopara PANS: the Baderi PANS would be allowed to state their case, and the body of Kond proprietors would then sit in judgement on them, make them pay for the damage, and punish them or accept their apologies. The Konds were to sit as a court, partly as a neutral body to adjudicate between the Jambopara PANS and the Baderi PANS, and partly as a group of masters determining what was to be done with unruly servants. As it turned out the Baderi PANS—not in so many words but more dramatically by their actions—did not recognize the Kond assembly as a court, assaulted one of its leading members, and then departed without trying to justify themselves and without even listening to the charges.

The Konds were thus forced to convene the second assembly not as a judicial body, but as a group meeting for political action against another group, whose equality they thus recognized implicitly while overtly denying it. They did not attempt to summon the PANS before them again, because they knew that such a summons would have been ignored. The Konds could no longer meet as a court to consider a breach of the law and to compel the offenders to submit to trial. There is no recognized legal procedure for dealing with the issues involved in this situation, neither in the law of the Administration nor in the customary law of caste, if I may call it that. For the latter is not framed to deal with a head-on collision between two castes as corporate groups, but only lays down the proper behaviour between a person of high caste and a person of low caste: the law is framed on the assumption that the low castes do not combine for corporate political action. Nor could the Konds have made use of the Government courts, even if they had considered such a course, since a village meeting of this kind is not a statutory body, and refusal to recognize it is not an offence. The meeting which assembled on 24.3.55 was not, therefore, a judicial council but rather, to use a metaphor, a council of war. At the meeting the Konds first set out to justify themselves before their own consciences, to make clear to themselves what offences the PANS had committed and what rules they had broken, and to declare other reasons which made counteraction necessary.

The principal complaint was that the PANS had behaved as citizens of the village equal to the Konds: '. . . they now no longer obey us. If we say anything to them, they just come out for a fight.' The Konds deny that the status of a PAN in the village is equal to their own: PANS have no ancestral right in the land, and inasmuch as they make their living in the village, their right to do so is the right of a dependent and a condition of their subordinate status. The main lineage of PANS was introduced by the grandfathers of the present generation of middle-aged Konds, specifically at the initiative of Ponga's grandfather. They had been given land on which to build their houses and they individually became the clients (*proja*) of the different Konds. They belong to the Konds and the Kond attitude towards them is that of an owner towards a serf, although they are not, of course, serfs in the eyes of the law. Liringa, in a moment of exasperation, said to me, 'Anyway, they're not *my* PANS. They're Ponga's. He should keep them in order.' Liringa himself keeps one of the PANS as his client and plough-servant, and his remark refers to the fact that the group was introduced to the village by Ponga's grandfather and not by Liringa's grandfather.

The group of PANS was brought to the village to serve two particular needs. Firstly, they provide musicians and scavengers for the village. The Konds of Baderi feel themselves polluted if they handle dead cattle or if they play musical instruments which in the Oriya village are played only by PANS or by other untouchables. These values are to-day found in most villages in the Kondmals and the Baderi Konds would probably be outcasted if they attempted to perform either of these tasks for themselves. Secondly, the PANS play an important part in the economy, as plough-servants and casual labourers, with whose help the Konds are able to manage at the time of planting the rice-seedlings and

K

again at harvest-time. Thirdly, the wealthier and more powerful Konds recruit their clients from among the PANS.

The correct traditional behaviour between a Kond and a PAN symbolizes their relative political and economic status. The PAN takes cooked food and water from a Kond: but a Kond cannot take these things from a PAN without being polluted. A PAN may not enter a Kond house, because his presence would pollute it and render necessary a ritual cleansing. Equally a Kond will not go into a PAN house, though in this case it is not the house which is polluted but the intruder. Touch defiles. The Kond addresses a PAN as 'son' or 'child' while the latter must reciprocate with 'father'. A PAN squats to converse with a Kond, if the latter is standing: or the Kond sits on a verandah, while the PAN must squat in the street. The PANS live in their own ghettoes. Their houses are smaller and meaner than most of the houses of the clean castes, and in the old street which adjoins Baderi hamlet the houses are crammed close together. The PANS may not use the village wells or bathing place, because they would bring pollution. Every aspect of their lives reveals the PANS in a position of ritual and social inferiority.

The complete and utter subordination, which this kind of behaviour symbolizes, is not found in the actual relationships between the Baderi Konds and their PANS. I have described the reasons for this change elsewhere[1] and I need only summarize them here. Wealth among the Konds is becoming concentrated into fewer hands than it formerly was. Fewer Konds are in a position to act as patron, and more of them have themselves to enlist as plough-servants or casual labourers. Within a more diversified economy, the Baderi PANS can make a living without depending so much on their former Kond masters. This process in Baderi is not nearly so advanced as it is in Bisipara. The Baderi PANS are Kond PANS and lack the initial advantages of speaking Oriya, living close to a good school, and dwelling in a village which is the economic metropolis for a large area.

All PANS in the Kond hills have a head start over their Kond masters in the race to benefit from the modern economy. They have always been middlemen, visiting markets in the plains, acquiring cattle for their masters, disposing of jewellery or buying it for them, and in the early days travelling far and wide to procure

[1] F. G. Bailey, 1957.

victims for human sacrifice. PANS still are middlemen in the remoter areas, where there are no Oriya villages, and where Konds still live a jungle-bound life. But the Baderi PANS have enjoyed these benefits less than the rest. Baderi is only two miles from Bisipara, and the Oriya traders from that village monopolize the trade in turmeric, while the Oriya PANS have an equally strong hold on the cattle trade. The Baderi Konds, living only two miles from Bisipara, the former headquarters of the Kondmals, and eight miles along the main road from Phulbani, the present head-quarters, are far from being so simple and gullible as their fellow Konds in the hills to the west of the Salki river.

But while the Baderi PANS are the losers in this respect, in another way they have benefited from their closeness to the centres of trade and civilization. Damodoro, the Oriya school-master from Bisipara, discussing this case, said, 'Of course, it's our PANS have started all this off. This Baderi lot have seen what happened in Bisipara. They know what it means to be a Harijan. Isn't one of them the son-in-law of our Jaya [one of the Bisipara PANS]?' Liringa too seized upon this: 'The Government calls them Harijans. They've seen that lot in Bisipara and that's where they learnt to behave in this way.' I think this reasoning is correct. The Baderi PANS do not number among them such strikingly rich men as those who lead the movement towards the emancipation of untouchables in Bisipara. Nor have they men with the pro-fessional achievements of the Bisipara PANS: none of them are schoolmasters and none of them are policemen. But they manage to ride along in the wake of the Bisipara PANS, and although the untouchable leaders in Bisipara did not take any direct hand in inciting the Baderi PANS against their masters, I think their example, coupled with a degree of economic independence, stimulated the Baderi PANS.

The Baderi Konds, under the leadership of Liringa, reacted in the way that the clean caste group in Bisipara reacted. They instituted a boycott. Bisipara is not the only village where this has happened. The Dutimendi Konds have ostracized their PANS and so have the Konds of Rasimendi village. But these boycotts are ineffective, for they cannot hit the PANS where it really hurts without also hurting the clean castes. In Bisipara and in Duti-mendi and Rasimendi the PANS have been deprived of their traditional privileges of music-making and of licensed begging at feasts and festivals. But this is not a mortal blow: it is no more than a pinprick. The PANS nowhere depend on their music-making for more than pocket-money. Their living is gained elsewhere.

The clean castes cannot deprive the PANS of their actual source of living, partly because it lies in a system over which the clean castes have no control, and partly because where they do have a measure of control, they depend for their own living on the labour of the PANS. The PANS supply that vital increment to the labour force which enables the cultivators to complete the work in the few short weeks of the planting season. I do not know what happened in Dutimendi and Rasimendi, but in Bisipara the leaders of the clean castes saw this fact clearly and no attempt was made to put a ban on the employment of PANS as plough-servants and as casual labourers. It was easy enough in Bisipara to get untouchables of a different caste to form the village band: but it would have been impossible to recruit enough labour to take the place of the PANS if the village had decreed that no PAN was to be employed as a casual labourer or a plough-servant.

Liringa and the Baderi Konds overreached themselves and would have made matters even worse, if it had not been for the intervention of Damodoro Bisoi, the Bisipara Oriya who was keeping the minutes of the meeting. Liringa insisted to me afterwards that the text was not written as he had wanted it to be written and as the meeting had decided. He said that they had put a ban on casual labour from among their own PANS. Damodoro told me that this had been put before the meeting but he himself had urged that it was well enough to deprive the PANS of their ritual privileges—music-making and begging: but how would they carry on their cultivation without casual labour? Liringa said that they could get labour from among the Bisipara PANS, or from the Konds of Kumeriguda, or that they could even bring out PANS from Phulbani. He insisted that in spite of what was written in their collective agreement, the Konds of Baderi would extend the ban to casual labour. As for the PAN clients he did not think that they should all be dismissed out of hand, but merely that property given to them should be resumed and that no new attachments of this sort should be concluded with their own PANS, other than the two households in Atisai and Majisai, who were 'good PANS'.

The argument could in fact be tossed to and fro in an academic fashion, since in March, April, May and the first half of June there is no work to be done on the farms. There is no employment for casual labour at that time and most plough-servants are laid off. Whatever decision was reached, it could not come into force until three months had passed, and I suspect that for this reason the meeting let Liringa have his way and did not feel it necessary to underline Damodoro's warning, even if they saw the force of his arguments and took the warning to heart. In fact every decision in that document was a dead letter, even the decree about fire, tobacco, funerals, and feasts, which is an idiomatic way of saying that the PANS would no longer be employed as music-makers. Neither Liringa himself nor anyone else dismissed his clients, who as individuals were certainly ready to dissociate themselves from the collective behaviour of the caste, if their living depended on doing so. Two months later the hamlet of Pandrisai employed the PAN musicians to play at a rite in their hamlet. Liringa said (when I asked him but not before) that the Pandrisai people would be taken to task for this and that Pandrisai had only done this to spite Baderi. But, whatever Pandrisai's motive, there never was any meeting and everything went on as it had always done. I saw Baderi PAN casual labourers working in the fields that season just as they had done in previous seasons. The Baderi boy-cott, having aimed to be more complete than the boycott in Bisipara, in the end came to nothing.

It came to nothing in the most literal sense of that phrase. There was no dramatic reversal of the decision. Liringa fought no rear-guard action. The document remained merely a piece of paper in Silu's possession and failed utterly to be a charter of Kond reaction. Neither side won a victory: there could be no victory, because, although a plan of action was drawn up, the battle was never joined. There was no need for any ritual of reconciliation nor any social medicaments: the sore healed over almost un-attended: and nothing was changed—at least nothing was changed ostensibly. On reflection, and remembering the tempests which followed when an untouchable struck a youth of clean caste in Bisipara, I find the smoothness of Baderi's return to normality amazing. This is the kind of incident which should be the prelude to a revolution: it almost was in Bisipara. Why should the temperature have been so much lower in Baderi?

The tension in group relations scarcely penetrated to inter-personal relations. On both sides there was a willingness to be Janus-faced. In the company of other PANS, a PAN would be militant and a revolutionary. With his master he would continue to display the usual mixture of familiarity and subservience. This is not simply hypocrisy. It is a form of social short-sightedness, an unwillingness to employ the syllogism, which is often found in social situations. All PANS are bad: Bilo is a PAN: but he is not bad because he happens to be Bilo, *my* PAN. The solidarity of the Kond group—or of the PAN group for that matter—was weakened and cut across by the ties between individuals. It was in their mutual interest that the relationships between the Kond master and his PAN client or plough-servant should continue undisturbed, and group-prestige did not prove a sufficient incentive to make individuals on either side sacrifice their profit or even their convenience.

In spite of the tone of the meeting and the desperate measures agreed upon, there is among the Baderi Konds a comfortable complacency about relations with their own PANS. I noticed this particularly in talks with Ponga. Ponga agreed that the PANS had got a bit beyond themselves, that the real trouble was that there were too many of them for Baderi to support, and that they had been stimulated by Government propaganda (again the word 'Harijans' was brought out with explosive contempt) and by the example of the Bisipara PANS. But he disagreed with the suggestion that Baderi was having the same trouble with its PANS as Bisipara had. The whole thing, he suggested, was Liringa's fault and if he had kept his mouth shut at the wedding or been more tactful in getting rid of the PAN youths, nothing would have come of it. I think he felt that Liringa had earned the slap in the face, and, considering Liringa's continuous challenge to his own authority as village headman,[1] was not unpleased by what had happened. He was particularly scornful about the elaborate plan to boycott the PANS. He did not say that it would fail, nor that he himself would refuse to carry it out: he supposed that they could get the Bisipara band, who are SWEEPERS and PANS of a different sub-caste from the Baderi PANS, to come and play. He would not say to me, an outsider, that the Konds of Baderi had not the solidarity to carry through the boycott, although he and everyone else must have known that this was so, particularly after Damodoro's

[1] See p. 222.

warnings. Ponga's scorn was directed rather to Liringa's mal-adroitness: all these elaborate plans for a boycott were quite unnecessary in Baderi. He said (I remember the tone and gist of his words but not the words themselves), "If Liringa hadn't gone off calling meetings I'd have waited a couple of days and then called the PANS over and said, "What's all this, hey? ", and we'd have talked it out and they'd have prostrated themselves in front of me and that would have been the end of it.'

I think that Ponga was probably right and that he could have handled the whole affair and had it finished within a day or two. The PANS, after talking themselves out, probably would have prostrated themselves before him, partly because he is the head-man and the richest man, partly because he has the genial self-assurance required to act the part of an indulgent leader, and partly because of his known violence and sudden bursts of un-controlled fury. No PAN would have slapped Ponga's face, for fear of immediate and savage retaliation. In this way Ponga, knowing that his personal authority had not been assailed, would have been content to let the whole matter pass with a purely symbolic demonstration by the PANS of their traditional sub-ordination. It would have been for Ponga a satisfying and insulting hint to Liringa that he was not in charge of the village, and for the same reason it would for the PANS have been a subtle revenge on Liringa.

But in another respect Ponga was wrong and Liringa right. Ponga and most of those who let themselves be bullied by Liringa into planning the boycott are complacent about their PANS and are unwilling to face the fact that change, if not already among them, is not very far away. Ponga, because he could manage PANS, believed that there was no PAN problem for the village: or, if there was a problem, then it was not so great that the old methods of dealing with PANS could not work. Although he recognized verbally such facts as the excessive population of PANS in Baderi and the corroding example of the Bisipara PANS, Ponga refused to see the incident as a manifestation of these social forces, so much as an instance of personal incapacity. Liringa had made a mess of things: and that was all there was to the affair. I have said that Ponga was wrong in this and Liringa right, because the disturbance was not merely the result of Liringa's maladroitness and self-assertion, but could also be a sign of the changing position of the PAN group in the structure of the village. On the other hand Liringa undoubtedly over-estimated the change, and took measures to meet a situation which had not arisen, measures which would have been excessive even if the PANS had been on the point of making revolutionary declarations about their future status in the village. Ponga, in the end, turned out to be right in his unspoken estimation that the old order was strong enough to persist.

In what does this change in the position of the PAN group consist? Ideally every PAN family has a master who employs not only the head of the family but the rest of them as well. In return for their work in his fields, he gives them daily food and perhaps one or two pieces of land, and other benefits—such as a *mahua* tree, from the flowers of which liquor is made—which they may exploit for themselves. In fact the situation is not like this at all. One or two PAN families are by tradition clients of particular Konds. But this relationship contains at first sight little more than the ceremonial trappings and in fact the clients make most of their living quite independently of their master. Some of the younger PAN men are employed as plough-servants, but the Konds generally prefer to have an unmarried youth for this purpose, since he will eat out of the same pot as the family and no provision need be made for his family responsibilities. The majority of PANS make their living as casual labourers, mostly for the Baderi Konds, but to some extent in the employment of public departments or of other villages. Through these three kinds of economic relationship, the client, the plough-servant, and the casual labourer, there runs a continuity, which I did not perceive to the same extent in Bisipara, and which still permits some Konds in Baderi to refer to certain PANS as 'my' PANS. The PAN family still holds the field or the *mahua* tree, although the master is no longer rich enough to give his client full-time employment. The plough-servant may come from the client family or be obtained through the agency of the head of the client family. Finally the master will endeavour to make use of his client's loyalties to see that when labour is scarce at the time of planting and harvesting he obtains at least the labour of his client's family. The bond is in evidence also at the ritual crises of life, and whether it is a death or a marriage or sickness the client will be in attendance to run messages, if the crisis is in the master's house, or, if it is in the client's house, the master will be expected to aid with advice, or money, or intercession with other people on his client's behalf. Neither the client nor the master depend absolutely upon one another, but the relationship is still to their mutual benefit, and is still sufficiently strong for both sides to accept as natural the traditional etiquette in which the subservience of the one and the dominance of the other are symbolized. This is the kind of relationship—a caste relationship—which Ponga proposed to use in restoring tranquillity after the disturbance in the village. He proposed to reprimand the PANS for failing to behave in this way, and he expected them to admit that this was the correct way to behave.

A relationship of this kind is a means of sharing out the produce of the land and seeing that those who do not own land receive a share of its products. For this relationship to function smoothly there must be an appropriate adjustment of population to land, and, in this particular system, an adjustment between the numbers of masters and clients. An increase in the number of masters, without an increase in the amount of land under cultivation or in the productivity of the existing land, may lead to a situation where the masters begin to do their own work or to employ one another, and to dispense with their clients and servants. Equally if the servant class multiplies then there may not be sufficient land in the village for them to be employed economically. If a man has managed an estate satisfactorily with one client-labourer, then his son is not going to provide employment for the three sons of the client and their families. Two of them must make a living elsewhere. Of course there is the possibility of adjustment within the system, in that while one servant is succeeded by three sons another two servants may die without sons. The probability of this happening within one village is not high, but the labouring castes and specialist castes are mobile and it is possible that the strains and stresses set up by differential increase can be adjusted by migration from one place to another, as in the case of HERDSMEN and SMITHS.

Both Ponga and Liringa remarked independently to me that the real trouble was that there were too many PANS: their street was full of husky young louts who had nothing to do all day but swagger about and look for someone with whom to pick a fight. This is true so far as the numbers go: in the 12 PAN houses in Baderi and Kamopara there are 12 youths between the ages of

12 and 20; out of 29 Kond houses in these two hamlets there are only 9 Kond youths of the same age. It is also true that the PAN population has swelled far beyond the point at which it would be possible for all of them to be joined in the intimate master-client relationship, even in the attenuated form which I have described. In other words, there are many PANS in the village who are in fact 'nobody's PANS', and who are not going to exhibit a generalized subservience when there would be nothing to be gained by it.

If the system were working in the way that Ponga and most other Konds would like to pretend, this surplus population would have had to go elsewhere and be absorbed into other villages. It has not done so. Not one of the Baderi PAN households has enough land to feed them for the year, let alone provide for their full needs. They work on the roads, when they are lucky enough to find employment. Out of the 12 houses 11 have a loom on which they weave cotton cloth, occasionally for their own Konds, but mainly either as piece work for a Textile Co-operative in Phulbani, or for sale in the open market. None of them produce the elaborate reserve-dye cloths which the Oriya WEAVERS make. They manufacture mostly small towels and plain cotton shawls. Either through this lack of skill or through the saturation of the market, none can do more than keep themselves alive. Two PANS have recently started turmeric trading and two have been trading for cattle, using money borrowed from rich Baderi Konds. One PAN is the village watchman at Rs.6 a month, and he owns a cart with which he contracts to do small transport jobs. Another one, who died in 1955, was the owner of a cart, a loom, and of more land than any other Baderi PAN, all of which he and his brother had received as gifts from their Kond patron, one of Dibi's widows. The Textile Co-operative, the open markets, work offered by public departments, contractual work open to carters in the employ of their fellow-villagers or merchants—in short the diversification of the economy, have all made it possible for the PANS to continue to live in Baderi although they are no longer able to derive their whole living as clients of the Konds, and therefore are no longer so closely under Kond control.

It must not be imagined, however, that the break is complete. In a sense both Ponga and Liringa are right in their estimations, although these are contradictory. Ponga was right in thinking that the traditional subservience could still be commanded and implicitly that the PANS were still an integral part of the village economy and were still dependent upon it. Liringa was right in that the PANS had sufficient independence of the Baderi economy to refuse on occasions to act out their subordinate role. But his actions imply an incorrect appreciation of the economic factors, and the same mistake, indeed, is implicit in Ponga's refusal to take the incident seriously. The Kond plan was arrived at by this kind of reasoning: 'The PANS owe a lot to us. We established them here and we have given them property and privileges. Yet they refuse to respect us and obey us. Very well, let them go it alone. We will withdraw our economic favours, and not expose ourselves any longer to their insults. We will have nothing more to do with them.' There is a punitive air about the proposed boycott, but there is more in it than just spite: it is designed as a restitutive sanction; and they hoped, no doubt, that the PANS would feel the pinch sufficiently to make them apologize and come back as humble servants. In fact the PANS came back, neither more nor less chastened than they had been before, and certainly they had no particular reason to regret having assaulted Liringa. What Liringa missed—and Ponga too with his easy assumption that the village economy and the village political organization were still to-day what they had always been—was that the Kond agricultural economy is subsidized by (among other things) the fact that the PANS for at least half the year support themselves in the new diversified economy. The labour force which keeps the village economy in motion during the peak periods in the cultivating season is, for at least six months in the year, supported elsewhere and is not a burden on the cultivators. The group of PANS, while too big in numbers to fit into the old type of relationship, is not too large during the months of cultivation: in fact at that time all the PANS are indispensable. Liringa realized that there were too many PANS for the village to support throughout the year and that the Konds could no longer command the simple homage which once they had enjoyed. But he did not realize that the village still depended on PAN labour and that no boycott could be effective without crippling completely the agricultural economy of Baderi.

Besides underestimating the degree to which the village depended upon PANS, Liringa over-estimated the economic independence of the Baderi PANS. In the early months of my stay I went through a list of all those who lived in Baderi and asked Liringa to estimate how much land they had. We used four categories: the first were those who had no land or virtually none; the second had some land but not enough to keep them alive for the twelve months of the year; the third could 'eat for twelve months' (this being a common phrase in the village); and the fourth were rich. Later I made a detailed survey of the Baderi lands and found out in fact how much land people owned. Liringa's estimate had been fairly accurate for the Konds. But in the case of the PANS he made a wild over-estimate. Out of 12 houses he put 2 (with a little hesitation) into the fourth or richest category: in fact they turned out to be well down in the second category. He put one into the category of those who can eat for twelve months, whereas it too should have gone into the second category: he put 2 into the second category, one of which has one small field, and the other of which has no land at all: with the remaining 7 he was correct in putting them into the first category of those which are landless or virtually so. In his beliefs about the PANS Liringa was all the time anticipating in Baderi the state of affairs which was coming about in Bisipara, where there are several wealthy PAN families, and where there is a sharp conflict between the clean castes and the PANS, much sharper than the conflict emerging in Baderi.

Kond hills society must always have been troubled by continued instances of an inappropriate ratio between landowning castes and servicing castes. The system, as I have said, contains its own corrective mechanism, in that when there are too many PANS in one village there may be too few in another village, and the balance may be restored by migration. Sometimes the Konds themselves take the initiative. Ponga's grandfather established the present lineage of PANS in Baderi. More often, when a PAN lineage is dying out, it will be joined by other lineages related as sister's sons or daughter's husbands, who come from a crowded PAN street to a village where their labour will have a scarcity value. This is happening at the moment in the large Kond village of Maseragando, which is isolated in the jungle-covered mountains to the west of the Salki river. But for various reasons this mechanism will not always operate without friction and it is not always enough in itself to cope with a large discrepancy in population. People do not like moving away, particularly to a place like

Maseragando. Many prefer to stay where they are and make a living somehow.

The present lineage of Baderi PANS have been able to stay on in the village, although they are too many to be supported by Baderi agriculture, because they can make part of their living in the new diversified economy. But their predecessors found a different solution, which kept them in Baderi for a time but in the end brought about a dramatic dispersal. None of that lineage (which I will call Kusnia's after the most prominent of its sons) are now to be found in Baderi. There is a hamlet in Besringia, called Kaulopara, which is peopled entirely by members of the Kusnia lineage and which is one of the rare untouchable hamlets which stands alone and is not part of another village. The other section of this lineage lives in a settlement established for them by the Administration in the neighbourhood of the Police lines in the headquarters village, Phulbani.

So far as the Baderi people know, Kusnia's lineage are their original Baderi PANS. No predecessors are known, and they were certainly in Baderi before the present PAN lineage which was introduced by Ponga's grandfather. I do not know whether the Kusnia PANS belonged to a particular segment of Konds in Baderi in the same way that the present group are said to be Ponga's (B3) PANS. The Kusnia PANS first came into prominence about the turn of the century. (I am not sure about the dates in this story nor about the order of events, since I was unable to gain access to Government records.) They were highwaymen and dacoits and achieved considerable notoriety. Baderi was well placed for highway robbery since it lay beside the old military road which connected northern Madras and the Orissa plains with the Central Provinces. This was one route by which traders passed to and fro carrying salt from Orissa and bringing cattle and other goods from middle India. It may also have been a pilgrim route to Puri, but I think that most of this traffic avoided the Kond hills and reached the Orissa coast by going through the valley of the Mahanadi. In any case by the time that Kusnia was a dacoit, the railways were built, and the old road would have been used mainly by traders.

The goods which were stolen by Kusnia and the men of the generation before him were passed to the Konds of Pandrisai, who acted as receivers. Where they went to eventually I do not know, but it may be presumed that the Pandrisai Konds provided only a convenient warehouse where the goods were stored until contact could be made with some outside receiver. Whatever the arrangement, both the Pandrisai Konds and the Kusnia PANS did well for themselves.

Kusnia and his brother Rungo, who were the ringleaders of the gang, lived in Kamopara. They used to steal cattle and goats, not only from other villages but also from their own Konds, and no-one who had a field near Kamopara ever got the full crop from it, since the PANS, going out at night in gangs, would cut the grain just before the harvest. Eventually Kusnia and Rungo were caught, sentenced, and put in the jail at Bisipara. (This shows that these events must have taken place before 1904, since the jail was moved to Phulbani, along with the rest of the headquarters, in that year.) Kusnia and Rungo broke out of jail and ran away to become outlaws. They operated for several years over the whole of the eastern Kondmals and the northern parts of the Ganjam Agency. Then part of the gang were captured in a village in Ganjam. The remnants escaped and set up a camp in the mountains behind Damopara. From there Kusnia and Rungo one day visited a festival in Gomapara village: they were recognized by the Baderi Konds, and were invited by Dibi to spend the night in Baderi and join in the festivities. They got drunk and Rungo fell into a drunken sleep. Dibi sent for the police and Rungo was captured. Kusnia escaped but gave himself up shortly afterwards, and both men went to jail. On the day that their sentence expired there happened to be a festival in Baderi. Kusnia and Rungo descended on this and with the help of their kinsmen in Kamopara thrashed the Balimendi Sirdar, who was attending the festival, and they also beat Dibi so badly that both men had to go to hospital. Kusnia and Rungo returned at night and set fire to Dibi's house and half of Baderi hamlet was burnt down. They were captured that same night and this time both of them and several of their kinsmen went to the penal settlement in the Andaman Islands. The Administration then moved the women and children and the few men in Kusnia's lineage who were not in jail to Phulbani, near the Police lines, where their descendants live to-day.

After one of their convictions—probably the last—Kusnia and Rungo turned King's evidence and revealed the names of the Pandrisai receivers. The Baderi Konds, who had suffered as much as anyone from the depredations of the Kusnia lineage, and who

in the latest incident had lost half their village, supplied corro-
boratory evidence and half a dozen Konds from Pandrisai went to
jail for periods of up to two years.

When one man turns criminal many causes are likely to have
contributed, and some of these will be psychological. But when a
whole community—and indeed a whole category of people, for
PANS throughout the Kond hills are a byword for lawlessness—
turns to crime, then the causes are to be sought in the constitution
and working of society. It seems clear to me that Kusnia and Rungo
and PANS elsewhere found in crime a solution to the difficulties
which their successors in Baderi have met by entering a diversified
economy. Whether Kusnia and Rungo preferred robbery to
working at a loom or labouring on the roads, or whether in their
day the economy was not sufficiently diversified to make room
for them, I do not know: but the reason which made it necessary
for them to find some source of income other than their dependence on the Konds, is the same both in their case and in the case
of their successors in Baderi.

There are two pieces of circumstantial evidence backing this
conclusion. Firstly the two PAN lineages seem to have overlapped
in Baderi. I have spoken of the present lineage as successors to the
Kusnia people. But they were in Baderi before the Kusnia lineage
was moved to Phulbani. It seems that the Kusnia lineage was
deeply involved with the Pandrisai Konds, was itself beginning to
acquire land, and in a period of arrogant expansiveness was not
what in Kond eyes a PAN group should be. Ponga's grandfather
may have introduced the present PAN lineage to do their proper
work: he may have brought them in so as to counter the growing
influence of the Pandrisai Konds. Alternatively it is also possible
that their presence aggravated the already difficult position of the
Kusnia PANS and may have been one of the factors turning them to
crime. I was unable to establish the exact course of events beyond
the fact that the present lineage must have been in Baderi before
the Kusnia lineage was removed. But, whatever the correct
sequence of events, Baderi could not have supported two groups
of PANS.

The second piece of circumstantial evidence is similarly marred
by my inability to date events. This evidence is the existence of another branch of Kusnia's lineage in a village in Besringia. The received opinion in Besringia was that this PAN settlement had been

established for several generations in Besringia and it is likely that they left Baderi before the dramatic events in which Kusnia and Rungo were concerned. But I was able to gather no story about their migration other than the usual one that they could not get enough to support themselves in Baderi, so that they came and begged jungle land from the Besringia Konds and made fields for themselves out of the jungle. If I could be sure that they left Baderi before Kusnia and Rungo set out on their career of crime, then this would be additional evidence that there was already an imbalance between the landowners in that village and the labouring population: and that this imbalance was solved by migration, a solution which was orthodox in that it did not lead to crime, but somewhat unusual for the Kondmals in that it resulted in the setting up of an independent hamlet of untouchables. Later, either by natural increase or by the introduction of the present lineage of PANS, the imbalance appeared again, to be solved this time by the forcible removal of the Kusnia PANS to Phulbani.

When a specialist caste grows too numerous it may abandon its specialization and turn to agricultural labour, and this is said to be part of that elasticity which gives the caste system its strength.[1] But there are many qualifications. Land is not unlimited and in Baderi at least, given the present techniques and land-tenure system, the land is continually coming to the point of saturation. At this point the dependent castes must take to other occupations —to crime or to various roles in a diversified economy—in which their traditional caste relationships with persons of higher castes need not be maintained. The change, as the events in Baderi show, is not abrupt. One might almost say that the social structure has its seasonal variations. In the cultivating season the PANS resume their traditional role, albeit under the guise of casual wage-labour. In the hot season they become entrepreneurs (of the humblest kind) in the modern economy. But the general drift is towards greater independence. Kusnia's lineage achieved considerable independence and before they were outlawed they had purchased several fields in Baderi out of the proceeds of their robberies.[2] When Kusnia's people were removed the present lineage of PANS began

---

[1] M. N. Srinivas in McKim Marriott (ed.), 1955, pp. 15–17.
[2] When they removed from the village the land had not been surveyed and the ownership of fields was not registered. The Konds simply resumed the fields which they had sold.

6. An educated Oriya PAN.

in a position of dependence, but by degrees they too are beginning to become economically independent. It is this future independence, when PANS may begin to own land and to employ one
another, which Liringa, with the example of Bisipara in front of
him, could see. Ponga, on the other hand, looked back to a comfortable past. On the whole the present in which both Liringa and
Ponga live, contains more of the past than it does of the future—at
least this is so in Baderi.

Baderi and Bisipara are within two miles of one another and the
Baderi Konds make frequent reference to the bad example set
before their PANS by the Bisipara PANS. In each village the PAN
population forms about a fifth of the total. The Oriya PANS in
Bisipara hold the same traditional position as do the Kond PANS in
Baderi, and suffer from the same, and indeed greater, ritual disabilities. They are bound into the village agricultural economy in
much the same way by interpersonal links, some long-lasting in
the mode of the old master-client relationship, but most of the
temporary and casual type arising from wage-labour. Like the
Baderi PANS they profit from the diversified economy and indeed
they have profited to a much greater extent. In Bisipara one hears
from the clean castes the same kind of complaints as the Konds
voice in Baderi: the Pans no longer know their place; there are too
many of them; when they came begging, not only those who
were entitled to come appeared, but the entire street; the village
can no longer afford to support them in the way that it could a
generation ago, since men are poorer to-day than they used to be;
the street is full of young louts, with nothing to do but make
trouble in the village; so-and-so is a good PAN, but collectively
PANS are beyond the pale of decent society; all PANS are thieves; the
PANS own all the fields in the vicinity of their street, because the
crops fell all into the hands of PAN thieves and the owners could do
nothing but sell the fields cheaply to PANS; and so forth.

But there are in fact many differences between the two villages
and the situations of the PANS in them. Bisipara is a large village of
nearly 700 people. Almost the whole of this population is concentrated in one area and is not dispersed like the hamlets of the Baderi
valley, in the whole of which there are less than five hundred

L

people. The dominant caste in Bisipara are Oriya WARRIORS who
have had considerable political influence in the area, both before the British came in the time of the rule (if it may be called
that) of the Boad Raja, and afterwards as servants of the Administration. The Konds had some political power in the time of the
Rajas, but since the Administration came they have been as
oppressed and helpless as the PANS themselves, until comparatively
recently.[1] Bisipara, almost from the time the British entered the
area in the middle of the nineteenth century until 1904, was the
seat of the headquarters. Bisipara is a village of traders and has
always had a number of merchant-shopkeepers, whereas Baderi
has been a village of agriculturists. Bisipara had a Middle English
School and still has an Upper Primary School, with three or four
masters on the staff and a brick schoolhouse, while Baderi has had
a Lower Primary School with a single schoolmaster and a mud-
and-thatch building. Bisipara is an Oriya village and inhabited by
Hindus, and it has within its boundaries three temples. The Konds
too are Hindus: but they are a different kind of Hindu—'backward
Hindus'[2]—and there was never a Hindu temple nor a BRAHMIN in
Baderi. Finally the people of Bisipara speak the Oriya language,
the language of the State and of the Administration, while the
Baderi Konds, although most of the men are bilingual, have Kui
as their first language and the language of the home.

The PANS of Bisipara are Oriya PANS while those of Baderi are
Kond PANS. This means more than that the language of the home
is different in the two groups. Bisipara PANS are vastly more
sophisticated. They all are PANS, certainly, and there was no
question of outcasting the Bisipara PAN whose daughter married
a Baderi PAN. It was felt that the girl might have done better for
herself, but no question of pollution was raised. They are the
same caste. Nevertheless the Bisipara PANS despise Kond PANS.
They are reckoned to be backward and jungly people, unable to
look after themselves in the modern world, and content with a
lower standard of living than that which befits an Oriya PAN. It is
for this reason and not because of sub-caste difference that there is
only the one marriage between the two groups. All other marriages
in the genealogy of the Bisipara PANS are with Oriya PANS living in
other Oriya villages in the Kond hills.

[1] See Chapter VII.
[2] G. S. Ghurye, 1943, *passim*.

There is in fact a difference in their standards of living. In the PAN group of Bisipara are numbered several wealthy landowners. Many of them are traders of substance, like Nrusingh Naik who is described elsewhere in this book.[1] One is a policeman: several are schoolmasters. If all the PANS in the Kondmals are to be considered one group, then the Oriya PANS, without question, are the elite.

There has been and still is going on in Bisipara a conflict between the untouchables and the clean castes, similar to that which appeared to be coming to a head in Baderi. I have described it elsewhere and here I need only recall the main events.[2] The conflict appears to have begun over Temple Entry. The Bisipara PANS demanded admittance, according to the law of the land, into one of the temples. This was resisted by the clean castes: the police intervened: the PANS were not in the end admitted, and the struggle seemed to die out. The Bisipara PANS went away and built a temple in their own street to the same deity. Sometime after this the clean castes of Bisipara ruled that the PANS were no longer to be allowed to provide music at the village festivals, and the privilege of licensed begging was withdrawn from them. This was done on the grounds that the entire PAN community used to come begging and the village could no longer afford to give on such a scale—an attitude which is implicit in Liringa's outburst at the wedding in Baderi. The PANS then set about reforming themselves: they proclaimed that they would be vegetarians and abstain from liquor (in fact very few of them lived up to this); they prohibited members of their community from scavenging and handling dead cattle; and they announced that from that time onwards they would be called not 'PAN' but 'Harijan'—'the children of God'—the name which Gandhi gave to untouchables. The final incident which I witnessed in this long-drawn conflict between the clean castes and the Bisipara PANS was similar to the incident in Baderi: a PAN assaulted a person of clean caste. But the circumstances of the assault, the status of the persons concerned, and the sequel were very different. In Baderi the assault took place in the middle of what was intended to be a judicial assembly. In Bisipara the incident happened at dusk in the fields, when the two persons were trying to pass one another on a narrow path. The Bisipara PAN is alleged to have pushed his victim off the path: in Baderi the

[1] See pp. 201–209.
[2] F. G. Bailey, 1957, Chapter XI.

incident was an open and unmistakable slap in the face, and could not in any circumstances be dressed up as an accident. The victim in Baderi was one of the leading men of the village: in Bisipara the offender was a senior PAN while the victim was a youth of fifteen. All things considered there seemed to be every reason why excuses should be made for the incident in Bisipara and why none could possibly be made for the assault in Baderi. The former might be smoothed over with hints about an accident or about provocation or about the respect which youth owes to age: the latter should cause an explosion of communal wrath. Precisely the reverse of this happened: in a few months the incident in Baderi seemed to have been forgotten: in Bisipara the echoes went on reverberating for more than a year. Even when this incident had died into the background, the ban on the PAN musicians and on the privilege of begging was still maintained in Bisipara. A few months after the ban in Baderi the musicians were playing for the hamlet of Pandrisai, and, so far as I know, they continued afterwards to be the music-makers for the whole village, as they had been before the incident.

There is an easy and immediate explanation why the ban on the Bisipara musicians continued and the ban on the Baderi musicians was lifted. In Bisipara the clean castes are solid and undivided over this issue: in Baderi the Konds appear to be divided. In Baderi there is only one group of untouchables (except for the two households in Atisai and Majisai which are apart from the main lineage): in Bisipara there are three other untouchable castes besides the group which was in conflict with the clean castes. As soon as the Bisipara PANS were deprived of the right to provide music their place was taken by SWEEPERS and a caste of PANS which came originally from the Ganjam Agency. They perform less skilfully than the original PANS, but the village is satisfied, and since they are much fewer in number, the clean castes are not incommoded by hordes of people begging for food at feast-times. The Bisipara clean castes, in other words, were able to exploit a division in the untouchable group. They had musicians on the spot ready to fill the vacancy. The Baderi Konds did not. The two 'good PANS' in Atisai and Majisai could not alone provide music, and the Konds would have had to hire musicians from other villages, who would without a doubt have exploited the awkward position in which the Baderi Konds found themselves.

The Baderi PANS seem to have benefited from a division in the Konds between Pandrisai people and the Baderi people. Liringa, when I asked him about the invitation which Pandrisai had given to the Baderi musicians, said that the matter would certainly be brought up because the Pandrisai people had done so merely in order to spite Baderi. Pandrisai is a hamlet which was founded from Baderi and is peopled mainly by the B1 segment.[1] There is an undoubted hostility between the two hamlets. But Pandrisai is still part of the Baderi cluster: they did, for instance, attend the meeting which was held to plan the boycott and the man who, with Liringa, was assaulted, came from Pandrisai. But there is a wider cleavage between Pandrisai and the rest than there is between any other pair of hamlets, and there is an undoubted, if still somewhat uninstitutionalized, hostility between them. I was told that this hostility dated from the time when the men of Baderi came forward to give evidence against the Pandrisai receivers, and it has continued through a series of minor conflicts, of which the latest was breaking the proposed boycott of the Pan musicians. I think that the ban would sooner or later have been broken in any case, both because of the difficulty of finding other musicians, and because the tension in Baderi between the Konds and PANS was in general far less than that in Bisipara between the PANS and the clean castes. The growing cleavage between Pandrisai and the rest of the cluster merely explains why it was the Pandrisai people who broke the ban, and not why the ban was broken in the first place.

There were no divided loyalties in the clean caste group in Bisipara, in spite of the fact that it includes different castes. The clean castes stood together: even the factional divisions within the WARRIOR caste were laid aside during the dispute with the PANS. Treachery was not inconceivable: stringent penalties were laid down for anyone who gave information to a PAN about the village's plans, or for anyone who refused to associate himself with whatever measures the village council agreed upon. But it was the individual traitor, the careless talker, and the eccentric, who were envisaged in these precautionary decrees, and the defection of a whole group of persons was not contemplated.

These are all reasons which strengthen or weaken the bitterness

[1] See p. 106.

of the disputes in the two villages and the degree of persistence with which they were fought out. The ultimate reason for the dispute itself is different. The Bisipara PANS are a formidable group of persons who constitute an actual and serious threat to the dominance of the clean castes in the village. It is just conceivable that the Bisipara PANS in five or ten years time—or even sooner—may win a local election and be at least in statutory control of the village, if not in actual and undisputed control. The same is not true of Baderi.

In Baderi the dispute was begun and brought to a conclusion within the village. Events and systems which exist outside the village (notably the diversified economy) affected the course of the dispute, but no-one concerned in it made a direct appeal to outside authority, and no action taken in the dispute was motivated directly by something which happened in the world outside. In Bisipara the cycle of conflicts was begun by the PANS invoking their rights under the Temple Entry Act, and they summoned the police in an attempt to have these rights enforced. Their reaction to the ban placed upon them by the village was to associate themselves with the All-India Harijan movement. They proclaimed that they were Harijans, and at the same time they laid down for themselves a standard of behaviour which conforms to the India-wide standard of respectability—vegetarianism, abhorrence of liquor, and so forth. When the WARRIOR youth was assaulted, the first PAN reaction was to call in the police and to try to make out a case that the WARRIORS had attacked their street. By their persistence they caused three judicial enquiries to be held, and in the course of these they petitioned a Minister in the State government. The very strength of these weapons would be enough to close the ranks of the clean castes.

Although in the end a decision favourable to the clean castes was reached—as in fact was inevitable since the clean castes had not attacked the PAN street as the PANS alleged—the very use of methods like these was enough to show that the Bisipara PANS were a force not to be taken lightly. They were able to use these weapons because they number among them men who are enabled by wealth and education to make use of the rights which the law gives them. There are schoolmasters and a policeman among them; there are owners of considerable landed property and men who handle large sums of money in trade and who are used to dealing with middlemen from the plains and with minor Government officials; one of their number is an agent in the permanent employ of the Congress party; another intends to stand for election as a Member of the Orissa Legislative Assembly. But in Baderi there is no-one like this. None of the Baderi PANS can write, though there are a few who can sign their name; none of them are wealthy; none are in direct contact with the political parties.

In part the sophistication of the Bisipara PANS is due to the favours which they, as untouchables, have received from the Administration. Jobs are reserved for them; they have special political representation; they are given every encouragement to fight against their traditional status of untouchability. The village is visited periodically by a person known there as the 'Harijan Inspector', a man of clean caste who publicly associates with the untouchables, though I was told that he purifies himself after-wards and does not eat with PANS, but this may have been the malicious gossip of the clean castes. He also reads a stern lecture to the clean castes of Bisipara saying that everyone should be allowed to use the wells and go into the temples and threatening that any-one who invokes untouchability will be fined Rs. 500. So far as the clean castes of Bisipara, who do not qualify for the reserved jobs, can see, the dice is loaded heavily against them, and the Govern-ment is all on the side of the untouchables. Hence the bitterness of the fight they put up—and in this case which they won. The per-sistence of the untouchables, and their readiness to invoke outside authority, is also to be explained by the privileges which the Government grants them and the favour in which they feel them-selves to be held. No 'Harijan Inspector' has ever visited Baderi, so far as I know. Nor do the untouchables feel themselves especially favoured by the Government, except in the light dimly reflected from Bisipara, since the Konds too have these differential privi-leges and are treated along with the untouchables as the favoured wards of Government.

The matter is peculiarly important in Bisipara since there was about that time a proposal to establish a statutory *panchayat*, the members of which would function as the local government for the village, taking over many of the powers of the village head-man and the Sirdar. The members and the president of this *panchayat* were to be elected, and there was an unhappy feeling among the clean castes of Bisipara that, since the *panchayat* would

cover an area larger than the village itself, the Oriyas now dominant in the village might not secure a majority, and that control
of the *panchayat* might fall into the hands of the undoubtedly able
men among the Bisipara PANS. An alliance between PANS and
Konds seemed unlikely, but the mechanics of an election are not
familiar to the village and there was a real fear that people so well
versed in the modern forms of democracy as the Congress agent
and the would-be Member of the Legislative Assembly might be
able to use both their skill and their outside contacts to gain control of the village. It is against such real issues as this that the pin-
pricks of banning the PAN musicians, and the protracted bitterness
of the assault case, are to be seen. But all this is remote from Baderi.
The Konds of Baderi cannot conceive of their PANS taking control
of the village, and they do not bother to think about the possibility of Baderi being included in a larger unit in which PANS
might gain control. Consequently the dispute in Baderi burnt
itself out quickly: there was no fuel to keep the fire alight.

Liringa's actions, although probably motivated by the indig-
nities which he had suffered, were designed to meet a situation
which had not yet arisen. Liringa was misled by the superficial
similarity between the Baderi PANS and the Bisipara PANS: the fact
that they were getting above themselves, and that there were too
many of them, and that their young men were forward and inso-
lent. He made a wrong appreciation and the plan based on this
appreciation failed. It would in any case have failed since it went
to extremes. Even in Bisipara there was no proposal to exclude
PANS from the economic life of the village. Ponga, and the other
Konds, looking to their own convenience, and sensitive to the
past rather than to the future, were right. In Baderi the rumblings
of change—of this particular change in the status of PANS—are still
below the horizon. In Bisipara the storm is about to break, if it has
not broken already.

CHAPTER VII

THE KONDS AND THEIR MASTERS

IN this chapter I discuss a wider political field in which Konds and Oriyas interact. The Kond and Kond-dependent political systems were complete, relatively coherent, and undisputed, in the sense that—roughly speaking—all the persons concerned would agree about correct behaviour. There were conflicts but there was no appeal against the system itself, no harking towards revolution, no denial of the rightness of the basic types of relationship. No-one, for instance, claimed that land in the Kond community ought to be given freely to affines and uterine kin: they gave land, but at the same time the recipients divested affinal or uterine status and assumed the rights and obligations of an agnate. The PANS from time to time refused to grant their masters the respect which the system demanded, but they did so on the grounds that their masters too were not fulfilling their obligations: they did not, until the recent campaign against untouchability, claim that the master-servant relationship was itself unjust or immoral.

But the distribution of land and resources between Kond and Oriya was not made within a single system upon the rightness of which all were agreed. I have called this chapter 'The Konds and their masters'. The Konds acknowledge that they have become subservient, but they deny that this is a proper relationship for a Kond. Konds and Oriyas have competed for several centuries to win control over one another. Konds have tried to make Oriyas conform to their system of political relationships, in so far as the difference of caste would permit. Oriyas (in particular WARRIORS) have tried to make the Konds behave as a dependent caste, subordinate to themselves in just the same way as Baderi PANS are by tradition subordinate to Baderi Konds. In this chapter I describe the history of this struggle and the different factors which at different times have favoured one side against the other.

The 1931 Census is the last which gives caste affiliation and is complete. The figures for the Kondmals are given in Table 6. Out of every eight persons five are Konds and less than two are Oriyas.

Even this figure, if we project it back before the Administration, is probably an exaggeration, for it must include the descendants of many who came to the Kondmals in the wake of the Administration. Before that time the proportion of Oriyas must have been even smaller.

These figures set two problems. At the present day Konds occupy fewer positions of power and responsibility in commerce and in the Administration than do Oriyas. Status as a Kond or as an Oriya has been relevant in the struggle for power, and positions of power are not distributed evenly throughout the population. In spite of their numerical preponderance Konds have been subordinated to Oriyas and still are to some extent to-day. The second problem concerns the distribution of population. There are at the present day (1951 Census) 1,243 villages,[1] containing 85,543 people in the 770 square miles of the Kondmals. Of these villages only thirteen contain more than one hundred houses, and in them

TABLE 6

THE POPULATION OF THE KONDMALS IN 1931

Category	Numbers	%
Konds	51,204	62·3
Other Adibasis	605	0·7
Untouchables	12,759	15·5
Oriya*	17,710	21·5
Total	82,278	100·0

* This figure is not given separately, but I have arrived at it by deducting the sum of the other three categories from the total.

live approximately one tenth of the population, 8,863 people. All but one of these large villages are Oriya. This does not mean that only Oriyas live there: there are also a few Konds and in all cases large communities of PAN untouchables. But the language of these villages is Oriya: the population is divided into many castes, and it is probable that no one caste comprises more than about a fifth of the population in any one village. These are multi-caste villages,

[1] A 'village' in the Census is more often a hamlet than a village-cluster. All the Baderi hamlets are listed separately in the District Census Handbook.

7a.

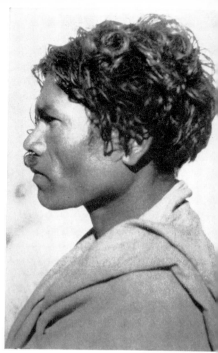

7b.

7c.

a. Kond.

b. Kond PAN.

c. WARRIOR.

while the Kond villages like Baderi are one-caste villages. Konds who live in Oriya villages are labourers and migrants, or else they are 'detribalized' like the Kond POTTER group in Bisipara. Approximately half the Oriya population is found in the thirteen largest villages in the Kondmals. The size of the village, as my discussion of migration between Kond villages indicated, is ultimately governed by the amount of land at its disposal. Oriya villages earn more from the diversified economy than does a Kond village, but they still are subsistence economies and depend on the land which surrounds the village. The large Oriya villages are sited in the wider valleys, where the greatest amount of land suitable for rice cultivation is to be found. They occupy the best cultivating sites in the valleys, while the Konds occupy sites which are smaller and in remoter valleys. Since the Oriya villages are sited in the broader valleys, they lie along the lines of communication. I have set out this argument in detail elsewhere and here I need only say that what was there said about Besringia *mutha* applies, *mutatis mutandis*, to the whole of the Kondmals.[1] The fact that they occupy the best land indicates that Oriyas have established a dominance of some sort over the Konds, who were unable to retain the best cultivating sites. How this dominance was established, what kind of relationships are contained in it, and how it is beginning to break down, will be discussed in this chapter.

KOND AMBIVALENCE

Oriyas treat Konds as a lower caste. No Oriya, other than the untouchables, will take food or water from a Kond—and some untouchables seek higher status by refusing food from Konds. But Konds are not treated as untouchables by any clean caste Oriyas, who enter Kond houses and move freely about the villages where Konds live and permit Konds to draw water from wells which Oriyas use. In Bisipara the meat at an untouchable wedding is often butchered by a Kond, since meat from his hands will be accepted by high castes, who would otherwise require an animal, whole and alive, from untouchables. Konds to some extent accept this position. They do not attempt to assert superiority over WARRIORS or HERDSMEN by refusing food and drink. The Oriya and Kond informants who worked with me in the hot weather of

[1] F. G. Bailey, 1957, Chapter II.

1955 at mapping the Baderi fields used to return at midday to make tea in the house of the Kond. Each day the WARRIOR (the Oriya) would go to the Kond well and draw water for the tea and then make it for the three of us to drink. One day he put his pot down and went outside to get the tea from my haversack. When he came in he picked up the wrong water-pot. 'Not that one, brother!' said the Kond quickly. 'That's ours!' Of course the Konds, like any other caste, do not accept completely the verdict of the rest of society on their position in the caste scale. They take food and drink from BRAHMINS, WARRIORS, and Oriya HERDSMEN, but refuse it from the hands of WEAVERS, WASHERMEN, DISTILLERS, and the rest. From their own PANS the Konds expect behaviour which symbolizes PAN inferiority and Kond superiority. In these ways they accept the ritual and symbolism of caste, and behave towards those above and those below, as if they were a caste.

The ritual ranking of caste corresponds to some degree with political and economic ranking. Ritual ranking is sensitive to political and economic changes except at the extremes, where the BRAHMIN and the untouchables are placed. Both in the political and the economic system, Konds are not and never have been in the same position of dependence on the dominant WARRIOR group as the other inferior castes. There is a corresponding ambivalence in the symbolic behaviour of Konds towards WARRIORS, whom they both accept and reject as their masters.

(Case 36)   (Time: traditional)
One of the Kond heroes was Olopo Malik. Olopo was a friend of the King of Boad. One day he asked the king for the hand of his daughter. The king was not a Kond: he was probably a BRAHMIN. This seems to have been a tactful king, for he said, 'You and I are two brothers. How could you marry a daughter of mine?' But he did not refuse outright: he set tasks. Olopo succeeded in splitting a large tree-trunk and passed the first test. Then the king paraded two women: one was his daughter dressed in filthy clothes like a woman of low caste: the other was a low caste woman dressed in all the finery of a princess. Olopo, being a simple Kond, chose elegance. All the courtiers standing around the king laughed and said, 'Now we know just how clever *you* are.' Olopo was covered with shame and seized the woman and went off to the Kondmals, where he killed her, cut the meat off her breasts and the meat off her thighs, and, as the text says, 'wherever there was any decent meat'. He took

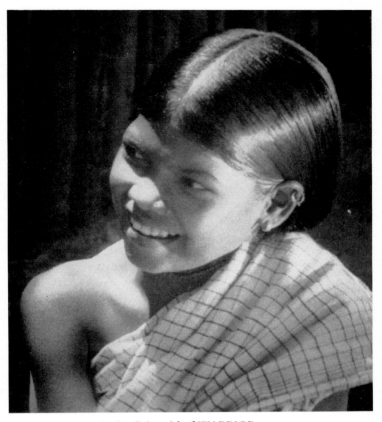

8. An Oriya girl of WARRIOR caste.

9. A Kond woman making leaf cups.

the meat to the king and told him he had killed a sambhur. The king ate it and was very pleased until he got a second message from Olopo telling him what the meat was and asking, 'Who is the clever one now?' Olopo then fled again to the Kondmals, for the king was hunting for him. He changed his name to Kohoro to confuse his pursuers, and on the way he said to himself, 'Now I've cleared out of Boad and I've come to the Kondmals. I might as well make a great name for myself in the Kondmals, mightn't I?' The story then relates how Olopo fired off four arrows and where they landed he made his kingdom, and the legend continues in this fashion, accounting for the names of several villages and *muthas*.

It is clearly not worth bothering about the historical accuracy of the legend. It is a portrait of a Kond as simple, brave, and strong; ingenious, but nevertheless outwitted by the Hindu king and mocked by his courtiers. Another element is that Olopo, who set out to found his own chiefdom, was a Kond. This fits with a persistent tradition among the Konds—and indeed among most Adibasis—that they have been driven out of the lowlands by the Hindus and forced to take refuge in the hills. But it is not so much that aspect with which I am concerned. The interesting thing is that Olopo at the beginning of the story is the trusted henchman of the King. 'You and I are brothers,' says the king. Olopo asks for the hand of the king's daughter, and this is an implicit claim to equality. The legend is saying, 'Konds belong to the same community as the rulers: Konds are a dominant caste: they have fallen because they are a little stupid and are unlucky, and have had to come and live in the jungle: but in origin they are warriors and the associates of kings.'

I met this tradition in other contexts. When I was talking about it with a man of WARRIOR caste and a Kond, the Kond suddenly looked away into the sky and said with an air of careful detachment that he had been told, although he would not like to say how true it was, that Konds and WARRIORS were really the same caste. They had both come to the Kondmals and the WARRIORS were those who had been successful, while those who were not so successful remained Konds. The WARRIOR did not deny it, and with a similar air of scientific impartiality remarked sententiously that you became what you were fated to become and the story might well be true. I do not think it is true: the cultural differences between Kond and Oriya are too great. The story must be taken as a legend in which the Konds claim equality with the dominant class among the Oriyas.

At times Konds deny high status even to the WARRIORS. An old Kond who lives near Bisipara was describing the arrival of the British, which his father's elder brother—so he said—had witnessed. When the conversation came round to the fighting qualities of the Konds I asked about the role of Oriya WARRIORS who appear in some of the earlier reports as leaders of Kond resistance. The Kond rejected this: 'What is their lineage name? Bisoi. What is that? It's *bisa* (a brass rod which is used as a weighing scale). That just shows what they were. They weren't soldiers and fighters at all. They're just traders. They came here for trade. We let them come, because we wouldn't lower ourselves by trading.' In fact 'Bisoi' was a title of service under the Hindu kings of Orissa. It is true that Oriyas are traders, and that their settlements are along the lines of communication, but these settlements occupy the best land. This fact, together with the many traditions of hard fights to win this land, disprove the old man's statement that Oriyas and WARRIORS were there only on sufferance. However there is a strong tradition among Konds that they are the real fighters, and the really dominant group, and that they have lost their dominance through the treachery and trickery of the Oriyas.

THE POLITICAL SYSTEM OF THE ORIYAS

The Kondmals form the most northern extension of the Eastern Ghats into the valley of the Mahanadi river. These mountains run down the coast of India to the valley of the Godaveri, but I am concerned only with the northern tip. This is a promontory of hills jutting into and surrounded on three sides by plains and river valleys. The hills are the home of tribal peoples. On the plains and in the valleys of the great lowland rivers live Oriyas, divided into a number of small kingdoms, which were classified until 1948 as the Feudatory or Tributary States of Orissa. To the north and north-west of the Kondmals is the kingdom of Boad: to the east of Boad and therefore to the north-east of the Kondmals lay Daspalla; south of this, to the south and south-east of the Kondmals, was the lowland kingdom of Gumsur. South of this was a small kingdom, Suradah, and south again lay Kimedi, Jeypore, and other states (Map 3). These Kingdoms were states composed of

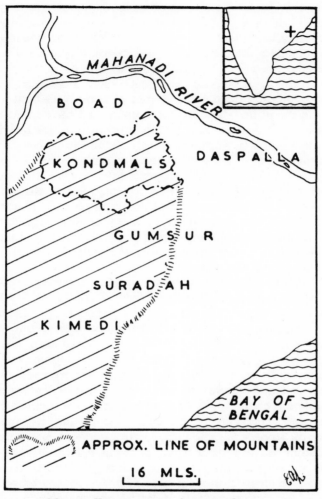

MAP 3.—KONDMALS AND ADJACENT STATES

smaller chiefdoms, the leaders of which owed allegiance to the king and held their land from him. The kingdoms were hostile to one another, and their history is marked by constant warfare, in which one king sought either to subdue his neighbour and make him a subordinate ally, or by conquest or bribery to detach chiefdoms from a rival kingdom and attach them to himself.

Geographically there is the clearest of boundaries between the hills and the plain. There are no foothills, and the descent to the plains is, on the west, north, east, and north-east of the Kondmals, so abrupt that it is appropriate to call the mountains a 'wall'. From the plains of Gumsur, for instance, within a distance of two miles, the height above sea level passes from 500 feet to 2,000 feet. On other sides the ascent is not so spectacular, but it is still sufficient to mark off the hills from the plains by the most distinct topographical line. The political line dividing the Kondmals from the surrounding Oriya kingdoms is not so distinct. For at least nine centuries—and I need not say that this date is uncertain—the Oriya peoples of the plains have established colonies in the hills, and have, through these colonies and directly, entered into political relationships with the Konds. From the point of view of the Oriya kingdoms the Kond hills were a frontier area, dangerous because it was inhabited by warlike tribes who not only fought among themselves but also raided into the metropolitan area. The lowland kingdoms protected themselves by establishing military colonies, by trying to settle tribal disputes, and by endeavouring to change tribal culture—in the broadest sense of that word—to resemble the culture of the settled and relatively pacified metropolitan area. This is one reason why, when the state had sufficient power, the frontier became a moving frontier: each newly pacified area had its own turbulent tribes on the new frontier. This is, of course, not the only motive for expansion. Protection often seems to be an incident to movements which are motivated in other ways. Many settlers have been land-grabbers : their migration was perhaps caused by overcrowding in the metropolitan area. Some were adventurers, soldiers of fortune whose ambitions could not be accommodated in the kingdom. In the small Oriya states these adventurers may have been rebels who were defeated and who went off, like Olopo Malik (Case 36: p. 160), to found a chiefdom in the frontier territory.

I compared the Kondmals to a promontory in a sea of Oriya

10 *a* and *b*.

Oriya musicians: clean caste

kingdoms. Each kingdom had its own frontier: all kingdoms established colonies and sought to extend their influence in the hills adjoining their territory. In this way one kingdom was brought into contact with others which lay on the other side of the hills. Of the kingdoms I have mentioned Boad's only neighbour on the plains was Daspalla. But it was in contact with other Oriya kingdoms across the no-man's-land of Kond territory. The moving frontiers of each of the kingdoms did not actually meet in the Kond hills. In a sense Boad stopped at the edge of the hills. The territory above the hills was in no way to be compared with the more settled chiefdoms of the plains. It was a no-man's-land, a buffer territory. No-man's-land was, of course, the land of the Konds. The Oriyas settled military colonies among them and endeavoured to control them. This movement had some success, but not spectacular success. The Konds remained very largely their own masters. Kings attempted to attach Konds by ties of allegiance and by the associated religious institutions. They tried to change Kond society, to pacify it, and to make use of the Konds in order to carry on the fight with other kingdoms. But they were only partially successful.

The basic relationship in the Oriya political system was between a lord and his dependent. The lord demanded allegiance and granted territory. Allegiance meant either tribute or military service or both, and a ritual dependence upon the patron deity of the lord. The system was held together ultimately by the concentration of force in one of its parts. So long as the kingdom continued in existence at a given size, so long did the king have the power to compel allegiance from his feudatories. This sanction was weakest at the frontier. The frontier chiefdoms were farthest from the king and his armies, and nearest to his rivals. They could change sides. This was not always and everywhere the case in the Kondmals because there were in some places large territories of no-man's-land in between the frontier territories of two kingdoms. But where conditions were suitable this did happen. Macpherson wrote in 1841:[1]

(Case 37)   (Time: *c.* 1840)

'A late event established unequivocally the true nature of this relation [between the hill people and the king]. The Khond district,

---

[1] W. Macpherson, 1865, p. 41.

M

or rather half-district of Hodzoghoro, lately transferred its attach-
ment from Boad to Gumsur. This affair was the subject of frequent
discussion while I was at Boad between the chief servants of the
Boad Raja, and the Khond chiefs who visited me. The right of any
Khond community to dissolve old and enter into new relations was
not disputed on the part of the zemindar [king]. He complained only
of the loss, through the arts of Sam Bissye, of an old subordinate
ally whom he had never injured. The idea of defection of a subject
society, far less the departure of a fief from its allegiance, was not
for a moment contemplated. *The rajah had, however, put forward very
different pretensions before I had an opportunity to institute exact inquiry.*'
[My italics.]

The text emphasizes that the Oriya hill communities (Hodzoghoro is in fact an Oriya district) were *subordinate allies* of the
king. They were not subjects. But, as the equivocation of the Raja
mentioned in the last sentence shows, he would have liked them
to be subjects. Distance and the presence of rivals prevented him
from asserting his claim and the hill chiefdoms were bound in
much more loosely than were the chiefdoms of metropolitan
districts. They were all but beyond the sanction of force. If they
paid tribute, it was likely to be nominal tribute and their allegiance
was uncertain.

The different subordinate chiefdoms from time to time attacked
one another, either raiding for loot, or to conquer territory, or to
attach another chiefdom in a dependent relationship. The same
process which went on between the various kingdoms also went
on inside those kingdoms. There were continuous struggles to
rearrange the ladder of lordship and dependency. In the metropolitan area these struggles were likely to have been inhibited by
the power of the king, by his watchfulness to prevent any of his
subordinates becoming sufficiently powerful to challenge him, and
by incipient bureaucratic administration. These struggles no doubt
went on, and many of the hill chieftains must have originated as
unsuccessful challengers to their neighbours or to their lords, or as
dynastic rivals within chiefdoms who rebelled and were defeated.
Nevertheless in the metropolitan territory there was some kind of
order. Relatively it was pacified. But this was not so in the hills.
The king could not be a policeman there, for he had not the
power. The Oriya colonies in the hills were not part of a co-
ordinated military force protecting the frontier. They fought one

another when it suited them to do so. The Domosinghi force which attacked Besringia was led by the Oriyas of Nuaga, who styled themselves as the 'Rajas' of Domosinghi. This force was opposed by the Oriyas of Bisipara, as well as by the Besringia Konds.[1] I have other stories of fighting between Oriya settlements. In the hills each settlement stood on its own[2] and owed loose allegiance to the Boad king and to no-one else. The settlements did not build up by allegiances into larger units. They were themselves maximal political segments.[3] There were no Oriya chiefdoms embracing large sections of the Kondmals and containing dependent chiefs, who were themselves masters of other dependent chiefs. The Oriya settlements were small and were separated by wide stretches of Kond territory. No chief was big enough or commanded

[1] See p. 61.

[2] There are a few agnatic connections between settlements arising from migrations but there is no structure of agnatic kinship connecting the villages into one system.

[3] Although there was no regional system based on relationships of lordship and dependency, there does seem to have been another kind of regional organization between the Oriya colonies, similar in some ways to the Kond region. Hodzoghoro appears in Case 37. This was a region lying to the south-east of the Kondmals and it is an Oriya unit and not, as the text says, a Kond territory. There are three other regions: Panchokuso; Barokuso; and Choudo-kuso. These are known together as the Four Forts. At the present day there are periodical meetings of the Oriya WARRIOR caste based on this organization. I have seen the minutes of recent meetings and decisions are recorded with this preamble: 'We of the Four Forts, sons and grandsons of the Ten Families, have decided. . . .' Each area has its own headman and nominates its representatives for the general meetings. These meetings to-day are concerned exclusively with caste policy and with punishing those who break the rules laid down about bridewealth, or who contract the wrong kind of marriage, and so forth. This—and here is its resemblance to the Kond system—is a meeting of equals, of kinsmen and potential kinsmen, and it meets to regulate kinship affairs. It is not organized on the Oriya principle of hierarchy and dependence. There are leaders but these are chairmen rather than lords: they are first among their equals and not lords among their dependents. To-day these meetings are not political. But it is possible that in the past they were used to co-ordinate military action. When the Boad king led an army across the Kondmals to attack the King of Kimedi (see p. 171), the hill Oriyas went with him, and they may have been mobilized in the pattern of the Four Forts. Macpherson's reference to the defection of Hodzoghoro suggests that the Four Forts were political groups. But I could get no confirmation from traditions about the Kimedi war, and I never heard a reference to the Four Forts which suggested that they were part of a military organization. I think they may well have been. But I do not know that they were.

sufficient forces to do more than grab small pieces of territory from another chief: they could not reduce one another to the status of permanent dependents. They could not rely upon the Konds to give permanent allegiance, for the Konds too were subordinate allies and no doubt likely to play off one Oriya chief against another.

The Oriya colony differed in structure from a Kond village. It was based on the interdependence of castes and not upon agnatic kinship. It was divided politically into two categories of persons— or, to be exact, one group and one category. The group was the dominant caste,[1] who in the Kondmals were WARRIORS (*Sudo*). The dependent category was made up of several castes—BRAHMIN, BARBER, HERDSMAN, untouchables, and others—who, while they were kinship groups, were not corporate political groups.

The internal structure of the WARRIOR caste-group in each Oriya village is similar to that of a group of Konds in a Kond village. It consists usually of a maximal lineage, with a fringe of small sister's son lineages attached, and one or two other small lineages. As in the Kond village there is evidence that much of the agnation is fictitious agnation and that the local group has been made up of people who have come from different places. There is a *de facto* village exogamy. This exogamy is not prescribed on a residential basis and occasional marriages take place between the sister's son lineages and the main lineage.[2] Marriage almost always is outside the political community, just as is the Kond marriage. The maximal lineage segments into a number of smaller lineages, which are equal in rank, although they may not be equal in power. One segment provides the chief, but this is in no sense a royal lineage. Any other WARRIOR segment can take its place, if it has the power to do so. In Bisipara the present chiefly lineage of Bisois supplanted a lineage of Naiks. Within the large Bisoi lineage itself the chieftainship seems to have remained in one line for the last five generations. The chief is first among equals and his relationship to the other WARRIORS is quite different from his relationship to people of other caste. At present WARRIORS form approximately

[1] For a further discussion of 'dominant caste', see pp. 257–263.
[2] The rule of *sapinda* exogamy, prohibiting connections within five degrees on the mother's side, makes it unlikely that the sister's son lineage can marry more than twice into the main lineage, until after a long time has passed. After the second marriage the whole of the main lineage is likely to fall into the prohibited category.

20 per cent of the population of Bisipara. In the last hundred years there have been many immigrants of other caste than WARRIOR and I would guess that the WARRIOR population would be at least half of the traditional village but this is little more than a guess.

The dependent castes are of two kinds, the community servants and the field workers. The former are BRAHMIN, BARBER, HERDS-MAN, WASHERMAN, and so forth. The latter are mainly PANS. The specialized community servants are likely to have been few in number, as they are to-day. I have distinguished them from the fieldworkers not by their specialization but because they are servants of the community, that is, of all the clean castes. They are attached to no one particular person or family, but their work and their payment is settled by the community in the village council. The fieldworkers were in a different position. Each family was attached as *proja* (subject) to a family of WARRIORS, who were in this relationship called 'king' (*raja*). I have called this the patron-client relationship. 'Who is he?', one may still ask: and the answer is, 'He is so-and-so's untouchable'.

We tend to think of caste-groups in a village as corporate political groups. Nowadays this is becoming true. In many villages the untouchables, for instance, are ranged as a political group against a dominant caste. But in the traditional system this was not so. There was only one corporate political group in the village and that was the dominant caste. Other castes were attached to it, not as groups, but piecemeal, if I may put it that way. In so far as an untouchable had political relationships with other persons of his own caste, or with persons of another caste, these relationships were mediated through the WARRIOR patron. As political groups, castes other than the WARRIOR had no corporate existence. Political ties went upwards towards the WARRIOR caste and not sideways towards their caste-fellows. If I may use an analogy which will be useful later, the dependent castes are like a conquered population which is split up and dispersed by individual attachments among the conquerors, and thus loses its corporate identity. I am making this point at length because it is important in understanding how the Konds fitted in the caste system. They were not the conquered and dispersed population: rather they were the subordinate ally which, after being conquered, retained its corporate identity.

KONDS AND ORIYAS BEFORE THE COMING OF THE
ADMINISTRATION

Many Kond lineage names are titles granted by Oriya kings:
Jhankero or Dehuri, indicating priestly office: Bisoi, Naik, Malik,
or Mahalik denoting leadership, and in particular military leadership; and various others derived from offices the nature of which
I do not know, such as Maji, Prodhan, Behera, and so forth.
There seems in theory to be a basic name in the caste which is not
connected with an office: for the WARRIORS it is Amato; for the
Konds it is Kohoro, although I have sometimes heard that the
latter too is a title. At the present day the only titles which continue to be assumed are the religious ones, Dehuri and Jhankero,
although this too happens only in a few cases. For most people the
name does not indicate office any more than does a name like
Chamberlain among ourselves. The great majority of the Konds
in the Kondmals are called Kohoro. The next most common name
is Malik. But in the eastern Kondmals, which is nearest to Boad
and on the most accessible route from the plains, Kohoro is comparatively rare and there are many Prodhans, Beheras, and Majis.
Here the influence of the Boad raja was stronger than in the rest
of the Kondmals.

One must not draw too many conclusions from the Oriya
titles among Kond lineage names. It does not mean that everyone
with such a title is descended from people who served the king.
Those who are called Prodhan say that they were given this title
because they were important (that is one meaning of the word) in
the king's service. Those who are not called Prodhan say that this is
nonsense: in reality the Prodhans are bastards descended of a
marriage between an Oriya called Prodhan and a Kond woman,
and the descendants have somehow got themselves accepted as
Konds.[1] Both stories about Prodhan are probably true. Some
Konds were granted the title, just as Olopo had at first the title of
Malik (Case 36). Other Prodhans are descended of mixed marriages. Others may have assumed the title.[2] I draw the minimum

---

[1] There is at the moment a SWEEPER family in Bisipara bearing the typically
SMITH title of Bindhani which they got from their SMITH father, while they
derived their caste membership from their SWEEPER mother.
[2] A. M. Hocart, 1950, pp. 57–63.

conclusion: that there were probably political relationships between Konds and Oriyas, and that some Konds may have served the kings and received titles from them.

A favourite story about the old days in the Kondmals describes a war between the king of Boad and the king of Kimedi. The king of Boad led an expedition across the Kondmals in order to seize an idol at Mahasinghi. His armies remained there for twelve years without success: then the Boad king obtained divine intervention, seized the idol, and returned home. At an Oriya village called Bondogarh he received another revelation and a tank was created by means of a miracle. Proceeding further towards home, when he came to the village of Bolscoopa, one of his dogs started a hare, but the hare, instead of running away, pursued the dog. This was a second revelation and the king established the idol at Bolscoopa. Until recently the deity of the Boad raja was worshipped annually, first in Boad itself, then at Bolscoopa, and finally at Bondogarh. The armies which made up the expedition consisted not only of hill Oriyas—and presumably Oriyas from Boad—but also of Konds. Most of these seem to have been drawn from the eastern Kondmals and from the Salki valley, although my investigations were not sufficiently extensive for me to be sure that Konds in other parts of the Kondmals did not go on the expedition. The backbone of the Kond contingent was the Six Lands (Case 24: p. 82). Bolscoopa, although it is an Oriya village, lies in the midst of their country, and the people of the Six Lands take an active part in the rites and are more concerned with the cult than are other Konds. But other Kond groups, which are the hereditary enemies of the people of the Six Lands, also went to Mahasinghi. Traditional enmities among the Oriyas also seem not to have counted. Both the Bisipara Oriyas and the Nuaga Oriyas believe that their ancestors took part.

Macpherson, writing in 1841, said that according to records in Boad—which I have not been able to trace—this expedition took place in the ninth century.[1] The Kond legends, the use of Oriya titles by the Konds, and the stories of the Mahasinghi war are sufficient to show that the Konds and the Oriya peoples both in the plains and the hills have been part of one political field for—if we accept Macpherson's date—at least nine centuries.

The Oriya supremacy and the powers of the Oriya chieftains,

[1] L. S. S. O'Malley, 1908, p. 72.

both in extent and in limitation, are shown clearly in the early records. Campbell, who fought in the Meriah Wars, had much to say on this, because it concerned the tactics to be employed in suppressing the Meriah rite. He wrote:[1]

> 'A [Kond] community is formed of a union of villages called a 'Mootah', and these again united to form a district . . . Districts again are governed by a chief of Oriya extraction, called "bissoi", the descendant usually of some daring adventurer, whose fallen fortunes drove him to the hills where, with his band of followers, he received a cordial welcome from the mountain tribes. The Khonds regarded such a warrior more capable to rule over them, and more fit to lead them on in battle, than one of their own tribe.'

None of this conflicts with the evidence I found, other than the 'cordial welcome'. Elsewhere he writes:[2]

> 'From long hereditary sway their chiefs exercized considerable influence, and had the power of moving to much mischief; or by precept and example smoothing the way and satisfying their people of the true object of our coming among them . . . The Ooryah chiefs, then, were my principal instruments for the suppression of the Meriah rite, and on them I chiefly depend for maintaining the ground we have gained.'

In a third quotation Campbell is explicit about the limited powers of the Oriya chief:[3]

> 'The "Bissois", the only people who could possibly be expected to second our views, have only a few peons in whom they could rely on such an occasion. The great mass of their subjects are Konds, their influence is the moral effect of habit, not of physical power; and men thus situated cannot be expected to aid in the compulsory abolition of a custom which all the surrounding tribes hold sacred.'

WARRIORS and their chiefs were superior in political rank to Konds and Konds were subordinate. But they were dependents in quite a different sense from dependents of other castes, like the fieldworkers. Konds retained their corporate identity in political groups. The Oriya chief commanded the allegiance of a group which was politically corporate in its own right. The chief was not the lord of individual Konds, as he was of some individuals in the

---

[1] J. Campbell, 1861, p. 12.   [2] *Ibid.*, p. 33.   [3] *Ibid.*, p. 1.

fieldworker caste. Nor did the other WARRIORS, who had *proja* among the fieldworkers, also have Kond *proja*. In so far as they had political relationships with Konds, they had them as corporate groups. In other words Konds were subordinate allies: and in this respect their dependence was not that which is typical of a caste system. The link between the WARRIORS and the Konds was not based upon specialization and was rather mechanical than organic, to use Durkheim's concepts. The Konds were, if I can put it this way, a kind of second dominant caste of landholders and warriors.

Kond political institutions continued to operate on many occasions as if the Oriyas were not there at all. The process of fission and accretion by taking on the obligations of brotherhood continued to keep the Kond population adjusted to the capacity of the land. It seems that the Oriyas were concerned in this, perhaps as arbiters, and perhaps, as Campbell suggests, and as happened in the war between Bisipara and the Nuaga people, as leaders. Indeed, it is as if the WARRIORS are on occasions drawn out of their own system of political relationships and compelled to act in terms of Kond political institutions. Conversely, on occasions the Konds are drawn out of their tribal political system and act within the Oriya system, as when they fought at Mahasinghi.

Localized Kond political systems, of the type which I described earlier, operate in a political field which contains also Oriya political institutions. At first sight this is true of any caste. For example the HERDSMAN caste has its own council and regulates its own internal affairs. It can be described as a system of social relations existing within a larger system of many castes. But the difference is that the HERDSMAN caste is concerned only with kinship and ritual and not with control over land and resources. HERDSMAN political relationships in the traditional system were mediated through WARRIORS. But the Kond system was also a system of political relationships: through these relationships Konds achieved control over land and resources. Politically the Kond was a member of a corporate group of Konds: the HERDSMAN was not in the same way a member of a corporate political group. This is one way of stating in institutional terms the difference between a tribe and a caste.[1]

For nine centuries the Konds lived under two different sets of political institutions: their own and the Oriya system. These

[1] See also pp. 263–266.

institutions conflict: they enjoin contradictory courses of action. Under the one system the Konds of Balimendi are the enemies of the Rupamendi Konds: in the Oriya system they are allies who go off together to fight the king of Kimedi. When there is a conflict of institutions of this kind we look for the means of resolving it: we feel that there ought to be consistency and that this will come about through the modification of one or the other set of rules. In this case, in the light of what happened afterwards we would have expected Kond groups slowly to divest their political function, and the Balimendi Konds and the Konds of Rupamendi to cease fighting against one another and come to fight only at one another's side. But for nine centuries this did not happen. What are the conditions which permitted this inconsistency to continue for so long?

One way of answering is to invoke situational selection. In some situations the Konds acted as if they were Konds: in others they acted as if they were dependents of the Oriya kings and chiefs. But this is only half-way to an answer: one must say what are the conditions which made it possible for the Konds to behave now under one set of rules and now under another. To do this is to analyse the weaknesses of the Oriya kings and Oriya hill chiefs: to say why they were unable to bring the Konds into their own political system in the way that other dependent castes were incorporated. The primary weakness of the hill chiefs, as the quotations from Campbell show, lay in numbers. Even at the present day, when there has been a vast increase in the numbers of Oriya settlers in the Kondmals, Konds are five out of every eight persons. In the traditional period they must have been a considerably larger proportion of the population. The Oriya chiefs depended on their services as soldiers. Oriya chiefs could conquer small patches of territory. But they had no forces at their disposal to conquer the Konds and to incorporate them as fieldworkers or non-military dependents.

A second weakness which ran from the top to the bottom in the Oriya system was internal conflict. Oriya hill chiefs fought against one another. They had to be careful with their Kond following, for fear of causing defections. The kings too fought against one another, and they in their turn were continually losing or gaining the support of subordinate allies. There was no concerted effort to pacify the frontier and bring the Konds to heel. The Oriya political system was too much fragmented to be capable of such an effort. Viewed as predatory states, the Oriya kingdoms were too much in conflict with each other and within themselves to become efficient imperialists. States of this kind are inherently incapable of operating in anything but small units. Only bureaucratic institutions could organize larger units and overcome the many difficulties of governing the Kondmals from a centre in Boad. The larger kingdoms of the Orissa coastal plain had judicial, military, and revenue officials, and there may have been such a system in metropolitan Boad itself. But there certainly was no political specialization of this kind in the hills. The Oriya chief did not hold an office: he held every office: and it was this fact which made it so difficult to control him from Boad, and made it easy for him to transfer his allegiance and his followers to another raja. But these same factors, which made him strong in the face of the Boad king, made him weak before the Konds. He stood by himself, certainly as the cultural representative of Boad, but not under Boad's protection as its political representative.

For nine centuries or more the Konds remained a tribe and did not become a caste because they lived in a frontier territory, protected from the political domination of the Oriya kings and ruling castes by their own remoteness, by their numbers, and by the weaknesses of the Oriya political system.[1]

THE ADMINISTRATION AND THE ORIYA SIRDARS

In 1836 the Raja of Gumsur, one of the lowland Oriya kingdoms (Map 3), became involved in war with the East India Company. The king had been tributary since the beginning of the century, and the occasion of the war was his failure to pay tribute. The rebellion was crushed, the king fled, and his kingdom was taken over and directly administered by the Madras Government. The raja fled into frontier territory taking refuge with the Konds. A small detachment of troops, sent to capture him, was caught in a defile and massacred by the Konds. Other forces were sent and in the course of operations the East India Company discovered

---

[1] As Case 11 (p. 42) and other cases show, the Konds are thoroughly imbued with the ritual values of the caste system. But in this book I am rather concerned with the degree to which they were affected by the economic and political relationships of the caste system.

that Konds practised a rite of human sacrifice. This was deemed contrary to natural justice and the Company, protesting that it had no wish to take over more territory, and grudging every rupee which its policy cost, spent over twenty years campaigning in the Kond hills to suppress both human sacrifice and female infanticide.

The Meriah Wars deserve a book in themselves.[1] Each year in the cold weather an expedition went into the hills. In their reports the officers in charge of these expeditions describe their own efforts to win the confidence of the Konds by persuasion, showing them the benefits of an orderly and settled administration, and convincing them by reasoned eloquence, that fertility and prosperity could be had without human sacrifice. In their remarks about one another's conduct the same officers describe how villages were burned, stores of grain destroyed, and the leaders of the Konds flogged or hanged. I said earlier that the Oriya kingdoms were too much in conflict to be efficient imperialists. The same seems to have been true of the Company. The Meriah Wars were a story of jealousies and spectacular confusion. In the early years the northern part of the Kond hills, including the Kondmals, lay within the jurisdiction of the South-West Frontier Agency of Bengal. Gumsur and the area to the south belonged to the Northern Circars of Madras. There were many complaints about the lack of co-ordination, which the Konds and the Oriya chiefs quickly learnt to exploit. When the Gumsur Konds had been terrorized sufficiently and were afraid to organize a sacrifice on their own land, they could always make a bootlegging arrangement with the Boad Konds; and vice versa. In later years this difficulty was overcome, but the conflict continued in other forms. There was a bitter struggle, which was prolonged for many years in print, between the two soldiers principally concerned in the Meriah Wars, Macpherson and Campbell. Macpherson himself had continuous difficulties from his immediate superior Bannerman, who had charge of the lowland areas in Ganjam. For various reasons Campbell and Macpherson alternated several times with one another. When Campbell had charge he reversed the arrangements made by Macpherson, and on one occasion succeeded in getting Macpherson and his entire staff put under

[1] I intend to describe in detail elsewhere the Meriah Wars and the annexation of the Kond hills. See p. 192, note 1.

arrest. When Macpherson had charge he removed and then imprisoned the Oriya chief Sam Bissye, in whom Campbell had frequently expressed his confidence. Reading between the lines Sam Bissye was making use of the patronage of Campbell to extend his own influence in the hills and crush his rivals. Other chiefs made similar use of Macpherson. The Oriya staff, which he brought with him from the plains, spent much of their time extorting bribes from the Konds. It is not surprising that the Konds themselves made use of this confusion. They fought with one another: they raided into the plains. Some sided quite early with the Company: others fought it to the end: many did not commit themselves until they saw which way the battle was going. Both Konds and Oriyas were equally involved, just as they had both been involved in the Meriah sacrifice. The Boad raja was drawn into the conflict, and he and his advisers also made good use of dissension within the Company's ranks. For some time the Company endeavoured to get its policy carried out in the northern part of the Kond hills by putting pressure on the Boad raja, but by 1855 it had become clear that he either could not or would not pacify the Kondmals and put an end to the Meriah rite. The Kondmals were annexed, and put in charge of a Tahsildar.

From the perspective of history the Meriah Wars seem a period of anarchy. One might think that the violence and the destruction of property would have destroyed all existing political and most social institutions, and wiped the slate clean for the development of the new form of society which the Company and a few years later the Government of India were bringing to the Kond hills. But this was not so. For many of the hill peoples this must have been little more than an intensification of the usual modes of political activity, set off by and somewhat complicated by the presence of the Company's armies. There is no evidence that during the period of the wars there emerged new groupings based on new institutions, and that the old allegiances to clan and to chief were destroyed. Certainly the structure was likely to have become more fluid, but it did not change. This is not surprising: both the Kond and the Oriya systems were warlike, and their institutions were adapted to making war. The radical changes that came later are to be traced not to the anarchy of the war years, but to peace.

For twenty years after annexation the Kondmals were ruled by a man called Dinobandu Patnaik, holding office as Tahsildar. For some years he was supported by soldiers, who were later replaced by a police force. Dinobandu is remembered for his demonic energy and calculated brutality. He extorted a fortune for himself, and in the process broke the warlike spirit of the Konds. Where duty might fail to move him, profit supplied the motive. His name means, I am told, 'friend of the poor'. The country was remote and Dinobandu ruled virtually unsupervised, three weeks posting away from his superior. He and his successors appeared much more appropriately as chiefs, having all the functions of government in themselves, controlling their armies (the police), and paying tribute to their superiors in the form of giving no trouble and keeping the district quiet. Such slender resources meant that the government had to be carried on through existing institutions, and Dinobandu, being himself an Oriya, made use of Oriya institutions, and, when possible, of Oriya men. He governed through Oriya chiefs, who themselves had virtually all the functions of government in the territories granted to them, and who owed allegiance to Dinobandu and gave him this by assisting in his exactions, and no doubt getting a share for themselves. The Oriya chiefs became, or were confirmed as, headmen in the administrative divisions (*muthas*) which themselves were based upon the Kond clan-territories. The new administrative divisions were also political communities, although they were no longer able to fight one another. Through membership of these divisions the people achieved command over resources. For many years the only specialization in government was between the police and the Revenue department. None of the many departments which are found to-day—Welfare, Excise, Agriculture, Medicine, Veterinary, and so forth—were then in existence. The *mutha* headman resembled his former self, the chief, in that he combined in his person all the offices of government, even, at this level, the police. The *mutha* was at that time a complete political unit. The headman was a lord (*raja*) and the people were his subjects (*proja*).

Loyalty to the headman persists. One of the *muthas* of the Six Lands has recently been put in charge of a Kond Sirdar: but, according to my informants, the Konds still obey and consult the Oriya headman, whom the Administration had deposed for peculation. They go to him to have their cases settled rather than

11. The wedding of a Headman's son.

As an act of homage the groom is being carried on the shoulders of a Bearingia Kond.

to their own Kond headman. Besringia provides a particularly good example of loyalty to a chief. The son of the Bisoi (this lineage name has become a synonym for Sirdar) was married in 1953. The Konds of Besringia came to pay homage on a scale and in a way quite distinct from the more sober expressions of good-will that came from other castes. They came in hundreds, a great winding procession dancing and swaying to the music of drums, blowing the horns which formerly played them into battle, armed with axes, firing off guns, dressed in the traditional war panoply of buffalo horns and peacock feathers. To my surprise I identified, in the middle of the dust and tumult, the WARRIOR head-man himself and half a dozen staid middle-aged WARRIORS dancing and shouting and stamping with the rest. None of the other Oriya castes joined in. This was an act of homage. It is something which no official, not even the Deputy Commissioner himself, can command: although similar shows are sometimes stage-managed for visiting politicians. A large Kond contingent, almost as large as that from Besringia, came from the neighbouring *mutha* of Jurapangia. Their leader explained to me that they were descended from the senior line of one of the founding lineages of the Bes-ringia clan. They now belonged to Jurapangia *mutha*.[1] But their Bisoi (the name of the chief's lineage) was the Besringia Bisoi: they were his subjects and he was their king: and, at the time of his investment, they had the right to bind the turban of office about his head. They had kept up this relationship for almost a hundred years, in spite of belonging to a different *mutha*. I suppose this is what Campbell meant when he talked of the 'moral force of habit'.[2] These attitudes were probably developed before the Meriah Wars, and such loyalty could probably be commanded by the successful Oriya chief even before the arrival of the Admini-stration.

Before the coming of the Administration the act of accretion involved ties of quasi-agnation, such as those of the Jiura-Malika people and the Damopara people in the Balimendi clan.[3] But, where there was a successful Oriya chief, then accretion must also have involved an act of allegiance towards him. The right of the incoming group to land, and their right to protection by the community they were joining, was validated in both systems.

[1] See p. 74.   [2] See p. 172.   [3] See pp. 48–49.

After the coming of the Administration protection of this kind was no longer required. There was neither the need nor the possibility of protecting one's own land or conquering other people's land by force of arms. Instead one bought the land and invoked the protection of the representative of the Government, who was the *mutha* headman, sometimes an Oriya and sometimes a Kond. This headman had many of the characteristics of a lord, and the division he administered was not merely a division, but also a community. The newcomers joined this community by offering their allegiance to him and they received from him, as the representative of the Government, protection and validation of their right to land. The Oriya headman—or his Kond counterpart —now ruled by something more than the moral force of habit: he had become a bureaucrat. But he still ruled the people as their lord.

This is the period in which there is for the first time discernible a curtailment of Kond political institutions. For many centuries the Kond communities, independent and with their own Kond institutions, existed side by side with Oriya communities. They seemed to be able to make occasional sorties into Oriya political life and yet maintain their own institutions and their corporate political existence. We traced this to the weakness of the Oriyas and to the nature of Oriya political institutions. Both systems allowed for warfare: and it seemed almost as if in the hills the Oriyas were drawn into the Kond political system. But after 1855 the bureaucracy, although meagre, was nevertheless able to keep the peace. It was—and this was part of the same process—strong enough to see that title to land no longer could be validated only in the Kond political system and by force of arms. The Kond political community began to be transformed into a community which involved Konds and Oriyas in a continuous relationship, which was activated in Oriya institutions, and of which the typical relationship was not that between brothers, but that between a lord and his dependent.

THE ADMINISTRATION AND THE KONDS

The Konds have always been recognized by the Administration as a category separate from the Oriyas, not to be governed as if they were ordinary Oriya cultivators on the plains. Bad communications, the evil reputation of the climate, and the expense in money and men of garrisoning the Kondmals—not to speak of the difficulties of guerilla warfare against the robust and turbulent Konds—all made the Company more than ordinarily conscious of the values of conciliation.

The Konds fought not so much because they wanted to preserve the Meriah rite, but because they feared their land would be taken or taxed. This fear was played upon by the more astute leaders of the Konds, particularly the Oriya leaders and the agents of the Boad raja. In 1855 Samuells, who had charge of the annexation of the Kondmals, issued a proclamation. The Konds would not be taxed: there would be no forced labour. The Government would not interfere in any way with 'the established usages and principles of justice of the Hill races, or change injuriously the hereditary authority and privileges of the Rajas, the Bissyes, the Mullickos, the Podies, the Konds and other Hill Chiefs'. The intention, clearly, was to conserve existing political and social institutions. That was the promise and the intention. The fulfilment was otherwise. Dinobandu Tahsildar first introduced the Kondmals to the benefits of regular administration. A 'torrent of eager exploiters' descended on the Kondmals. Just as the Oriya chiefs could disregard the Boad king, when they wanted to do so, so Dinobandu and his subordinates and personal followers could evade the Government's promise to respect Kond rights and Kond property.

In 1891 the Kondmals were made a sub-division of Angul District. Angul is separated from the Kondmals by the Mahanadi river, and in that time it was separated also by the Tributary State of Boad. Although his immediate superior was nearer, the Kondmals Magistrate continued to be virtually independent. The Angul Deputy Commissioner made an annual visit, but the difficulties of travel and the Kondmal's own brand of malaria made sure that this inspection was, as one sardonic Sub-Divisional officer said, 'a hurried scamper'. In 1897 the Angul Regulations passed into law. The Magistrate in the Kondmals was allowed great discretion in applying regulations: and he was permitted to make his own regulations without further formality concerning sanitation, public health and communications. Legal protection was given to the Konds and an attempt was made to compensate for their disabilities in a formal system of law. Civil cases could be initiated without a formal petition: cognizance of crimes could be taken on

N

verbal statements alone: no legal practitioner could be employed without the permission of the Magistrate, and cases had to be argued by the litigants with the help of their articulate friends: Kond forms of oath could be used in the courts: the Magistrate was permitted and advised to refer cases for judgement to councils of tribal elders. In short, an effort was made to make the law easy of access and to strip it of the formalities which make it so much easier for the rich and sophisticated to employ the letter of the law to evade the intentions of the legislator. To put it crudely, the Magistrate had sufficient latitude to administer what he thought was justice rather than merely the law. If he liked the Kond and thought the Oriya a rascal—and the European Magistrates often did think in this way—then he could let this influence his judgement to a much greater extent than could a Magistrate in one of the Regulation Districts. The Angul Laws Regulations also provided economic protection for Konds. Interest on a debt could not exceed 24 per cent per annum. The total of accumulated interest could never exceed the sum lent. Land could not be transferred by sale, mortgage, or gift from a Kond to a non-Kond without the permission of the Magistrate. I have not the material to say in detail how far these measures[1] achieved their intention and how far they failed. The inundation of Hindu settlers, which swamped parts of the Gond country, never took place in the Kondmals, and this may be attributed to legislation, as well as to the deterrent climate and the shortage of rice land. On the other hand I know that the regulation about the transfer of land has been frequently evaded, either with the connivance of the Oriya clerks in the Record Office, or, more simply by not registering the transfer. My informants said that there were great abuses of this law at the time of the land settlement.

---

[1] The motives which led the Government to protect the Konds are clear. First there were the difficulties of conquest and subsequently the fear of uprisings. Later this motive receded in importance and became replaced by a vague idea that Konds were somehow more deserving than Oriyas. This attitude is found in any alien colonialist Government: it is the distinction drawn between the 'educated native' and the 'noble savage'. But it is also an attitude of mind more complex than this alone. People like the Konds were admired by Europeans for their manliness, their lack of subtlety, and for their avoidance of the forms of servility. At a less conscious level the educated native is disliked because he is challenge, but this could scarcely have been the case in so backward an area as the Kondmals.

The Administration set out to protect Konds from their Oriya exploiters. This was a negative policy: a reaction to trends unwittingly started. But throughout the same period there is discernible the germs of a policy which has the same object in view—protecting the Adibasi—but by different means. Both Campbell and Macpherson in their reports pressed for roads and markets. Campbell was anxious to see missionaries at work. The country should be opened: it should be made uniform with the rest of the Province: the Konds should be educated. This policy was carried on by those who came later. In 1875 the Konds were persuaded to pay what is called a 'voluntary' tax of three annas to the plough. The government doubled the sum so raised each year and this money was used to make roads. Some of it was used to build schools. After the turn of the century an Industrial School was built to teach Konds, and 'deserving persons' of other castes, crafts by which they might support themselves and improve the standard of living in the Kondmals. Much of this work was done by the local Magistrate, in particular by Ollenbach who served in the Kondmals between 1901 and 1924, and who was the very epitome of paternal government. Recently this has become the declared policy of the Government. The Konds are to be educated and equipped to hold their own in the modern economy and in the modern political arena. For the moment they are protected. If anything, the protection has been intensified. Kond land is still untaxed: it still cannot be alienated. Jobs in the Administration are reserved for Konds. There are scholarships for Konds. A number of Ashram schools have been founded, where Kond boys are boarded and given both a general and a vocational education. The Konds of the Kondmals have their own member in the Legislative Assembly of Orissa. The key word is 'uplift'. The Konds are to be made the cultural and social equals of the Oriyas, both those in the Kondmals and those in the plains. But for the moment they are protected.

For the last hundred years there have been two broad trends in Government policy towards the Konds: one is protection and conservation: the other is assimilation. But, whatever the end in view, the Konds have been treated as a separate category, and granted special privileges. This is one of the reasons why they are to-day emerging as a separate political community.

KONDS AND THE DIVERSIFIED ECONOMY

In the modern economy a number of accidents have combined to give the Konds a common economic interest against people of other communities. A proportion of all minor Government posts are reserved for Adibasis, providing persons with suitable qualifications come forward. But I was told that there are not many Konds who reach even the minimal standard required for a messenger. Very few qualify for clerical posts in Phulbani, but I believe that near the Baptist Mission at Udaygiri there are more Konds with the required qualifications. There are some Kond schoolmasters but, proportionately to their numbers in the total population, they are few compared to Oriya schoolmasters and those recruited from the untouchable castes which speak Oriya. Most of those who have found jobs in the Administration come from the Oriya-speaking eastern plateau in the Kondmals. There are better schools in Oriya villages, which are larger and on the lines of communication. Konds, on the other hand, live in remoter valleys, where either there is no school, or where the schoolmaster is less likely to be visited by inspectors and consequently takes his duties less seriously than do those who live near the bus route, and in villages which can be reached easily on a bicycle. In this way a smaller proportion of the Kond, and a larger proportion of the Oriya, population goes to school. A third reason is the competition offered by Oriya-speaking untouchables, like those who live in Bisipara. These have the same privileges as Adibasis and can compete more effectively: they grow up speaking Oriya and they live in the villages where the schools are built.[1]

The Konds have also failed to take advantage of the diversified economy to the same degree as Oriyas and Oriya untouchables. In Bisipara every Oriya and every untouchable makes something out of commerce. Old women peddle salt and spices around Kond villages. Men trade for turmeric and oilseeds. Some make and sell parched rice and paddy. Some are middlemen in the markets. Untouchables trade in live cattle and in hides. But between 1952 and 1955 I met only two Konds who worked as middlemen, and even they did so to supplement an income gained in other ways.

[1] This does not, of course, apply to all the untouchables, for many of these are Kui-speaking and live in Kond villages.

One was a Kond who had lived from childhood in Bisipara. The drunken headman of Baderi said to him one day in 1955, 'Hey you sod of Kond! Are you a Kond? You're the sort who destroys our customs, aren't you? Although you are a Kond, yet you come here trading for turmeric' (Case 38: p. 197). The other Kond trader had spent several years in the Tea Gardens of Assam, and he went about the bazaars and festivals selling mirrors and small trinkets. The Konds despised these two men. Their work was beneath the dignity of a Kond. Proud Konds say that trade is work for Oriyas and untouchables: humble Konds say that they are too stupid to trade and would be outwitted by Oriyas. This is true: in the turmeric trade the Oriyas combine to keep one another in business. It pays a Kond who lives half-a-mile from the merchant to sell his turmeric to an Oriya middleman. The Oriya still makes a profit, because the merchant will give the Oriya a better price than he will give to a Kond. It is in the merchant's interest to retain agents who help him by combing the hinterland and diverting turmeric which might go to other merchants. Nor did any merchants retain Kond agents, so far as I know, other than the detribalized man in Bisipara. Many Konds have no reason to break into the ring of traders, for they can get cash by growing turmeric. They alone grow turmeric. No Oriya regularly grows it, although a few experiment from time to time. Oriyas say that the work is not worth the return; that they can get money by trading and in other ways; and that they need not lower themselves by growing turmeric like a Kond. There are other reasons. To protect young turmeric plants from the sun the field must be covered with a thick layer of leafy branches. Most Oriya villages stand clear of the jungle and the branches would have to be carted long distances. Kond villages, especially in the remoter valleys, lie against the jungle.

Konds are ranged as a class of producers against Oriya middle-men. They have a common interest in opposition to trading classes. The bureaucracy recognizes this cleavage. Regulations governing credit and alienation of land help to preserve the distinction, by maintaining the Konds as a separate economic class, when otherwise they might have been reduced to labourers in the service of Oriya merchant-landowners. Konds have, against the local Oriyas, a common economic interest which is recognized by the Administration. They have an incentive to act in concert against local Oriyas and to maintain the privileges and safeguards which the Administration gives them. They have, in other words, a motive for becoming a political group. In the modern representative democracy numbers count, and the Konds are learning to organize themselves to make effective use of numerical superiority.

THE WIDER POLITICAL ARENA

Dibi Kohoro (the strong man of Baderi), by establishing the right relationship with the Magistrate, was able to make himself a power in his village and, indeed, in the eastern Kondmals (Case 28: p. 95). But even in Dibi's lifetime the centre of power was moving away from Phulbani. After Ollenbach left in 1924 there was a relatively rapid turnover of officials, none of whom learnt to speak Kui or established the same close personal relationships with Konds. They came and went quickly, and for some years before independence the Magistrates were Indians, who, I think I am right in saying, took a less romantic view of Konds and were more sympathetic to Oriyas. Dibi himself, towards the end of his life, attempted to get himself appointed *mutha* headman (Case 28: p. 95). The Oriya occupant of the post organized the Konds of Balimendi to petition against Dibi, who, not surprisingly, had made many enemies in his ascent to power. Dibi failed to make an impression in Phulbani and went to Cuttack in order to lobby there. The Oriya claimant went too, and won his case: Dibi failed to become headman. That the contest went out to Cuttack is significant. Such a parochial matter would never have gone outside the Kondmals in the reign—that is the right word—of Ollenbach.

At the present day an ambitious man would not try to become *mutha* headman. Political power is achieved in a different system. The steps in the ladder now are first to be active in the Kond caste, by working with an organization which is called the Kui Samaj, to get into the inner ring in this organization, to be employed as a 'social worker' by Congress or one of the other political parties, and eventually to reach the top by becoming a Member of the Legislative Assembly. There is evidence that in his long career Dibi did much to help his fellow Konds against Oriyas, and even, on one occasion, against the Magistrate himself (Case 28: p. 95). But these good works were, in a way, a by-product. Some of those who seek power to-day are no doubt driven by motives as personal and selfish as those of Dibi, but their activities are directed primarily into championing the cause of the Konds. The MLA, who was elected in 1952, fought a long and successful case against some Oriya merchants who were exploiting the ignorance of Kond peasants. A deputation from the Kui Samaj went to the State capital some years ago and complained that the Magistrate was allowing Oriyas to take and register Kond lands in payment of debts. I heard of a case at secondhand and I am not clear whether the complaint was against the Magistrate or against the venality of his subordinates. But the result of the deputation was that it is no longer possible for an Oriya to register such land. (This I was told by a rueful Oriya informant.) Oriyas often get land because Konds do not know their rights: but they cannot register it in their own name and their title is not secure.

The increased effectiveness of Konds in the larger political arena arises from the vote and from their numbers. The political parties cultivate Konds and the present Government maintains the privileges which the Administration has always granted to Adibasis, not only from motives of justice and altruism, but also from self-interest. They need votes. It is in the interest of the Konds to organize themselves and make their vote effective by voting as a community. They are no longer individuals under the paternal care of the Magistrate. They are committed as a group in a wider political arena.

But this is not yet a fully functioning representative democracy. The local officials and their subordinates still have great powers— as in any bureaucracy. The Konds (and other villagers as well) are still largely ignorant of their democratic rights and completely unskilled in exploiting these. The Kui Samaj is far from representing all Konds. It does not influence or represent all the Konds even in the Kondmals. The centre of activity is the Oriya-ized eastern plateau, and most of the members come from that area. In 1955 I met Konds who were trying to set up an allied organization in the western half of the Kondmals, at the instigation of a rich man of that area who had political ambitions. Eventually the movement will spread to the rest of the Kondmals and will meet and join similar organizations in other parts of the Kond hills. But it has not yet done so.

The Kui Samaj is not primarily a body organized for activity in State politics. Only recently has it begun to take 'on these functions. In origin it is like a caste Samaj, and much of its work is concerned with enforcing marriage regulations, settling disputes, outcasting, and promoting Sanskritic custom—or, better perhaps, promoting Oriya custom. At first sight it is scarcely a political organization at all: it is concerned with cultural uplift—with seeing that Konds behave more and more like BRAHMINS. It seems strange that a movement which is involved in a European-type bureaucracy and in parliamentary politics should be so much engaged in promoting a culture which is typical of quite a different type of political system—that of caste. How do these two activities fit together? What is the significance of Sanskritization[1] in the modern political scene?

As a cultural phenomenon Sanskritization is, of course, peculiar to India and countries which have derived their civilization from India. But there is nothing peculiarly Indian about its social significance: it represents a means of claiming higher social status: it is a mechanism for social climbing. In the caste system it can function as a safety-valve, enabling those who are economically and politically qualified for power to achieve recognition. Sanskritization by a dependent caste is a sign that it is challenging the dominant caste and either trying to take its place or at least to be recognized as equal. Such a movement does not necessarily mean the decay of the caste system. It might be a means by which the system is adjusted to meet economic realities, just as fission and accretion kept the tribal society adjusted to natural resources. Sanskritization does not represent necessarily a change in structure: positions in the structure change but the type of relationship which characterizes the structure does not change. An example

---

[1] No-one seems to like this term. Even its author is prepared to discard it 'quickly and without regret', once a better term or terms are found (M. N. Srinivas, 1956, p. 495). However inept, 'Sanskritization' is still in use, and I do not think time would be well spent in justifying the use of a different term. As I use 'Sanskritization' it means, roughly and without stopping to make qualifications, 'social climbing by conforming to an all-India standard of respectable behaviour', or, for the Konds, 'social climbing by following standard Oriya behaviour'.

I emphasize that this is not a general discussion of 'Sanskritization', but only of the part it plays in contemporary political changes in the Kondmals.

See also pp. 233-5.

of this would be the history of the Boad DISTILLERS which I have given elsewhere.[1]

Nevertheless there are in Sanskritization certain elements, which, from the point of view of an ordered and stable caste political system, may be disturbing. The outcome might be a return to equilibrium, of the type I have described. But it might also be structural change—an arresting of the move back to equilibrium, at the end of which there emerges not one dominant caste, but several castes, all of which have some—but not a complete—claim to dominance. Such a system is still called 'caste' and it is this type of system which is found in most villages in the present transitional Indian society. But this type of society is different from the classical pattern of dominant and dependent castes.

Firstly and most obviously Sanskritization is an attack on the hierarchy. We have noted that such an attack is not necessarily revolutionary, but may merely be a rebellion which changes positions in society but does not change its form. Secondly Sanskritization is sometimes a corporate activity with political implications by what was formerly a dependent caste with no corporate political existence. The most striking examples of this are, of course, the assiduous attempts of the untouchables to Sanskritize their behaviour. The third element in which Sanskritization appears to be inimical to a caste system is in the general levelling of culture. It is true, of course, that the protagonists do not see the process only in this light: an essential motive is to assert their superiority over others, and not merely to claim equality with the highest. But, whatever the protagonists think, in the long run the process tends to eliminate the diacritical differences between castes, which reflected and helped to maintain the hierarchy.

Sanskritization is said to have been going on for hundreds of years without impairing the structure of caste.[2] But Sanskritization to-day is often a sign that the political institutions and political structure of India are changing. Whatever was happening in the past, when castes to-day seek to Sanskritize themselves, they may be working in a new political system.[3] In the example described

[1] F. G. Bailey, 1957, Chapter IX.
[2] M. N. Srinivas, 1952, p. 30.
[3] I do not imply by this that political advancement is the only motive for Sanskritization: the new culture is, no doubt, conceived of as a value in

by Dr. Cohn in Senapur, are we to say that the untouchable Chamars are seeking to replace the Thakurs as the caste of dominant landowners, and to reduce the Thakurs to the status of dependence without a corporate political existence?[1] This is clearly nonsense. The two castes are both trying to establish themselves as effective political groups in the new democracy.

Sanskritic culture is the culture of the nation. It is a claim to respectability not only in the local caste structure, but also before a wider audience. It is a criterion of respectability acknowledged with varying degrees of sincerity throughout India; even beyond the bounds of Hinduism. It had a particular value during the struggle for independence and it still has a value in giving a home-spun covering to the European institutions through which the country is governed. This, I think, is why organizations like the Kui Samaj, which start with the object of improving group status with their neighbours and in their own locality, continue and even intensify these cultural activities when they move into the larger political scene. In order to compete effectively and to command respect the Konds, being very much in a minority in the new arena, must take on Oriya culture and try to become the cultural equals of the Oriyas. Just as they have to learn the Oriya language, so also they have to learn Oriya etiquette.

The readiest way of describing the political change that is occurring now in India, and has been going on for the last hundred years, is to say that territorial cleavages are being replaced by cleavages between castes. The struggle is no longer between clans or chiefdoms or kingdoms, but between castes—between, for instance, the Okkaligas and the Lingayats for control in Mysore.[2] When the Communists put up a candidate, even they have to see that he comes from the caste which is numerically dominant in the area, even though that caste may be a sink of reaction.[3] From all over India there is evidence that castes, organized to the width of the linguistic region, are politically

---

itself. However, I am arguing that the aims of the cultural reformers do, in the cases I note, conform to the political ambitions of their community, and are a ritual expression of those ambitions, even though many of those who conform to the new standards may not realize the political expediency of doing so.

[1] Bernard S. Cohn, 1955, pp. 53–77.
[2] *Economic Weekly*, 1956, pp. 859–64; M. N. Srinivas, 1957, pp. 541–2.
[3] M. N. Srinivas, 1955, p. 137.

active and courted by political parties.[1] 'Caste', wrote Professor Srinivas, 'is an institution of prodigious strength and it will take a lot of beating before it will die.' [2]

The term 'caste' is appropriate for these political groups. But, nonetheless, the differences between caste in this form and caste in its traditional political form must be recognized. The traditional system contains one dominant caste which alone has a corporate political existence: the other castes are its dependents and are not politically corporate.[3] But in the modern system all castes which are large enough to make their wishes felt are corporate political bodies. In other words, the political structure in the two cases is completely different. Secondly the cultural paraphernalia which symbolized the hierarchy in the old system are absent from the new system. The untouchable in the traditional system accepts his disabilities. But the Harijan member of a legislative assembly is not disqualified in this way. There is no untouchable dining room in Constitution House in Delhi. The system is designed to make, and policies are directed towards making, the untouchable and the Adibasi as good politically as any other man. The system works towards cultural assimilation, while the traditional caste system promoted cultural disparity. Thirdly the new political system is infinitely wider than the old one and the economic system tends to promote spatial mobility, and this fact in itself must lead to the decay of many essential elements of the old caste system. The traditional caste system, with its usages of pollution and avoidance, can, as Dr. Marriott says, only be conceived of as working in 'small packages'.[4] There is no untouchability on trains because no-one knows who are the untouchable travellers. Caste in its traditional form can only flower in small-scale societies, and in the absence of extensive spatial mobility.

The basis of Kond unity in the modern political system—a unity which is as yet potential rather than actual—is their common economic interest, shaped partly by the accidents of the new economy, partly by Kond traditions, and partly fostered by Administrative policy. The basis is not cultural uniformity: it is not Kond culture: for Konds are trying all the time to make

[1] M. N. Srinivas, 1957, *passim.*
[2] M. N. Srinivas, 1955, p. 133.
[3] For a further discussion of 'dominant caste', see pp. 251–6.
[4] McKim Marriott, 1955, p. 191.

themselves similar to the Oriyas. It is misleading to say simply that they have learnt to act together as a caste. They have not: they are learning to combine as a political group, recruited for the moment on the basis of caste, but which, even in the near future, is likely to be widened to include all Adibasis in Orissa. By a stretch of terminology such a group can be called a 'caste'. Its badge is caste culture: but that is not the basis of its unity. In size and in internal organization it does not resemble the traditional caste. It operates in a political system radically different from that of the traditional caste system.

CONCLUSIONS

As an analysis of social history this chapter is inadequate.[1] I have described in outline the relative command at different periods of Konds and Oriyas over material resources and over one another. In the earliest period, before the Administration, numerical superiority enabled the Kond clans to maintain their integrity, and to be the chief alignment through which a Kond protected his right to land. After the Administration came, the right to land was validated not by membership of a clan, but by allegiance to a Sirdar in the first instance, and ultimately to the Government. Since many of these Sirdars were Oriyas, and since the Oriyas in general were much closer to the Administrators

[1] This chapter contains some wide generalizations about political developments in Orissa and elsewhere, and I would have difficulty in substantiating all of them. Firstly some of them are forecasts (I have made clear in the text what is actuality and what is forecast): secondly some of these generalizations are not based on intensive and detailed analysis of cases. There are many topics which I have not been able to cover adequately, sometimes for lack of space, but more often for lack of material. Important in this category are the Kui Samaj, the modern system of representative democracy, and the modern region-wide 'castes'. I hope to fill in some of these gaps in later studies which will begin with the Meriah Wars and the annexation of the Kond Hills, examine in greater detail the Administrative developments outlined in this chapter, and concentrate upon the relations, not only in the Kondmals but also in Orissa generally, between a bureaucratic administration and a parliamentary democracy based upon universal adult franchise. I justify the inclusion of this inadequate and somewhat superficial outline on two grounds: firstly I think that I had sufficient material to propound hypotheses which may stimulate further discussion: secondly, without the material given here, it would be impossible to understand the significance of many events discussed in the following chapter, and in the concluding chapter.

than were the Konds, and since they were better able to exploit the opportunities which the commercial economy brought to the Kond hills, the Konds slipped back into a subordinate position, and the political relationship through which they achieved control of land began to resemble that in which a dependent caste achieves a share in the resources of the land in the caste system. But before this process could be carried very far, the balance swung back in favour of the Konds, firstly because caste *as a political system* (not, of course, in its cultural entirety) began to be undermined by the modern economy and by the presence of the Administration, and secondly because the Konds, again through their numerical superiority, are able to compete more effectively than the hill Oriyas in the modern representative democracy. Putting it simply, the main political alignments for a Kond have been firstly the clan, later the *mutha* under the rule of a Sirdar, and recently the 'caste' in its modern form as a political category and an emergent pressure group.

In the following chapter I return to the narrower field of Baderi village and show that all three alignments are still to some degree effective. Change is taking place; but it is not abrupt; it comes slowly.

PART THREE

STRUCTURES IN ACTION

CHAPTER VIII

A DISPUTE IN BADERI

KONDS operate in three different political structures or systems: with their fellow Konds; with dependent PANS and dependents of other caste; and with the Oriyas who are regarded somewhat ambivalently as masters. Each structure can be described as a whole in itself. Relationships within any structure are not always harmonious and each contains conflicts, but, except in the case of Kond-Oriya relationships, there are corrective mechanisms which make for continuance and equilibrium.

In order to describe any one of these three systems as a whole, complete in itself, one has to make abstractions and hold many things equal. But in fact, when a Kond competes with another Kond for power within the traditional Kond political system, his role in other systems, with Oriyas, or with PANS, or with the Government, cannot be ignored. He is able to make use of these outside relationships to influence his relationships within the Kond system, which has been presented as if it were a whole in itself. We can describe 'the structure' standing by itself: but if we are to describe the 'structure in action', we have to think no longer of *the* structure, but rather of several structures, which together set a limit to the possible ways of behaving, but at the same time permit the individual to pursue his own ends by choosing to use whatever relationship he finds most advantageous at that particular time. Choice of this kind exists, of course, within systems—there is no structural means of explaining why the Damanikia people chose to side with Balimendi rather than with Gondrimendi (Case 14: p. 49). But here I am concerned rather with the existence of choice between different systems of political behaviour. To illustrate this I present a case which was written down for me by the Oriya schoolmaster, Damodoro Bisoi, who also wrote Case 35 (p. 128), and who was himself concerned in the events.

(Case 38)   (Time: 1955)
    'On March 17th 1955 Ponga Kohoro, the headman of Baderi

village, drank palm wine in the morning. When he came back from the forest, where the grove of palm trees lay, he drank arrack and by mid-day he was thoroughly drunk. While drunk he became violently angry over something which Goneswaro Bisoi, the Sirdar of Balimendi, and his *paik*, Nrusingh Naik, both of our village [Bisipara] had done.

'This was the reason for his anger. Some days beforehand Nrusingh Naik had been to Baderi to collect the Watchman Tax and the Plough Tax. Manda Kohoro of Baderi handed over Rs.6/4. Manda had not paid his tax for three years, and he promised to hand over another year's tax, and so bring himself up to date, in a few days' time. Nrusingh took the money to the Sirdar, Goneswaro, and said, "Manda has handed over Rs.4/8 and says that he will give the rest in a day or two." Goneswaro wrote down that Manda had paid Rs.4/8.

'The next day Goneswaro Bisoi went to Baderi to hand over receipts for the money he had received. When Manda's name was called, he said that he would produce Rs.3 in a few days time. Hearing this Goneswaro said, "You have four ploughs. That makes As.12 each year. For the Watchman Tax you pay As.9 for each plough and that makes Rs.2/4. So every year you pay Rs.3. If you are also going to pay the additional 2 pice to the plough that makes four annas, and so every year you have to pay Rs.3/2. You have handed over to me—or rather to Nrusingh—Rs.4/8. Three years tax for you is Rs.9/6. So that makes Rs.4/14 to come."

'Manda at once replied, "On Ponga's verandah, in the presence of Ponga and Arjuno, I am giving Rs.6/4 for the two years. How is it that you have written down Rs.4/8? Ask these people whether or not I handed over Rs.6/4!"

'At that time Liringa, Karika, Ginda from Pandrisai hamlet, and Chunomali were there. After they had argued for a time Liringa said, "Manda gave Rs.6/4. Lots of people saw it. Write out a receipt for Rs.6/4!" Manda said, "Your Worship, I handed over two years tax. Please write a receipt for Rs.6/4." Goneswaro replied "Nrusingh gave me Rs.4/8. I will ask him about it, and I will give you a receipt afterwards." Then Liringa said to the old man, "You write for us—that is, for Manda,—a statement that you received Rs.4/8 from Nrusingh, as coming from Manda. Get on with it and write it out quickly. We'll go to the Magistrate with it. You and Nrusingh will soon find out what it means to be Sirdar of Balimendi." He poured out a stream of abuse of this kind on Goneswaro Bisoi. [In English Liringa's words sound too mild to be called 'abuse'. But there is a difference in Oriya, the language in which the text was written, and in which the quarrel was conducted.

Manda, the victim, had used the plural forms of respect in addressing the old Sirdar—forms which could be translated 'Your Honour' or 'Your Worship'. But Liringa used the single form which is properly employed for children, intimate friends, servants, and animals.]

'The old man Goneswaro was cunning and said that he would write no receipt until he had asked Nrusingh about the matter. Then, fearing that if he stayed in Baderi, he would get more abuse, he went off as quickly as he could, to Pandrisai hamlet.

'On the morning of March 17th, Ponga Kohoro, who had heard about Manda's taxes, was talking with some other drunken people in the street in front of his house, when along came Nrusingh Naik. Nrusingh had agreed the week before to buy a heap of turmeric which Ponga had for sale and he had come along to have another look at the pile, for which he had promised to pay Rs.80. The moment Ponga saw him he went into a furious rage, and began, "So you eat for yourself the money we pay to the Government ..." Nrusingh saw at once that he was drunk, and he fled to another part of the village. Ponga chased him to the end of the street and then stood there for a full half-hour, spitting out abuse after him.

'I closed the school at 12 o'clock and went into the village into Ponga's street, and I sat down in Manda's grain-shed to talk with Arjuno [Ponga's son], Manda, and Tuka. At this time Kosira Kohoro and Norendero Behera, both of our village Bisipara, had come to Baderi to try to buy turmeric. When they saw me Kosira said, "O mother's brother, let us go home to the village together." I told them to wait for a minute and I would be with them. Kosira and Norendero sat down in the grain-shed and waited for me.

'At that moment Ponga arrived, looked over the half-wall of the grain-shed, saw who was inside, and began upon Kosira, "Hey you sod of a Kond! Are you a Kond? You're the sort who destroys our customs, aren't you? Call yourself a Kond, and yet you come here trading!" He went on like this for a long time. When he had finished with Kosira, he turned on Norendero Behera, "Sod of an Oriya! What are you here for? Have you come just to show me that gold chain round your neck? You've come here just to show me one gold neck-chain have you? I've got *six* for every one of yours. Clear out, you rotten sod!"

Kosira and Norendero didn't wait for me, but they fled. Then Ponga noticed me and said, "You sod of a schoolmaster! You're the one who teaches Nrusingh to cheat us of our money. Sodding WARRIORS sods! Being a sod of an Oriya and a sod of a Bisoi you know how to cheat the people out of money. So you're a schoolmaster like your father. He taught you to cheat, you rotten bastard. A sod like you gets money by choking it out of your subjects. You rotten sodding thief!" Saying this, Ponga snatched a yard and a half of cloth that I was wearing round my shoulders, and went off to look for Nrusingh to give him some more. I was frightened and went off and hid in Tuka's house. Manda begged my cloth off him and brought it back. We all fled. He abused everyone he met, and thrashed his own son, Arjuno. But Arjuno just kept quiet and didn't answer back.

'That same evening he kicked Arjuno and his daughter-in-law out of the house. He beat Arjuno as well. They fled to Gomapara village to the house of their preceptor, Datia Das, and stayed the night there. In the morning they brought their preceptor to Baderi. He gave a lot of good advice to Ponga and prohibited him from drinking arrack. Ponga agreed to this and said he would not drink it again.'

It is, perhaps, difficult to follow this text at first reading, for it contains many proper names, both of persons and places, and it arises from a simple, though detailed, monetary calculation. But the action is neither complex nor subtle. A minor Government functionary seems to have attempted to embezzle a small sum. This alleged peculation was detected. Another man, not directly concerned in the matter, being drunk and uninhibited, made use of it to say what he thought about various individuals and categories of persons, both those who had offended and those who in this case were free from blame. The drunken outbreak was finished in a day, and although it was not forgotten, it led, so far as I know, to no serious consequences. I do not know how it was settled in the end and I suspect that the missing Rs.1/12 are still part of Balimendi's enormous arrears of tax. But the episode had apparently blown over within a week. Nevertheless, although the action was simple and the affair ended in a short time, the social relationships, a knowledge of which makes it possible to understand the motives and intentions of the persons concerned, are of very great complexity, and need to be seen against a long period of history. The incident, trivial in itself and in no dramatic sense altering the course of history even in that village, should not be regarded as a mere eddy in the stream, but rather it is a chart—admittedly a confused chart—of the winds and currents of social life. The persons in the case know what they want and where they want to go, but like sailing ships they are bound to make use of wind and current over which they have no control.

All the participants, other than the narrator, the Sirdar, Nrusingh Naik, the man with the gold neck-chain, and the preceptor, are Konds. There is also a third social category, the Administrators, formerly British and now Indian, who do not appear in the case, but whose presence is implicit in all its parts. I shall discuss the status and actions of each of the protagonists in turn.

NRUSINGH NAIK

Nrusingh Naik, like the Sirdar and the narrator, lives in the Oriya village of Bisipara. He is an untouchable of the Oriya PAN caste, and he is the client of Goneswaro Bisoi, who is a WARRIOR. This relationship has nothing to do with the fact that Goneswaro is a Sirdar: it is a relationship between the two families, a highly personal one, in which the client (*proja*) is almost a part of his master's family and is addressed as *pila* (child). Oriyas of WARRIOR caste, who are not Sirdars, also have these clients. But Nrusingh is also an appointed assistant of Goneswaro Bisoi in the latter's capacity as Sirdar of Balimendi. Nrusingh is a *paik*, one of the hereditary landed militia, who once made up the armies of the Oriya kings. For his work in assisting the Sirdar he receives a grant of tax-free land, and he commands a measure of delegated or reflected authority. From the point of view of the Sirdar there is nothing incompatible in the two roles which Nrusingh plays. Both as his assistant (*paik*) and as his client (*proja*) Nrusingh is his servant, and I have no doubt that he chose Nrusingh for his *paik*, because he was already a client. There are two relationships, different but on the whole complementary: in both Goneswaro Bisoi gives the orders and Nrusingh obeys.

Nrusingh appears in the incident in a third role—as a trader in turmeric. Nrusingh is, in fact, a man of considerable wealth, who deals both in turmeric and cattle and who possesses land besides that which is attached to his office. His standing as a man of substance is in contradiction to his roles as an untouchable and as the client of Goneswaro. His duties as *proja*, like those of most other *proja* in Bisipara, have become little more than token services offered on ritual occasions and at times of crisis in the master's household. Authority in the master-client relationship depended among other things upon the fact that the master controlled the livelihood of his servant. In fact Nrusingh is not wealthy enough to wish to drop the income he gets from his Government land, but his comparative affluence, together with a strong personality, makes him into an indisciplined and self-willed *paik*. He is nicknamed *sana Sirdar*—'the little Sirdar'.

The actual relationship between Nrusingh and the Sirdar is a rope of many strands. It is more than the simple and abject subservience expected of the untouchable client towards his master, although this is the relationship which, on the whole, is paraded overtly and in the forefront of the interaction of the two men. Nrusingh's manners towards the Sirdar are not those of an official towards his senior, still less those of a successful entrepreneur towards a landed aristocrat. He exhibits that odd mixture of familiarity and deference which marks an old and trusted family retainer. Indeed it looks in the incident as if Goneswaro is trying to cover up for his servant's misdemeanours when he refuses to give a receipt which could be used to bring Nrusingh into court. But this is clearly not the whole story: it is not affection for Nrusingh which stays the Sirdar's hand. For several reasons Nrusingh is in a strong position, and the old man cannot bend him absolutely to his will.

This is shown in the refusal to give a receipt. Firstly it must be understood that no-one doubted that Nrusingh was in the wrong. It is expected of such a man that he will cheat. Assuming, then, that Nrusingh had taken the Rs.1/12, what were the courses open to the Sirdar, who, like everyone else, believed that Nrusingh was guilty? Firstly he might give a receipt for the amount he had actually received, as Liringa suggested he should. But this course has its dangers. If the Konds complained to the Magistrate, then at the best the inefficiencies of Goneswaro's Sirdarship are exposed. At the worst Nrusingh might swear that he had handed over the whole sum, and the Sirdar thus would have run the risk of being himself charged with peculation. It is in the joint interest of Goneswaro and Nrusingh to keep the matter within the *mutha* and not to let it go to higher authorities. Secondly Goneswaro might have given a receipt for the full amount, Rs.6/4. The Konds could no longer complain, and the matter could not have been brought to the notice of higher authority. But, firstly, this might set a precedent for dishonest Konds, who might in the future claim that they had handed over to Nrusingh more than they had actually done. Secondly the Sirdar would have had to extract from Nrusingh the difference between the amount written on the receipt and the money which Nrusingh had handed to him, or else make it up out of his own pocket: and this too would set a precedent which might encourage Nrusingh to cheat not the Konds, but his own master. I think that Goneswaro anticipated difficulty in getting the money out of Nrusingh: Nrusingh is not a trusted retainer, although he is an old one: for two reasons Goneswaro does not command the sanctions which the word 'retainer' suggests. Firstly Nrusingh finds the association profitable, but he does not depend absolutely for his living on his master's goodwill, since he is a man of substance in his own right. Secondly he holds an official position as *paik*, a position which is confirmed by the Government and marked by a grant of land, and he cannot be dismissed arbitrarily, as can a personal servant. Goneswaro would have had to make out a case before the Government and the lands would have had to be resumed in order that they might be granted to the new incumbent: and in this situation Nrusingh might be able to manipulate the officials with whom the decision lay, as effectively as could Goneswaro.

The relationship between Nrusingh and the Sirdar is complex, made up of relationships some of which complement one another and some of which contradict one another. So also is the relationship between Nrusingh and the Konds neither simple nor whole and consistent. Firstly Nrusingh is a PAN and an untouchable, while Konds rank as a clean caste. Nrusingh should treat people of clean caste with deference. He should address them in the honorific plural and use the polite forms of teknonymy. Conversely they are entitled to call him by his name and address him in the normal familiar plural forms, or even, if they want to stress their respective statuses, they could address him in the singular forms, and Nrusingh would have no right to take offence. Nrusingh should avoid getting too near them, so that they will not be polluted by contact. If he meets a man of clean caste on a narrow pathway, then good manners demand that Nrusingh should turn back or descend into the field and make way for the other man. The forms of behaviour proper to an untouchable symbolize the fact that he has no authority: that he is a servant: that he is socially and ritually inferior to people who belong to the clean castes.

But the other roles which Nrusingh plays in his relationships with the Konds of Baderi and other Konds are on the whole roles which demonstrate superiority, or at least equality. Firstly he is a *paik*. He is a minor official. He bears the title of an office which once belonged to the landed militia of Orissa—that is, to persons of property who had the right to bear arms. The military connotations of this office are now virtually defunct, and the *paik* is in fact a minor official, paid with a grant of land, under the control of the Sirdar, to be used to collect tax, to attend the Sirdar on his journeys when he himself goes out to collect taxes, and to act as a messenger summoning people to the Sirdar when higher officials come to visit the *mutha*. Nrusingh carries in his office of *paik* a reflected and delegated authority, immediately from his Sirdar, and ultimately as a representative of the Administration. He gives orders. It is true that he is merely passing on these orders and that they derive ultimately from a higher authority, but in fact they are delivered as orders and Nrusingh does not hesitate to browbeat and threaten if the recipients show signs of disobedience. When Konds come before the Sirdar, or before a higher Government official, Nrusingh attends and behaves exactly as a Sergeant-Major, marshalling people before his Commanding Officer. He behaves, in these circumstances as a person of rank superior to the Konds—as indeed, in this particular hierarchy, he is: he is an official: they are peasants.

Nrusingh uses his office to compensate for his disabilities as an untouchable. He parades his authority in a way which is not typical of *paiks* who are not untouchables. In the area with which I was familiar, by far the greatest number of *paiks* are of clean caste. They are apt in the presence of high officials occasionally to bark at their fellow-peasants but they do not carry on the systematic hectoring which is a feature of Nrusingh's behaviour. They do not need to do so. They behave as near equals of the Konds (most of them are Oriya HERDSMEN or Kond POTTERS), which socially they are, and Konds are on the whole willing to treat their occasional lapses from good manners as an incident of their office rather than as a sign of a loutish character. They do not need to compensate for ritual disabilities by emphasizing their superior position in the administrative hierarchy, as Nrusingh does.

In an earlier paragraph I sketched out the behaviour which is proper to an untouchable in the presence of people of clean caste. But in practice the relationship is not so simple as this. I have written it as a Kond would claim the relationship ought to be. An Oriya PAN would give quite a different picture. The Konds stand somewhat outside the group of clean castes. There is no doubt that they are clean: but the Konds are not in the same position vis-à-vis the untouchables as are the other clean castes. There are two essential differences. Firstly the PAN untouchables who live in the Kond villages have quite a different function in the village from that of their brethren who live in Oriya villages. In the Oriya village in its traditional form the WARRIORS were the landowners and masters of the village, while the PANS were their serfs and clients. In the traditional Kond village the PANS had a similar position in that they were mainly agricultural labourers: but the additional duties which they performed made them much more independent and much more powerful than the PANS in an Oriya village. The Konds are by tradition agriculturalists and warriors, and they had, and still have, contempt for those who engage in trade, and for those who have any dealings at all with foreigners. The PANS were servants who performed these two functions: they traded in cattle, provided victims for the rite of human sacrifice by kidnapping or buying them from distant areas, and acted as middlemen and even as interpreters when the Konds had to deal with foreigners. When the armies of the East India Company first came into the area in the third decade of the nineteenth century, the military reports speak of two village officials: one is the Kond headman; the other is the 'Digaloo' or interpreter, who could speak both Kui, the language of the Konds, and Oriya, the language of metropolitan Orissa. In fact there never was such an office. 'Digaloo'—or, more properly, 'Digal'—is a PAN lineage name and would probably be borne by all the PANS in the village. The 'Digaloo' was thus not a person in authority in the Kond village: he was merely a person put up in front by the Konds to traffic with outsiders, because he could speak their language and had travelled about and seen something of the world. Essentially, for the Konds, this was a means of retaining their dignity, and they regarded the task of the Digal as a menial one. Outsiders were considered to be of low rank and it seemed proper to deal with them, not directly, but through a person of low rank. Nevertheless the position gave the PANS considerable influence and independence, unrecognized by the Konds, but nevertheless real.

This is still true to-day. Many Konds employ PANS in this way. PANS act as agents to buy and sell cattle or jewellery, or to collect or to contract debts. The trust which the Konds are compelled to place in the PANS is said to be abused more frequently than not and there are innumerable stories of the ways in which Konds are cheated by PANS. The PANS are intermediaries, necessary to the Konds for reasons of status, but untrustworthy: for the PANS, the Konds are slow-witted masters, who are entitled to the forms of respect, but not to actual respect.

Nrusingh's actions, in the incident described, must be seen against this background. His attempt to appropriate part of the tax money is not simply an attempt to cheat the Government, but is also an extension of the normal behaviour of a PAN in monetary dealings with Konds. If it is true that he cheated deliberately and did not make a simple mistake, then he probably hoped that Manda would not—or could not—read what was on the receipt. It was a measure of stupidity or a miscalculation that he chose to try this trick on one of the most sophisticated and aggressive Kond villages in the neighbourhood. There are, of course, other factors which might have entered into his calculations: the lax system of accounting; his strong position against the Sirdar which I described above; and the probability that even if he were discovered, then the worst that could happen would be that he would have to make good what he had taken. Here I am only concerned with the relevance to his actions of the general pattern of Kond-PAN relationships, and I think that it would be true to say that Nrusingh would have been much more chary of trying this particular trick on an Oriya.

The second factor which complicates Nrusingh's relationships with the Baderi Konds is that he is an Oriya PAN and not a Kond PAN. He grew up in an Oriya village: he speaks Oriya: he is advanced and sophisticated to a much greater degree than are Kond PANS. He therefore enjoys a share in the general dominance and social superiority which the Oriyas have over the Konds. His connection with the Oriyas gives him a status which works against the disabilities of being an untouchable. He is a representative—in Kond eyes a poor representative—of the culture and civilization towards which the more advanced Konds are striving.

He is identified with the dominant group; and like them he is identified with the Administration and the forces of modern commerce, and much more able to manipulate these forces than is the average Kond peasant. It is the Oriya PANS who are most skilled at exploiting the determined shyness of the Konds, and the tendencies which are apparent in the relationship of Konds to Kond PANS are much magnified in the relationship between Oriya PANS and the Konds. The Konds think of their own PAN as a cheat: they regard the Oriya PAN as a bigger and cleverer cheat.

Finally Nrusingh appears in the incident as a trader in turmeric. He bought from Ponga a heap of turmeric roots for Rs.80 and he had left it in Ponga's house to be stored until he had arranged transport to take it to the merchant's shop in Bisipara. He was probably waiting in the hope that he would be able to buy enough from different people in Baderi to make up a cartload. The relationship of these two men, as buyer and seller, is not directly dependent on their other relationships in the caste system, or in the Administrative hierarchy. PANS in the area of Bisipara do not have a monopoly of turmeric dealings, as they have of cattle trade: indeed they play a minor part in this traffic compared to the part played by the Oriyas of clean caste. Nor does Nrusingh's position as *paik* help him directly in his business, although it does have for him an incidental use. The major social cleavage represented in this transaction is between the Konds and the Oriyas.

The Konds grow turmeric, but never act as middlemen. The Oriyas never—or very seldom—grow it, but monopolize the trading. At first sight Nrusingh appears in this role not as an untouchable nor as a Government functionary, but simply as another Oriya, in competition with his fellow villagers and Oriyas from other villagers to buy turmeric in Baderi.

But in fact, both in this incident and in general, Nrusingh's role as a trader cannot be divorced from and set in a compartment separate from his other roles. I have already described how his affluence, to which turmeric-trading contributes, gives him an independence of his master Goneswaro, in contradiction to the traditionally subservient role of the PAN client. In the same way he becomes a person more formidable to the Konds than would a poor man in the same position, although his wealth is not so great as to give him much influence on this score. To anyone, Kond, clean caste Oriya, or even the Administrators, a rich

untouchable is a person to be treated, if not with respect, at least
with caution. From the other direction, Nrusingh's position as a
paik is of advantage to him in trading. Like the Oriya schoolmaster of Baderi, who described the incident to me, Nrusingh
spends much of his time in Baderi on official business. The Konds
never advertise openly the fact that they have turmeric for sale.
They treat the market as a seller's market and it is difficult for
the Oriya middlemen to discover even who has already harvested
and dried his turmeric. Nrusingh and the schoolmaster are well
placed in this respect in Baderi, the schoolmaster because he is
there every day, because he can use the boys as his intelligence
service, and because he has many friends and is well-liked in
Baderi, since he helps the people when they require letters or
documents to be written in formal and correct Oriya. Nrusingh
too is well placed in that he is frequently in a position in which
he can ask for favours, and if people on whom he is putting
pressure do not want to sell him their turmeric, or have none,
they can at least let him know who else in the village has turmeric
for sale. This is probably why Nrusingh, almost alone of the
Bisipara PANS, all of whom are Oriya PANS, has any substantial
dealings as a middleman in turmeric.

But the interpenetration of these roles is not to be exaggerated.
All the different roles do not come automatically into play on
each occasion. For instance, it is clear that in the incident the
vehemence of Ponga's attack was not in any way lessened by the
fact that he himself had just concluded a deal with Nrusingh, and,
so far as I know, the turmeric was in fact handed over to Nrusingh
later. There was no question of trying to penalize Nrusingh for
his peculations by preventing him from trading or by organizing
a boycott. Trading is, in a way, something which is treated as
incidental and outside the normal run of social life. The Konds
do not hesitate to rub in Nrusingh's untouchable status when he
visits them as a *paik*: and Nrusingh compensates by over-playing
his role as a *paik*. But neither of them would let the animosities
which run in these two relationships interfere with a bargain
which both sides find satisfactory.

Neither in his relationships with the Sirdar, nor in his relationship with the Konds, is Nrusingh playing a single unitary role,
within one structure of social relations. In both cases Nrusingh
operates in two or more social systems. To the Sirdar he is at

once an untouchable client, a junior official, and a relatively well-to-do entrepreneur. To the Konds he is a PAN, an Oriya PAN, an official, and a trader. To each of these roles is attached an appropriate form of behaviour: that is to say, in the case of Nrusingh and the Konds, he may behave as a PAN, an official, or a trader: and conversely the Konds may treat him as any one of these three, but not all three at the same time, because the roles are in some situations contradictory. For instance the greeting to an official is not also the appropriate greeting to an untouchable, for the one demonstrates inferiority and the other superiority. In every situation the actors have an element of latitude and may choose the way they will behave in order to further their own ends. The Konds can humiliate Nrusingh by treating him as an untouchable or they can flatter him by treating him as an official, whichever suits their purpose. There is no single system into which can be placed all the relationships in which Nrusingh is concerned. Rather there are a number of alternative systems, from which people can choose how they will behave.

GONESWARO BISOI

Goneswaro is an old man of commanding height, with a face and manner apparently matured in authority. But this authority is an air: he has the forms but not the reality of power. Compared to his neighbour, the Sirdar of Besringia, Goneswaro is much less able to manipulate the formal authority which he has inherited, so as to shape events to his own advantage. Goneswaro's weakness may indicate a defect of character or constitution, a lack of that energy and force which successful managers of men have; it may arise from a combination of various accidents which are personal and idiosyncratic to Goneswaro's life; or, thirdly, the weakness may be in the position he occupies in society, which may be such that no amount of personal drive and ability and no history of personal success could give him real authority. It is in the third of these factors that I am primarily interested, and I have neither the training nor the knowledge to make anything more than superficial comment on Goneswaro's character. However his character is clearly of importance and I must take account of it in my arguments. I shall therefore set out to show the way in which the form of society as it is now, and the various social forces at work to change it, tend either to circumscribe or to magnify the Sirdar's power and I shall assume that Goneswaro's success or failure within the limits set by social factors is the result of his personality, which my analysis must take as given.

The signs of incapacity as a leader are obvious enough, once one gets past Goneswaro's patriarchal appearance. He has a bad stammer. He cannot speak well in a meeting. This, in itself, is not a serious handicap for the Besringia Sirdar too is a poor orator. But he has henchmen who put his points for him, and he confines his part in a council to brief, staccato, authoritarian pronouncements, only made after he is sure that his mouthpiece has brought the meeting round to the right frame of mind. Goneswaro, on the other hand, cannot contain himself on these occasions. He speaks in the same staccato way, but he is often incoherent, and he sometimes cannot finish what he is saying before another person starts to speak, either to answer him or to finish his sentences for him. A second personal factor is that the other Sirdar, although in late middle age, is physically active and—for the Kondmals—healthy and vigorous. Goneswaro is an old man, crippled by rheumatism: he walks with a stick and is frequently unable to walk at all. He is unable to visit his *mutha* frequently and he has to rely on his *paik* Nrusingh. In any leader physical weakness is a handicap to be compensated by other qualities: these Goneswaro lacks. Thirdly Goneswaro's life has been, by the standards of the Kondmals, a failure. He is a member and could be the head of a large and wealthy lineage of WARRIORS: but he has quarrelled with his collaterals so many times that he has little influence. He has no son, a sure sign that he was born under an unfavourable star: he has at least once adopted a son from his lineage, but the old man's bile drove the son away again. Now, in his old age, Goneswaro is disposing of as much of his property as he can and passing it to his daughter and her son, who live in a distant village. This, in its turn, alienates his lineage brothers, who consider themselves reversionary heirs. His office as Sirdar would have been inherited by a son, but now no-one knows who will succeed him, and it is unlikely that the office will go to a reversionary heir in the lineage. As he sells his land and property, and as he displays a conspicuous lack of interest in who will succeed him, Goneswaro is acknowledging his failure and is dissolving his social personality while he is still alive.

That is all that I can say about Goneswaro's character and personal history. I now have to show how Goneswaro, like Nrusingh and everyone else concerned in the incident of the stolen tax-money, has roles to play in different social systems; how he selects different roles on different occasions to compensate, so far as he can, for his weaknesses; and how other people are able to manipulate social relationships so as to exploit these weaknesses.

This is clear enough from what I have already said about Nrusingh. Through the Sirdar's physical weakness Nrusingh is indispensable to the running of the *mutha*. Some people bring their tax: but many have to be bullied and harried into paying, and Goneswaro cannot do this, since the more remote villages in his *mutha* are five miles from the village where he lives. Nrusingh is also secure because, as I have said, he cannot be arbitrarily dismissed, as could a personal servant: he is Goneswaro's subordinate, but not Goneswaro's servant. Nrusingh is also sufficiently wealthy to free himself from absolute economic dependence on Goneswaro. It would be best for Goneswaro if Nrusingh could be made to behave only as a *proja*—a personal dependent and retainer. In fact Nrusingh has two other contradictory roles which he can use to strengthen himself in this relationship. This is one reason why Goneswaro cannot, so to speak, throw his servant to the wolves by giving a receipt for the amount he had actually received and thus providing written evidence of Nrusingh's peculations. This is also one reason why Nrusingh could risk bringing about a situation which might—and in fact did—embarrass his master. He had nothing more to fear than his master's anger.

Nor, evidently, have the Baderi Konds much cause to fear the Sirdar's anger. In the incident of the tax-money the only Kond who behaved according to the traditional code of manners was Manda. He was quiet and restrained in the presence of the Sirdar, although he was the person most concerned in the peculation and the one most hurt by it. He addressed the Sirdar in honorific forms, and he appealed for his protection, acting the role of a dutiful person of lower rank. The proper forms, which a Kond ought to observe in conversing with a Sirdar, are those which show inferior rank and exhibit respect. But other Konds in Baderi stood up to Goneswaro and abused him, and although he did not give in, he was without the authority to ride the storm and settle the matter there and then. He abandoned the attempt to collect taxes and went off to another hamlet. No Kond would have dared to speak like this to the Besringia Sirdar. Once some drunken Konds were passing through Bisipara on their way back from a wedding. They were not drunk enough to have lost complete control over themselves, but they were in a state of unusual garrulity, and were explaining to me the relative effects of palm-wine as against *mahua* liquor. I had never met them before and I was surprised that they should talk to a European so easily about this topic, when all strange Europeans are identified with the Government, and when the district was dry and all liquor illicit. Suddenly the Besringia Sirdar appeared and the talk stopped abruptly. I went on asking questions: the Sirdar, who knew what the talk had been about, grinned: but the Konds remained silent, and after a short time went away, walking up the path very stiffly in a comical attempt to appear sober. Every Kond drinks: and everyone knows that they drink. The rigours of the law come down mostly on those who deal in drink and not on those who make it for themselves. To my knowledge the Besringia Sirdar has never reported anyone for being drunk, and investigations and prosecutions are undertaken directly by the police and the Excise Inspectors. Yet, in spite of the fact that they must have known that they were at least as safe talking to the Sirdar as they were talking to me about their drinking exploits, in his presence they were overcome with embarrassment and got away as quickly as they could. The Konds of Besringia—and of other neighbouring *muthas*—were afraid of the Besringia Sirdar. They did not simply obey him as a Sirdar: they feared him as a man. Goneswaro, with exactly the same formal powers, and the same structural position in the society, they came near to despising.

A Kond is expected to give material tokens of the Sirdar's rank. The 'additional' two pice, which enter into the calculations of Manda's tax are a 'voluntary' payment to the Sirdar, about which the Administration officially knows nothing. The Sirdars are paid by a 12 per cent commission on the tax which they collect. But in fact they collect—or nowadays try to collect—not only the two pice, but also many other forms of '*mamul*' (perquisite). At harvest the Sirdar and his agents tour the *mutha* collecting not only the Government's tax and the two pice, but also a contribution of grain from each house, and their expenses while touring the *mutha*. The Sirdars claim a gift when there is a feast in their *mutha*, and they used to receive dues at the funeral of a rich Kond, amounting sometimes to several head of cattle. Conversely, on important occasions in the Sirdar's own house—especially at the marriage of his eldest son or at the latter's succession on the death of his father—the Konds of the *mutha* are expected to make substantial contributions to the feasting, to attend in person, and to show themselves off as the retainers of the Sirdar.

Ideally there is in this relationship between the Sirdar and his Konds an element of positive acquiescence, a feeling that he is their chosen and accepted leader. When a Sirdar succeeds to office the Konds have a right to make formal his investiture by binding about his head the turban of office, and by making various other signs of allegiance. This right is said to be recognized by the Administration—although I have no cases to demonstrate it—and Konds believe that their intercession can prevent an unsuitable person from succeeding to office. In Balimendi I have taken part in discussions about whom the Konds should choose to succeed Goneswaro. There is no formal election and no regular demo-cratic procedure: but the Balimendi Konds believed that they could in effect make their own choice by presenting petitions to the Magistrate in support of or in opposition to particular candidates.

It was in these discussions that I learnt what kind of personality the ideal Sirdar should have and what duties he should undertake. There are two main parts to these duties. The first is that the Sirdar should be able to intercede on behalf of his subjects with the officials, and should be able to protect them against outsiders. There were, for instance, occasions when the Besringia Sirdar sent his *paiks* or his *proja* to help Konds of Besringia who had been cheated, usually by PANS from other *muthas*. This is not done so often now, since the Konds themselves recognize that their own Sirdar's intervention is seldom effective in another *mutha* and that it is better either to indulge in some modified form of self-help, or to go to the police and the Magistrate. The second part of the Sirdar's duties is to settle disputes within his own *mutha*. This service is appreciated by the Konds, and in Bisipara I have seen many councils presided over by the Sirdar settling land, marital and inheritance disputes. His decisions were not always effective and sometimes were taken on to the Government courts, particu-larly when substantial amounts of property or money were

P

involved. But the Sirdar's court was popular because it was cheap and swift and its procedures were simple and easily understood.

That is the ideal role of the Sirdar in relation to his Konds. They are *his* Konds and they owe him loyalty, even affection: he is their king, chosen and accepted by them to lead, to represent them against outsiders, and to settle their disputes. In reality every Sirdar plays not that role but also several others.

Not all Sirdars are Oriyas, but both Goneswaro and the Sirdar of Besringia are, and this factor can be held neutral between them, as a determinant of power. But it would be impossible to understand the attitude which the Konds held towards Goneswaro and Nrusingh in the tax dispute, or the epithets which the drunken Ponga threw at the Oriya schoolmaster, without also taking into account the generalized relationship between Kond and Oriya and what stereotypes the Konds have about Oriyas.[1] The attitude of the Baderi Konds towards Goneswaro was coloured not just by the fact that he is their Sirdar, or that he is the representative of the Administration, but also by the mere fact that he is an Oriya. Indeed Ponga's drunken remarks are in effect an accusation that Goneswaro was behaving not like a Sirdar, like a king, or even like an official, but like an ordinary money-grabbing Oriya. He knows how to 'choke money out of his subjects'. He knows how to cheat them and exploit them. Goneswaro and the schoolmaster are here being lumped together with the Oriya merchant classes, with the shopkeepers and merchants and turmeric traders.

In the case of Goneswaro this accusation is not justified. The old man is no longer interested in making money. He is running down his estate. He does not trade in turmeric or take part in any kind of commerce. The Sirdar of Besringia, on the other hand, persuades some Konds in his *mutha* to hold back turmeric until the market is paying scarcity prices, and then sell it to him at the price ruling in the time of plenty. But his Konds do not shout public accusations about 'choking money out of his subjects'. This is because he fulfils fairly efficiently his other duties as Sirdar and because he has a commanding personality, whereas Goneswaro, who is relatively innocent of extortion, fails on both these counts. The accusation about extortion is not just a specific accusation: it is also a reflection of the economic cleavage between Kond and

[1] See Chapter VII.

Oriya[1] and a reflection of Goneswaro's general inadequacies as a Sirdar.

There is a further role which all Sirdars, and particularly the Oriya Sirdars have, in contradiction to the ideal relationship between king and subject. The accusation that the WARRIORS—the caste to which the hill chiefs belonged—'choked money out of their subjects' is not an idle one. The list of *mamuls* (perquisites), which to-day is dwindling fast as the Konds become politically more sophisticated, was very considerable even as recently as a generation ago. The reality of this extortion, by people who have derived political power from the presence of the Administration, is not so much to-day, but the memory and the stereotype of the ruthless Sirdar remain in the Kond mind.[2] This role detracts from the ideal relationship between the Sirdar and his retainers. In becoming a servant of the Administration he has been able to ignore some of his traditional obligations and he is no longer constrained by the traditional sanction of desertion or rebellion. He acts not as a king, as 'the father of his people' (that phrase is used), but as a bureaucrat.

The relationship between the Sirdar and his people is complicated because they are both actors in another system of political relationships—in the bureaucratic administration and recently in the representative democracy. Absolutely in the latter, and to an increasing extent in the former, the Sirdar and his subjects are equals. They are equal before the courts. The Konds can—as they threatened to do in the tax case—appeal to the Magistrate against the decisions and actions of the Sirdar. The modern administration, particularly since the growth of political representation, is hostile to the Oriya Sirdars, and the latter can no longer be sure, as once they could, of the backing and support of the local officials. Alternative forms of Government are arising and it is clear that administration through *muthas* and Sirdars is about to give way to a more representative system of local government.

The Sirdar, in his relationship with the Konds, cannot be just the Sirdar and nothing more. Inevitably he has also to play other roles towards the Konds: and even if he does not (as Goneswaro does not go in for trading), the Konds may accuse him of doing so or act towards him as if he did, or make use of him as an incumbent

[1] See p. 184.
[2] See p. 181.

of one of these roles, although in fact he may remain completely
passive. Success and power are achieved not by playing one of
these roles to the exclusion of others, but by using one to make
good deficiencies in the others. The Besringia Sirdar is skilled in
doing this. He tries cases and fulfils his judicial functions better and
more fairly than most Sirdars. But this alone would not give him
the power that he has: he has two other sources of power. He
keeps on good terms with officials and has a reputation of being
a just and efficient Sirdar—relatively so, at least. Having this reputation he can in fact be a good friend or a dangerous enemy to his
subjects. The second source of his power is that he has a close and
intimate contact with the people of his *mutha*. He tours personally
to collect taxes and *mamuls* and does not leave this task to his
paiks. Even his trading activities contribute to this nexus of social
relations and bind him closely to individuals in his *mutha*. He is
accessible in a way that Goneswaro is not: it is worth while bringing a case before him because if he comes down on your side, he
may be able to do something to help you and to harm your
opponent. He is able to help or to harm people not only because he
is a Sirdar: he gains wealth and influence through trade and by
other means: he makes adroit use of divisions in his *mutha* so that
he may rule. To divide is to rule. Goneswaro, now an old and
sick man, is incapable of working in this complex of social relationships. He is physically unable to travel about his *mutha*.
Now that he has grown old he is not interested in settling disputes,
and he is in any case a poor man in a council. Even if a case comes
to him he does not wield the power and influence in the other
systems—trade and power derived from the Administration—
to be much help to those who come seeking his favour. Consequently they do not come. The Administration regards him—
so a Revenue Inspector told me—as an incompetent and dishonest rascal, who would have been removed had he not been so
old and likely to die in any case in a short time. It is a consequence
of this that a case involving a few rupees should blow up into
violence and abuse in his *mutha*, while in Besringia things of
greater magnitude never come to the surface. The Besringia
Sirdar by skilfully using the actual power which he has in other
roles, is, in his traditional role of Sirdar, able to preserve the forms
of authority and respect. In fact he derives his power from the
modern and not entirely from the traditional system.

There is a final and very important factor in assessing the capabilities of the two men. Besringia is a much easier *mutha* to manage by the system of 'divide and rule' than is Balimendi. Besringia *mutha* contains many more immigrant lineages than does Balimendi. In Besringia the group of Konds is not united to the same degree by ties of agnation as is the group in Balimendi. The title which the immigrant people hold to land is derived from the Administration and the closest representative of the Administration is the Sirdar, particularly an active and subtle Sirdar like the man in Besringia. The Balimendi Konds, whom Goneswaro has to manage, still behave towards him as a corporate clan towards an outsider—as, presumably, they would have done before the Administration came to the area.[1]

MANDA KOHORO

Manda Kohoro is a young man, slightly corpulent for a Kond, with a puffiness about the eyes and cheeks that is a sign of internal disorders caused by protracted malaria, He is frequently ill, and this may be the reason why his fields are not well cultivated and he is reputed to be a slovenly farmer. He is occasionally taken by a fit, and he has acquired a reputation as a diviner and healer. He is well-to-do, as standards are in Baderi, in spite of his poor cultivation. He is also shy, quietly spoken, and is considered a friendly, inoffensive person, but not a fool. It may have been his docility, combined with a slight affluence, that caused Nrusingh to choose him as the victim of his peculations. The qualities of moderation, humility, and restraint are also apparent in the part he played in the affair. He spoke in a quiet and reasoned manner to the Sirdar, and although he was the victim, he was neither aggressive like Liringa, nor violent like the drunken Ponga. It was Manda who begged back the cloth which Ponga had snatched away from the Oriya schoolmaster.

In this situation there were three ways in which Manda could behave. His aim, clearly, was to see that the money which he had handed over should find its way to the Government, so that he would not have to pay it again. The first course open to him was to insist on his rights at law, ultimately on his right to bring a complaint before the Magistrate about the conduct of the Sirdar

[1] See pp. 170-5.

and his subordinate. He could, that is to say, have conducted himself as a citizen, and as a person who stood equal with Goneswaro and Nrusingh before the law. A second course would have been to remind Goneswaro of his obligations as a Sirdar—as Manda's 'king'—and his duty to protect Manda from an unscrupulous minor official. Manda would then, in words and by his behaviour, emphasize his dependence upon Goneswaro, and, by implication, his continued faith in the latter's probity. The third weapon in Manda's armoury was to invoke the support of his fellow Konds and by their joint pressure to cause the Sirdar to straighten the matter out. These three courses are not, of course, exclusive of one another and in fact Manda, either willingly or under pressure of circumstances, followed all three; but it seems to me that he relied mainly on the second course, while his comrades favoured the first, and drew Goneswaro's attention to the third factor.

Manda himself only made an excursion into the first course by asking that he should be given the correct receipt. The point of this receipt, of course, is that ultimately it can be used if the case goes before higher officials. But he did not, like Liringa, make this an open threat. To make use of a threat like this is in many ways a game of poker. Goneswaro knew that the sum involved was less than two rupees. He also knew that it would cost Manda much more than this even to start proceedings before the Magistrate. On the other hand Goneswaro knew that if a complaint was laid, it would cost *him* a lot more than the missing Rs.1/12, in terms of time, trouble, and money to clear himself and to make sure that the incident did not damage him irreparably before the Government. Manda too knew this, and all the Konds knew that Goneswaro's reputation did not stand well in official circles. Against this, Manda would have had the trouble of marshalling witnessess, and although it is likely that all his fellow villagers would have backed him, their expenses of attending court would have had to be paid by Manda, in the form of providing meals for them while they were in Phulbani. Nor could he have been sure that Goneswaro would not have been able to exert himself sufficiently to find a Baderi Kond, who, for reasons of spite against Manda or against someone supporting Manda, would provide evidence favourable to Goneswaro and against Manda. Finally both parties have in their lifetime seen people ruined by getting caught up in the judicial machinery, and in spite of what is said about the litigiousness of the Indian peasant, in the Kondmals at least the peasants much prefer to try to settle their cases without making use of the Government courts. All in all, I think that both sides realized that to go to court over Rs.1/12 would be a grave mistake.

The advantage, at this stage, lay with Goneswaro. He could be sure that the Konds were bluffing. Nevertheless he refused to write a receipt for the lesser amount (Rs.4/8) because this could have been used by Manda not to make a formal appeal before the courts, but to produce as evidence before the Revenue Inspector who tours periodically in the villages to investigate cases of pro-longed failure to pay tax. An appeal before this man, backed by the evidence of his fellow-villagers, would have cost Manda little, since the first enquiries would have been conducted on the spot and might have been enough to settle the case in his favour. But again, he ran the risk that Goneswaro in the meantime might have been able to find witnesses to speak against Manda.

I do not think that Manda had worked all this out, step by step, as I have written it. It is much more likely that a person as diffident and inarticulate as himself, would simply have ruled out any course of action which would involve him with the official machinery and might eventually land him in the courts. He went no further than to ask for the correct receipt.

Manda, then, preferred to act as a *proja*, speaking respectfully and with moderation. He did so, as I have said, probably because it was in his nature. But even this moderation, this presentation of himself as a reasonable and moderate man, has implications for a future recourse to higher authority. It would be in Manda's favour to be able to show that he had conducted himself correctly throughout. Otherwise Goneswaro might have claimed that he would have written out a receipt on the spot and corrected a simple error of calculation made between him and his subordinate Nrusingh, had not the Konds become violent and abusive and made it impossible for him to explain the mistake to them and set it right. In fact, after Liringa's interjection, the atmosphere be-came so charged that Goneswaro simply ran away and left matters where they stood.

It is hardly likely that Goneswaro, and still less Nrusingh, would have been influenced by Manda's reasonableness. They are more likely to have despised him for it, and had Manda stood alone, he would have represented a serious threat to neither of them. But Manda did not stand alone. He may well have been content with his own reasonableness because he knew that there were other forces working on his side. There were other Konds in Baderi, notably Liringa, who were eager to follow a more aggressive course, partly because they liked Manda, partly because he was their 'brother', partly for reasons of justice, and partly to further their own ends. Secondly the incident clearly aroused in Baderi the Kond esprit-de-corps, the feeling that they must stand together against the Oriyas and protect themselves from exploitation. What Manda was unwilling or too diffident to do for himself, the group might have been willing to do for him, not because of the Rs.1/12 involved, but because Manda stood as a symbol of Balimendi nationhood, if I may call it that.

Liringa Kohoro

Liringa intervened in a way that was characteristic of him. He avoided the uninhibited and self-destroying frenzy of Ponga: but he struck more sharply and decisively on Manda's behalf than did Manda himself. His aggression was calculated not only to disturb Goneswaro and to voice the inarticulate feelings of the Konds around him, but also to enhance his own position among the Konds of Baderi. By serving one end he could also serve the other: the two aims, in other words, although in two different social systems, were complementary: and Liringa made use of his opportunities, neither underplaying them nor overplaying them, with the same assured political competence that the Besringia Sirdar displays.

Liringa's intervention was the more disturbing to Goneswaro because he knew that not only was Liringa a more determined, a more resourceful, and an altogether tougher person than Manda, but also because he was much more capable of carrying out his threats than any other Kond in Baderi. He is a man of about forty, ambitious in village politics, shrewd, and very articulate, but without the wealth and lacking that blundering charisma which keeps Ponga in the first position in the village. He was educated as far as the eighth standard in a Middle English school, a qualification far in excess of any other Kond in Baderi: and he reads and writes fluently and correctly in Oriya. He can present a case with force and clarity, and had the matter come before the Revenue Inspector, it would have been Liringa, and not Manda himself or the village headman Ponga, who would have spoken against Goneswaro and Nrusingh. As advocates neither Nrusingh nor Goneswaro could have matched him in debate, and both Goneswaro and Liringa himself knew this.

Liringa's ability to appreciate the situation rapidly and seize upon the weaknesses in his opponent's position is shown in the few short sentences which are recorded in the text. Manda would have been content to receive a receipt for Rs.6/4: he was not interested in embarrassing Goneswaro or in using the incident to strengthen the position of the Konds against the Oriyas. He was willing, implicitly, to let Goneswaro extricate himself from a difficult position without too much loss of face and without material harm. But Liringa did not ask for a receipt for Rs.6/4. He first demanded an explanation for the fact that the receipt offered to Manda was for Rs.4/8. He knew that Goneswaro could have only two answers to this: either he could say that he or Nrusingh had made a mistake: or else he could say—and this seems to have been the truth—that this was the first he knew of the affair and Nrusingh must have been deceiving him. Liringa could then have said that a Sirdar ought to be able to control his subordinates, or that a WARRIOR ought to be able to discipline an untouchable. In fact Goneswaro said that he would ask Nrusingh about the affair, implying that he, as Sirdar, knew nothing about the matter but would straighten it out as soon as he had seen Nrusingh. This would probably have been enough for Manda: but it offered Liringa an opportunity to probe into two of Goneswaro's weaknesses—his ambiguous relationship with Nrusingh, and his bad reputation with the Administration. Liringa asked the Sirdar to write a receipt for Rs.4/8. Such a receipt would, at first sight, have cleared Goneswaro himself of any complicity in the peculations. But Liringa correctly appreciated that the Sirdar would be unwilling to arraign Nrusingh, because Nrusingh was both indispensable and capable of putting up a fight against Goneswaro himself. He also appreciated that Goneswaro would not relish having the affairs of his *mutha* subjected to the close scrutiny which would be entailed in an enquiry. I do not think that Liringa expected to get the receipt for Rs.4/8. His real purpose in asking for it was to embarrass the Sirdar, and to let him know that

Liringa at least knew where the Sirdar was most vulnerable. The final subtlety in Liringa's questions is that he raised the suspicion that Goneswaro and Nrusingh were in fact acting in collusion. This is the implication of Goneswaro's refusal to give a receipt for Rs.4/8 and so arraign Nrusingh, and Liringa drove it home by talking as if they were hand in glove: 'You and Nrusingh will soon find out. . . .' Liringa was correct in thinking that the Sirdar could not afford to let Nrusingh down: but he managed to insinuate as well that Goneswaro was concerned in this particular peculation. Goneswaro had no answer to all this: all he could do was leave Liringa victorious in the field.

This was indeed a victory for Liringa rather than for Manda. Had the Konds pressed for a receipt for the full amount, they might have got it. The Sirdar, alone in an assembly of Konds who were clearly in the right, might in the end have yielded to cajolery, flattery, and threats, and given them what they wanted, especially as the amount was so small. It is true that this might have been a dangerous precedent, but it would have allowed him to come out of this particular situation with the minimum loss of face. He was not given the chance. Before the process of persuasion, which is a long and well-tried technique among these people, could get under way, Liringa stopped it by losing his temper—or appearing to lose his temper—and shifted to another tactic, which was calculated not so much to serve Manda's ends, as to strike a blow in the protracted conflict between the Sirdar and the Konds, and between Oriyas and Konds in general, and to exhibit Liringa himself as the leader and champion of the Baderi Konds. Goneswaro clearly was down: Manda would have allowed him to acknowledge defeat gracefully and retire from the ring: Liringa, on the other hand, was determined to strike the Sirdar when he was down, and to be the one who struck the blow.

Liringa, in fact, was using this incident to validate his claim to be the real leader of the Baderi Konds in the place of Ponga. I do not know whether Liringa wants to hold the official position of village headman. This post carries no salary and no perquisites, although it does, of course, carry some prestige. Liringa may well be aiming rather for the reality of power, and even if he gets the opportunity may prefer not to go to the trouble of competing with Ponga's son—supposing Ponga were to die—for official recognition. But he is ambitious for power in the village. He

claimed to me that he is the senior person in the founding lineage
of the Baderi Konds. He said that his ancestors had always been
the chiefs in the village, but his grandfather, who had fallen on
hard times, relied too much on the wealthy and powerful grandfather of Ponga. This man got himself appointed joint headman with
Liringa's grandfather, and in the next generation it was Ponga's
lineage alone which held the headmanship. Liringa claims, in fact,
that by descent he is the real head of the village. He loses no
opportunity of showing up Ponga's shortcomings, which are
frequent and spectacular. Liringa's weakness is firstly that he is a
much poorer man than Ponga: and secondly that his fellows
mistrust his cool subtlety which, as a factor in leadership, is no
match for the expansive bullying geniality of Ponga.

The incident of the taxes gave Liringa an ideal opportunity to
show his prowess. He has the required forensic abilities and a
sufficiently subtle insight into human relationships and human
nature to be able to drive the Sirdar into a corner and at the same
time arouse the corporate spirit of his fellows: 'You and Nrusingh
will soon find out what it means to be Sirdar of Balimendi'.
Ponga, drunk or sober, would merely have lost his temper and
by his excesses would have exposed himself to the insinuation that
if he had kept his mouth shut they might have got Goneswaro to
sign a receipt for Rs.6/4. He would not have been able to high-
light the Sirdar's points of weakness, as Liringa did, and would
probably have attempted merely to shout the Sirdar down. (He
was not, I believe, in the village when Goneswaro came to hand
out the receipts.)

Liringa's position in this incident is the obverse of that of
Goneswaro and resembles, in some ways, the position of Nrusingh.
Liringa's skills are conspicuously those which Goneswaro lacks,
and resemble the skills of the Besringia Sirdar. All these people
have to cope with several different systems of social relations.
Goneswaro is handicapped because Nrusingh is not merely his
proja, but is also a Government servant and a prosperous trader,
while Nrusingh can use these last two roles to strengthen his
position against his master. Liringa was able to make use of a
dispute which arose in the system of relationships between Kond
and Oriya, and between a Sirdar and his subjects, in order to
strengthen his own position against a rival in quite a different system,
the political system of a Kond village. A more subtle and energetic

man than Goneswaro might have been able to make use of this cleavage in the Kond system. Had Goneswaro been in control of the situation he might have quietened Liringa by asking why he, and not Manda himself or the village headman Ponga, was doing all the talking. He might have demanded that they should postpone discussion until Ponga was present, and then it would not have been difficult for him to cause Ponga to take the bit between his teeth and trample down Liringa in the process. But Goneswaro lacked either the insight or the energy to follow this course.

The various systems and structures, so to speak, are to some extent neutral. Goneswaro's weakness is only partly in his structural position: his weakness is also that he is too old and too tired of life to manoeuvre within the limits which are set by his structural position. Like the winds and currents in the metaphor I used earlier, the different social systems are there as the ultimate regularities in social life. The actors cannot go beyond a fixed limit. Neither side in this dispute, for instance, could hope to gain its ends by the use of force: Goneswaro could not call in the police or an army of private retainers to beat down Kond objections: nor could the Konds attack Goneswaro or transfer their allegiance to another chief. But within the limits of structures and systems, there is room for choice and manipulation, and those people are successsful who have both the necessary energy and who perceive the alternatives open to them.

PONGA KOHORO

In the face of events both Manda and Goneswaro remained largely passive. Things happened to them: they reacted with the minimum of movement and neither took any but the most obvious courses of action which the situation offered to them. For them it was an affair of the missing tax money and the receipt and nothing more. Liringa on the other hand was active and turned the situation to his own advantage, making it serve his ends in other fields. I do not think that Manda saw clearly what could be involved in the situation. Goneswaro probably saw the implications of the moves made by Liringa, but he was unable to start counter moves, even the obvious one of probing into the cleavage between Liringa and Ponga. Ponga reacted violently, but he thought with his heart rather than with his head. He was undoubtedly very drunk throughout the day, and if he made any calculations these were rather instinctive than rational. I shall discuss the various alternative courses of action which he might have taken, and I shall give reasons why some of the things he did were to his own advantage, but it must be remembered that, drunk as he was, many of his actions obstructed rather than furthered his ambitions and his intention to help Manda. If I can put it this way, while Liringa picked a careful path through the social maze, Ponga blundered about into every corner of the maze and did not in the end find his way through. But from the very vigour and extent of his actions and words, an analysis of the part he played in the dispute gives a much wider picture of society and the forces at work within it.

Even sober, Ponga is subject to demoniacal rages. On this day he was drunk, and undoubtedly the reasons why he reacted so violently to the presence of Oriyas and a renegade Kond in his village were simply that he is a violent man and had drunk too much. But whether he realized it or not, it was in his interest to make some kind of mark in the dispute. Ponga had been away from the village when the dispute first was aired before Goneswaro and the running had been made entirely by Liringa. Liringa had spoken up as the champion and protector of the village and Ponga had done nothing. In fact what Ponga did on this day probably did not help either his own cause or Manda's. Had he stopped short at the point of abusing Nrusingh, his actions might have been in his favour. But it was a mistake to turn the attack on to the others. The renegade Kond and the Oriya trader did not matter so much: they are nonentities so far as the Baderi Konds are concerned, and no-one worried because they ran up against the sharp end of Ponga's temper. But the Oriya schoolmaster is a moderate man and popular in Baderi and it was a mistake to involve him in the general condemnation of Oriyas. The other two men from Bisipara fled. The schoolmaster took refuge in the house of a friendly Kond, and Manda himself recovered the shawl for him. Finally it was a mistake to vent his anger on his own son and daughter-in-law. It obscured the significance of Ponga's attacks on the Oriyas. It made it seem that Ponga was not really concerned with championing Manda and the Kond cause, so much as with letting his temper run riot.

Ponga is concerned in the dispute in three main roles. Firstly he is the subordinate of the Sirdar, both in the Administrative system as a village headman, and in the traditional system as a subject of Goneswaro, his 'king'. Secondly he is the representative of, and the spokesman for, the Konds of his village. Just as he has to transmit, in theory, the orders of higher officials, so also he has to present the views of his people and stand up for them before the Sirdar and the Administration. Thirdly he appears in quite a different role: that of a seller of turmeric. I will discuss this last role first.

Although the transaction by which Ponga sold Rs.80 worth of turmeric brings him into direct contact with Nrusingh, and although Ponga is the only person who at the moment has this contact, yet this relationship seems to have had little bearing on the course of the dispute. It so happened that Nrusingh fell foul of Ponga on an occasion when the trading relationship had brought Nrusingh to Baderi, and in this historical sense the trading relationship is relevant to the dispute. Had Nrusingh not appeared at that moment, then Ponga might have drunk himself into a state of quiet insensibility, and the rest of the drama would not have taken place. But the relationship was irrelevant to the dispute in a sociological sense, as distinct from an historical sense, because neither Nrusingh nor Ponga tried to make use of it in this particular dispute. There would have been little point in Nrusingh trying to do anything. I am sure that he thought that the incident in which Goneswaro had been involved a day or two before had blown over: otherwise he would not have come to Baderi, because no-one in that position would go looking for trouble. It is possible that had the dispute been of more serious proportions, and had Nrusingh felt that the incident might bring real trouble down on his head, he might have tried to use his relationship with Ponga to split the Konds and get some of them on his side against Manda. But Nrusingh has probably ridden out many storms of this kind, and it is unlikely that he was much worried by what happened to Goneswaro and what had been said in Baderi.

Nor does it seem to have occurred to Ponga—drunk or sober—that he might use this relationship with Nrusingh either to help Manda or to put Liringa in his place and show who was the real leader in Baderi. There were two ways in which he might have done this. The more subtle and more difficult course would have been to offer to help out Nrusingh, by hindering Liringa or by encouraging Liringa to overreach himself: and he would expect in return more favourable terms for his turmeric on this and on future occasions. This course would have the advantage of increasing his profit and of making things difficult for Liringa. I doubt whether this would have occurred to Ponga, even sober, and given time to think the whole thing out. He has a rugged simplicity and directness, which would make the course distasteful and which renders him incapable of successful double-dealing of this kind. Liringa might have been able to do it, if he had wanted to: but not Ponga. Secondly, while Ponga's conscience might have allowed him to try duplicity of this kind in concert with another Kond, I doubt whether he would be willing to make such a deal with an Oriya PAN, both because he would think it beneath his dignity, and because to be caught out in such an association would give his enemies a very useful weapon against him. The second and more direct way in which Ponga could have used his special link with Nrusingh to help Manda in particular and the Konds in general would have been simply to refuse to sell the turmeric to Nrusingh, and perhaps to try to organize a village boycott of Nrusingh. He did neither of these things, not because actions like this are unknown—boycotts against shopkeepers or individuals are common enough (and are known by that English word)—but for other reasons.

It is clear that Ponga acted entirely on the spur of a drunken moment. Between the time that the scene with the Sirdar occurred and the time that Nrusingh came to the village two days had elapsed, and Ponga had done nothing about it, beyond gossip with his drunken cronies. The Konds were waiting to see what the Sirdar would do next: in fact neither he nor the Konds did anything, and still had done nothing when I left the area eight months later. Ponga had struck a good bargain with Nrusingh over the turmeric. He had persuaded Nrusingh to buy it without weighing it, judging the quantity by sight alone: and in fact Nrusingh had come to the village because he wanted to look again at the heap in order to see if he had made a mistake, or if Ponga had been taking any of it away. Ponga would not want to break this bargain because one of his villagers had been cheated of Rs.1/12, especially when it appeared that the Sirdar and Nrusingh might in any case climb down.

But there is more to it than this. There is a definite feeling, although it is not put into words, that trading and commerce are in some way outside the ordinary systems of social relations. I had noticed this in Bisipara, at the time of the bitter conflict between the clean castes and the untouchables. In spite of this conflict none of the personal economic links between clean castes and the untouchables—mostly wage-labour—were in the least disturbed. While a case was being fought before the Magistrate and oaths of secrecy were being extracted by their leaders from each side, the normal economic intercourse went on undisturbed.[1] I think that in the Baderi case everyone concerned—Nrusingh, Ponga, and the Konds of Baderi—would have thought it a sign of madness had Ponga attempted to bring pressure on Nrusingh in such a way as to jeopardize their trading relationship.

I have gone to some length to describe the things that Nrusingh and Ponga might have done, but did not in fact do, in order to bring out the element of choice in the situation. There is a temptation to assume that because two persons are connected in several different relationships, then these different relationships must always act upon and modify one another: to assume, for instance, that Liringa's ambitions to be a man of importance in Baderi must always and inevitably influence his actions towards the Oriyas, as they did in this dispute. But this is not so: for reasons of conscience, or expediency, or any other reason, it is sometimes possible for the individual to insulate one system from the other, and deliberately to set one relationship to one side and see that it is not brought into play. This is exactly what Ponga and Nrusingh did with their relationship as seller and buyer of turmeric. The different systems of social relations are not inevitably and inextricably connected with one another but are connected only when someone chooses to connect them.

The element of choice is again illustrated in the second role which Ponga might have played in this dispute. Ponga is the village headman. He is thus part of the same hierarchy as the Sirdar, being in charge of a village, while the Sirdar has charge of all the villages in a *mutha*. Nrusingh too is part of this hierarchy, but while the other two have charge of stretches of territory and fulfil most of the functions of Government at that level within their territories, Nrusingh is a functionary proper having a specialized duty within the *mutha*. It is not possible to

[1] See F. G. Bailey, 1957, Chapter XI.

allot him a place in the hierarchy in which Ponga and Goneswaro are placed. Between Ponga and Nrusingh there is an inherent ambiguity in rank in the administrative system: it is the same uneasy relationship as that which can exist between a superior's personal assistants and his inferiors in the hierarchy—as, say, between the Deputy Commissioner and the Governor's secretary. Indeed part of the trouble with Nrusingh is that he arrogates to himself—or has delegated to him—too many of the actual functions of the Sirdar: that he is not merely a messenger; that he does not behave like a messenger, but has taken on so many of the mannerisms of a Sirdar that people have come to call him the 'Little Sirdar'. While it might be proper for the Sirdar to interfere in the affairs of a village, it is not proper for his messenger to do so. Whether Ponga thought or not in his drunkenness, it would have been entirely reasonable for him to humiliate Nrusingh, since the latter's arrogance is an attack on Ponga's authority in the village.

As the Government intends the system to work, the Sirdar should make his contacts with the villages through their headmen, just as the higher officials should make their contacts with the *mutha* through the Sirdar. In fact the large erosion of the Sirdar's powers in recent years arises from the fact that he is by-passed both informally, and in newer structures of administration (as for instance in the specialist departments of agriculture or veterinary science), and most of all in the modern political democracy, all of which have reference to the individual directly and not to the individual as the subject of particular Sirdars. The same process seems always to have gone on in the relationship between the Sirdars and the village headmen. The ideal relationship is one of personal loyalty from the subject directly to the Sirdar and not mediately through the village headman. The best and most successful Sirdars, like the head of Besringia, are those who have a network of direct contacts with many individuals in their *mutha*. It would be difficult to work through the Kond village headmen, because they are closely identified with the people of the village, and invariably of the same caste as the majority of their people and closely related to them, and are not in a position to exercise the authority which this kind of administration demands. Furthermore there is no real need for the Sirdars to delegate powers to any great degree since in none of the *muthas* which I know is any village more than one day's walk from the village in which the

Q

Sirdar resides. However, in spite of this, in theory the village headman is responsible to the Sirdar for the good conduct of his village.
The headman of the village is, in theory, the most junior official,
if I can describe a post which is hereditary and unsalaried by that
term.

In the tax dispute Goneswaro made no attempt to employ
Ponga in this rôle. Ponga was not consulted, as, officially, he
might have been—indeed, ought to have been. It might well have
been good tactics for Goneswaro, as I pointed out earlier, to bring
in Ponga in his official capacity, in order to split the Konds. But
he did not choose to do so, perhaps because the habit of direct contact between the Sirdar and the Konds was too strong.

The role of the village headman is in fact made up of two
different relationships. On the one side is his official relationship in
the hierarchy to the Sirdar. He is an official, whose duty it is to
represent the Government to his villagers and to transmit the
orders of the Government. In the other direction the headman
represents his villagers to the Government. He is their spokesman
and protector, and it is this role which can give a headman authority, much more than can the fact that he represents the Government. In other words, the headman is scarcely a bureaucrat at all
and derives very little real authority from the bureaucratic system.
This may be why Liringa appears to be seeking informal power in
the village rather than the forms of authority: and it would have
been a good reason for Ponga, if he thought about it at all, to
break out into a show of violent opposition to authority and to
non-Konds in general. The headman, if he has authority at all
over his villagers, has it because he can effectively represent
their interests against higher authority. In the structure as the
Administration intends it to be, the village headman occupies one
of those awkward and ambivalent positions in which he has to
look both ways. In fact, if the headman of a Kond village looks
upwards to his superiors, or even if he attempts to look both
ways, he is lost. His real power is all to be found behind him:
either he is the champion of his village: or is he a nonentity: or he
becomes a virtual outsider like Sudersun (Cases 31: p. 97 and
34: p. 112).

Liringa, I think, could appreciate this analysis. With Ponga,
behaviour calculated to give himself power in the village is in his
heart rather than in his head. It is instinctive: and his reactions are

not always adjusted to particular situations but are apt to emerge in a generalized hostility towards non-Kond outsiders. Liringa's tactics were directed towards that particular situation. They were calculated specifically to help Baderi village and in particular Manda Kohoro. His words and actions were relevant to one particular occasion and were to some extent effective. Ponga's explosion, on the other hand, although it was sparked off by Manda's dilemma, did not confine itself to that alone, but erupted as a savage, incoherent comment on the generalized relationship between Konds and Oriyas. It did nothing to help Manda. On the other hand, had Ponga not gone to ludicrous extremes, it might have been a better assertion of leadership than Liringa's more rational actions. Liringa brought in the other Konds of Baderi by threatening that they would stand behind Manda: 'We will show you and Nrusingh what it means to be Sirdar of Balimendi. . . .' Ponga, on the other hand, gave voice to a general grievance. He was not merely speaking for Manda. The very amplitude of his comment and his coarse emotion are likely to impress the Konds and drive home to them that they all have grievances of the same kind as Manda. He did not merely say that they would stand behind Manda: he voiced the reasons why they should do this. He lifted the situation out of the particular into the general: and by doing so he called not only on the sense of justice of the Konds, but also upon their self-interest. This is leadership: it is true that it is the leadership of a demagogue, but it is not the less effective for that. In fact if it was ineffective and did not in the end enhance Ponga's standing in the village, this was because he did not know when to stop. He attacked the wrong Oriyas: he thrashed his own son for no reason at all. In this way his excesses exposed him to an *argumentum ad hominem*: Ponga was not really a champion of the Konds because he attacked everyone indiscriminately. Nevertheless, in spite of his mistakes, Ponga had made an instinctive appreciation of the social relationships which give a Kond authority in his own village. The Administration does not give its village headman sufficient powers to let him drive his villagers: he has to be a leader.

The sentiments which Ponga expressed in the half-hour while he ran amok in the village, and which are implicit in the actions which he took the following morning, are filled with contradictions. Predominantly he attacked what might be called Ponga's idea of what the Oriyas value. The Oriyas are portrayed, with a coarse invective, as liars and thieves who live only to make money by cheating others. Nrusingh eats the money taken for the Government. The schoolmaster, like his father before him, is occupied in teaching people how to cheat. In a very indirect sense this is true. More Oriyas than Konds go to school, partly because they realize that the skills which they learn in school are of use to them in commerce and in their other dealings in the modern world, and partly because few Oriya villages and many Kond villages are without a school. In commerce or in dealings with the Government the literate man is in a much better position than a man who cannot read or write. To this extent, then, there is truth in what Ponga said: part of the skill of the Oriyas in commerce is the result of their better education. Konds like Liringa, who are better educated than the average Oriya, are much less likely to be cheated than those who have not been educated.

Ponga, then, accused the Oriyas of misusing the political authority which they have in order to extort money from their subjects. He directed his attack on the WARRIOR caste, from which the Sirdars are drawn, and the schoolmaster came in for the invective because he was a WARRIOR and an agnatic relative of both Goneswaro Bisoi and the Besringia Sirdar.

These are two facets of a single grievance—cheating in commerce and cheating by the abuse of political power—which every Kond is ready to talk about. It is their standard complaint and it is in this area of social relations, rather than in culture, that they see themselves different from and opposed to the Oriyas.[1]

The obverse of Ponga's attack on the supposed Oriya values is his implied eulogy of Kond values. Konds abhor trade—at least they abhor the role of middleman—which, as I have explained above, they relegate by tradition to their untouchables.[2] Kosira Kohoro, who lives and was born in Bisipara, is undoubtedly a Kond, but he is attacked because he has come as a middleman in search of turmeric: 'Are you a Kond? You're the sort who destroys our customs. . . .' This is Ponga's comment on change and decay. It is his lament for lost Kond values, for the decay of the Kond way of life, for, indeed, the old standards of morality. It is said—even by the Oriyas—that in the old days you could leave a bag of gold coins in a Kond village street, and come back and collect them a

[1] See Chapter VII.
[2] See pp. 134 and 205

year later: but not nowadays. In the old days Kond customs and Kond morality prevailed. Now contacts with the Oriyas have changed that. Ponga, the natural demagogue, reminds the Konds of their fallen virtues, at the same time blaming others—Oriyas and renegade Konds like Kosira—for the fall. He says 'our customs', meaning that the people in Baderi still uphold them and still are virtuous, in spite of the exactions of the Oriyas and the defection of Kosira and other outsiders.

Up to this point Ponga has presented a consistent, if distorted, picture of society in the Kond hills and the forces at work to change it. It is, of course, inaccurate in the way that any caricature or stereotype is, but it contains no contradictions. The Konds—that is to say Ponga and the people of Baderi and of other places, not including men like Kosira—are honest and abhor commerce and are virtuous farmers: and they are under constant attack by thieving and unscrupulous Oriya traders and merchants and officials, whose sole measure of virtue is wealth.

But even at this point Ponga is not entirely consistent. He is not content to taunt Norendero Behera merely for being an Oriya. 'What have you come for? Have you just come here to show me that gold neck-chain? You've just come here to show me *one* neck-chain, have you? I've got six for every one of yours. . . .' Ponga suddenly switches from the line he had taken in the attack on Kosira. He no longer talks of 'our customs' with all that implies, but suddenly declares that he, as a Kond, can beat Norendero at his own game, which is making money. The Konds are cheated and oppressed, but they aren't such fools after all. Ponga is six times as wealthy as Norendero: and so forth. We no longer have a picture of the proud and downtrodden Kond, who, by reason of his ancestral virtues, falls an easy prey to the unscrupulous Oriya. A Kond can excel in the pursuit which the Oriyas value most— the pursuit of wealth—and yet still be a good Kond and an ob- server of Kond custom. Konds, in other words, are not necessarily failures at all: they are just as good as Oriyas, and can match the Oriyas even in the field chosen by the Oriyas themselves.

The dramatic contradiction in Ponga's day of drunkenness and morning of repentance was the visit of his Oriya preceptor. Ponga, drunk, spent the day abusing Oriyas indiscriminately for their worldliness: sober on the next day he listened patiently and hum- bly to the advice of an Oriya whom Ponga himself employs as a spiritual adviser. The preceptor, Datia Das, lives in the Oriya village of Gomapara, which lies in Balimendi *mutha* about a mile and a half away from Baderi. The preceptor is not merely a good man to whom people turn for advice: he makes a profession of it. He has a large clientele in the eastern half of the Kondmals, both among the Konds and among the Oriyas. He makes a regular tour, when he is fed by his clients, and receives gifts of money from them: from these tours he is popularly supposed to return with two or three hundred rupees in his possession. Liringa told me that four people, including himself and Ponga 'kept' (he used the Oriya word *'rokhiba'*, which is also used of a servant or an employee, including those on *jejemani* service) the preceptor. Fundamentally his task was to 'teach the Konds the Hindu way of life'. (Liringa himself compared this preceptor's role in the Kondmals with the role of Gandhi in India.) He gave them advice on points of Hinduism. He was willing, for a fee, to invest them with a cotton thread (*poita*) which would protect them from sickness and misfortune and he could recite certain prayers (*mantra*) for the same end. He is more than simply a specialist who sells his skills. He is, for instance, a 'father' to Liringa, so much so that he would not act as preceptor for Liringa's child, since the proper relationship between a man and his grand-daughter is not a disciplinary one, but a relationship of friendly indulgence. Finally he is called in to read a moral lesson to backsliders like Ponga, very much as a clergyman is among ourselves. This was the man whom Ponga respected and to whose advice he would listen.

I am tempted to resolve the contradiction between Ponga's sweeping condemnation of the Oriya way of life and his affection for 'Kond customs' on the one hand, and his respect for the Oriya preceptor on the other hand. An obvious way out would be to say that the preceptor is not really an Oriya at all, but that his saintliness lifts him above caste and ethnic divisions, in the same way that Gandhi was above caste. If this were true, then Ponga's relationship with his preceptor would not conflict with his proclaimed hatred of Oriyas. But it is not true. Firstly the cynics of the Kondmals readily point out that the preceptor makes a very good living out of his traffic in holiness. He is just as worldly, in his own way, as anyone else. Secondly he is not above the division of race and caste: he is frankly and wholeheartedly an Oriya. His task—as Liringa said—is to teach the Konds the *Hindu* way of life.

His mission, in other words, is to eradicate Kond barbarities and instil Oriya values. This does not mean, of course, that he preaches the value of worldly success, as one would expect from Ponga's caricature of the Oriya character. It means rather that Hinduism has values which the Konds themselves recognize as good, and which they are anxious to acquire.

The contradiction is really there. Ponga is in fact playing two roles which directly contradict one another. In one role he is the champion of tradition, of Kond tradition, of the Kond way of life: in the other role he is one of the 'new Konds', who discard as fast as they can the barbarities of being a Kond and assume the manners and customs of a Hindu gentleman. It is not simply that Ponga was drunk on one occasion and sober on the other, and that he is atavistic when drunk, and, when sober, progressive. His life, like that of many other Konds, is guided by both values and he oscillates between them.

In this analysis of the part which Ponga played in the tax dispute, I have shown that he had several alternative courses of action, from which he could select. He chose to ignore the relationship which he had with Nrusingh as a trader, because he thought, if he thought about it at all, that it was in his interest to do so. In the same way and for the same reasons, he did not choose to exploit his role as an official in the service of the administration. Analysed *ex post facto* his actions show an instinctive preoccupation with the leadership of the village and the championing of what might be called the Kond 'cause'. But in the final event in the drama he turned away from this role of being a Kond traditionalist and put himself under the guidance of his Hindu preceptor.

His immediate reason for doing so was simply that his son Arjuno brought the preceptor along to Baderi on the morning after Ponga had been drunk. Ponga accepted the advice with humility because he knew that he had made a fool of himself, and he knew that he had behaved badly. But these reasons do not explain why Ponga should 'keep' a Hindu preceptor in the first place, if it is important for his authority in the village and for his prestige that he should appear as the champion not only of Konds but also of Kond traditions. Nor, if power and prestige in the village are the sole objective, does it explain why Liringa too should keep the same preceptor, when he has the same ambitions as Ponga.

The explanation is that both Ponga and Liringa have yet another role in another different system. This system, much wider than the village and the *mutha*, is the one in which Konds are involved in the struggle for control of the modern forms of power in the representative democracy. It is an advantage in this struggle to be a Hindu gentleman and not an uncouth aboriginal.[1] Both Ponga and Liringa are on the outermost fringes of this system, but it does affect them sufficiently to make them want to conform, in their dealing with the more sophisticated Konds, to a standard of behaviour different from the traditional one. Neither Ponga nor Liringa is ever likely to make any mark or achieve any power in the wider system, but they have, so to speak, at least entered their names for the race, and that is why they employ the preceptor. The behaviour which he teaches them, and the façade of Hinduism, are appropriate in some situations whether they are dealing with Oriyas or with Konds: it is behaviour which will help them to gain the ends, remote though these are, at which they are aiming in the wider system.

In the situation in which the Baderi Konds found themselves opposed to Goneswaro and Nrusingh, it would not have been appropriate for Ponga to emphasize his aspirations to become a Hindu. It would have provided a relationship with the Oriyas and an identification with Goneswaro and Nrusingh which would have obscured the sharp division between Konds and Oriyas, and might even have placed Ponga on the wrong side. In other words Ponga can best gain his ends in this situation—these ends being authority in his own village—by playing the role of a Kond traditionalist.

There is one final complication. I have spoken as if the local situation, in which it is appropriate for Ponga to act as a Kond traditionalist, and the wider situation, in which he can aspire to gain his ends by being progressive in the direction of Hinduism, are completely separate and completely insulated from one another. Clearly they are not: the very fact that such untravelled men—untravelled in the widest sense of the word—as Ponga and Liringa employ a Hindu preceptor, is clear evidence that the wider system penetrates down to the level of the villages. To some extent everyone in Baderi, even the old men who are frankly uninterested in reforming their manners and who still enjoy a

[1] See p. 190.

12*a*. Kond buffalo sacrifice, now rarely performed.

12*b*. Kond men, dressed in women's clothes, dancing at a festival.

discreet meal of buffalo meat, accept the new values and respect those who adopt them. The preceptor is not regarded as an icono-clast (from the point of view of Kond tradition) but simply as a good man.

It followed from this that Ponga did not lose status by employ-ing the Hindu preceptor. Nor did the people of Baderi think that there was anything particularly illogical in following a drunken outburst of Kond patriotism with a visit from a Hindu, whose profession is to impart the Hindu way of life. It showed that Ponga is—as I have heard him described both by Konds and Oriyas—a 'good man at heart'.

The contradiction between Kond traditions and the Hindu way of life is still there, and it exists now not only for Ponga and Liringa, but to some extent for every Kond. Their lives are guided by two contradictory groups of values, and like Ponga, they move from one to another. We cannot resolve the contradiction and claim that it is an apparent one by saying that one value guides the people in one field of social activities, and the other value is found in a different field of social activities. At the very broadest level of survey, one can say that Hindu values 'belong', in some sense of that word, to India, while Kond traditions 'belong' to the Konds of south-western Orissa. But in the Kond villages both values are found and in a single social field. Ponga's prestige and authority are maintained by, among other things, being at the same time both a traditionalist and a progressive.

CHAPTER IX

TRIBE, CASTE, AND NATION

THE CONCEPT OF 'STRUCTURE'

THERE are two assumptions in this book which the reader may challenge, and for this reason I discuss their usefulness and limitations. The first of these is the identification of 'structure' with ultimate consistency, and the second is the admittedly crude estimate of political motivation, which is an easy target for superficial criticism, although I think it is less easy to impugn its pragmatic usefulness.

Structure, in the way that I have used the term, is of course an abstraction, a set of generalizations abstracted from regularities of behaviour or from statements about what ought to be regularities of behaviour. It is possible to use such a structure as a model, and to 'set it working' while assuming that other factors are 'equal' and do not affect the working of the model. This is, so to speak, to work upwards towards further and more remote abstraction. I have not done this: I have looked downwards and related structure to the realities of behaviour—in other words I have considered as many variables as possible.

Rules which may not be inconsistent with one another at the level of 'static' structure, may in practice (in a dynamic analysis) conflict with one another. In a static analysis there is no inconsistency in the two rules that a man must be generous to his own sons and to his sister's sons. In practice, when we take into account the fact that wealth varies from man to man and that some men may not be wealthy enough to meet both obligations, the rules may conflict with one another. This is not a contradiction at the level of static 'structure': it is a conflict apparent not in a static but in a dynamic analysis.

Structural analysis at the dynamic level consists in showing how, in spite of conflict, the static structure presented still remains an illuminating description of social life. There are various ways of doing this; the rule is dramatized and reinforced by the punishment of deviants; conflict in smaller groups may bring into action—

perhaps even into existence —larger groups;[1] and there are various secondary rules designed to cope with conflict and prevent it from changing or destroying the structure.

'Contradiction', as distinct from 'conflict',[2] is primarily an heuristic device used to diagnose the presence in a social situation (or social 'field') of more than one structure. This means that a contradiction cannot be recognized immediately upon its perception. Nor can it be recognized at the level of static analysis, because there it is by definition ruled out. Conflict appears at the level of dynamic analysis: and it can only be recognized as a contradiction by the absence of self-regulating factors, such as those mentioned above. Thus a man allies himself to group B and in doing so defects from group A. If the result is to bring into action a larger group of which both A and B are part, *and yet which is in some sense neutral between them*, and if this larger group settles the conflict, then we are not here dealing with contradiction. The case can be stated with the same result in terms of rules and institutions. If a man follows rule A and deviates from rule B, and if there is a third rule or institution designed to settle such situations on the grounds that *in this particular situation* one or the other rule is appropriate, then this is not contradiction. The phrases in italics are of particular importance. If the group which comes into action is not neutral between A and B but is in fact one of the sanctions of B (or A, as the case may be), and if it is effective, then there is a contradiction between the two allegiances and not merely a conflict. Similarly if the third rule or institution is simply an assertion of one or the other rules as being invariably and automatically the right one, then this is contradiction. An example is provided by the first case given in this book. This is a contradiction between the Kond rule of landholding and the Administration's rule. There is no body or institution neutral between these two for settling the conflict: the following of one rule is automatically the negation of the other.

The assumption of 'consistency' as a part of the definition of structure is a means of enabling us to use the idea of structure for the study of social change. The first step is the identification of a logical consistency between the rules of behaviour: this I have called a 'static' analysis. The second step is to identify those

---

[1] M. Gluckman, 1955, especially Chapter III.

[2] See p. 7.

institutions which seal off conflict and which tend to keep behaviour in conformity with the logical model: this I have called a dynamic analysis. The third step is to move from a 'conservative' towards a 'radical' approach in the study of society[1] and to study conflicts which are not contained or sealed off within one structure. I cannot emphasize too strongly that without the 'fixed points' which are provided by a static structural analysis, we have no means of describing the change that is taking place. In the last resort the description of all movement—even walking across the room—must identify two or more points if the direction of movement is to be conveyed, and more than the bare fact of motion is to be noticed.

While the concept of a static structure is necessary for a description of social change, it also has its dangers and its inadequacies. It is to meet some of these that I have used the concept of substructures, and the concept of a 'field'.

It is all too easy to assume that in some way one structure can fill all fields of social activity in any given society and that one may speak of *the* social structure. Indeed any analysis begins with this assumption because it is heuristically necessary. The corresponding error in studying social change would be to assume that the different structures follow one another serially and as wholes, each in turn filling the whole field of social activity. Because there are places where caste no longer functions politically, it is not to be assumed that caste is just as dead in every other social field. If it were true, there would be no need to invoke more than one structure in any total social field, and there would be no contradiction, no bridge-actions,[2] and the task of analysis would be much simpler.

While one needs whole structures in order to establish the direction of change, one cannot analyse the process of change without dealing with sub-structures, because the immediate contradiction is between these sub-structures rather than between total structures. For example the tribal system of kinship is not in contradiction with the caste system. I have pointed out their similarities, and, indeed, the caste system walls off one set of kinship relations from another. Similarly Kond rites and beliefs are not, on the whole, in contradiction with the Oriya rites and beliefs. There is rather a mutual accommodation, and these are

[1] R. Bendix and S. M. Lipsett, 1954, pp. 9–14.
[2] See p. 252.

two ritual sub-structures which do not conflict with or contradict one another. The contradiction between the two structures was localized in their political and economic sub-structures: this was the point of impact between them. It is for this reason that in the political field the Kond tribal structure has all but passed out of existence, while at the same time it remains in full existence as a kinship structure and important as a ritual structure. This would to some extent be true of the caste system, where problems of change are brought to notice by the incongruence of ritual behaviour and political behaviour between high and low castes. Social change, then, must be conceived of not as the replacement of one *total* structure by another, but by changes in sub-structures within one or another field. The change and contradiction, in other words, is not between total structures or systems, but between sub-structures within one social field.

This gives rise to difficulties. At the level of static analysis it is enough to point out the logical consistency between different rules of behaviour. In a dynamic analysis, which is concerned with self-sealing mechanisms and mechanisms of adjustment, the writer must show not merely that one rule entails the other, but also that at the operational level these rules sanction one another. This is the point of continuing to use the word 'structure' in a dynamic analysis; the Earth cult of the Konds sanctioned political behaviour and vice versa.[1] Why, then, if structure has the systematic character which I have assumed, does not the destruction of one sub-structure (e.g. the political) lead to the destruction of the other sub-structures? It does, of course, lead to the destruction of the total structure, since this has been defined as the relationships between the different sub-structures. This phenomenon—differential rates of change—has been most noticeable in the ritual field, and to ritual is ascribed some kind of cultural 'inertia'.[2]

The different sub-structures seem to have some kind of autonomy independent of the total structure. This is not a perfect autonomy: I am not throwing away the fundamental heuristic postulate that all aspects of social life are connected with one another. If the point of impact has been—as it usually is—in the politico-economic field and in this field sub-structure A gives way to sub-structure B, then the other sub-structures in the total

[1] See p. 52.
[2] D. Forde, 1954, p. viii.

structure A in the end either wither away or become modified so as to make them consistent with the total structure B, or indeed they may already be largely consistent with it.

But the time-lag involved in this process brings in its train more difficulties. I have spoken of only two structures, using the signs A and B. But in the analysis I have dealt with three—the tribal structure, the caste system, and the Administration—and I could have brought in at least one more in greater detail, namely the modern representative democracy which is in many important respects in contradiction with the system of Administration. My interest has been in the political field and in the three (or four) political sub-structures. The process of change in the political field is once again not to be conceived of as in series, but the different systems overlap with one another. I have shown how all four are relevant to an understanding of political activity to-day. But at this point my difficulty is in the fate of the other sub-structures: kinship and ritual. I have postulated as 'fixed points' the various total structures, conceived of as static. But from the point of view of the Konds (or of the Oriyas) these fixed points cannot be thought of as stages in a course of development or evolution, through which they must pass. This is true from several points of view. Firstly there is no evidence that the Oriyas ever went through a 'tribal' stage. Secondly, although there was a time when the Konds came near to the Oriya political model, their total social structure never was the same as that of the Oriyas. To-day, when their political activity is centring on the Administration and the political democracy, their kinship system is still consistent (for instance in scale and in rules of exogamy) with the tribal political system which now is all but defunct. If and when the Kond kinship system changes to the small-scale system which seems—in India at least—to fit with an expanding capitalist society,[1] it will have 'by-passed' the caste system. The kinship sub-structure will, so to speak, have missed out a stage through which the political sub-structure passed.

It may be that in lighting upon Kond hills society in the last hundred years, I have encountered a situation of unusual complexity. It may be that the Oriya colonization, the Meriah Wars, the subsequent infiltration of Oriya mercantile classes, the growth of the Administration, and finally Indian independence and the

[1] K. Gough, 1952, p. 82.

coming of a system of representative democracy have induced an unusually large degree of 'anomie' and created an unusually extensive field of political choice and an unusually severe degree of conflict and contradiction. In these circumstances the analysis of political behaviour as part of a single consistent structure—as a substructure in a total structure—is certainly impossible. Yet I do not think I could have brought even this slight degree of order to the enormous heterogeneity of social activity without the concept of structure, as a system of logically consistent regularities of behaviour. The search for consistencies clears away, so to speak, much of the primary disorder, and lets us see where in fact the contradictions lie, where are the points of impact, and what is the direction of change. What it does not do is provide abstractions which are useful in understanding the process of social change. This does not take place at the level of total structure but within one field between sub-structures and ultimately at the level of individual choice.

The Political Field

Political relationships are concerned with the distribution of resources and power. 'Distribution' includes not only those situations in which men co-operate with one another to achieve control over territory, or to protect their territory against outsiders, but also a wider field in which people do not co-operate but instead compete against one another for the control of resources. In other words a 'relationship' does not mean only harmony and co-operation regularly practised, but it can also mean relationships of institutionalized (i.e. regular) hostility and competition.

In presenting the relationships in which the Baderi Konds are engaged I have tried to move from the simpler to the more complex. In the first part of the analysis (Chapters II-V) I began to discuss competition for power and control over resources, and the way men combine with one another so as to compete the more effectively, as if the only people in the arena were Konds. The 'Kond political structure' as a 'structure'—that is, as a set of generalizations—is complete in itself and it can be satisfactorily analysed without reference to the relationships which Konds in fact have with their own PANS as dependents, or with the Oriyas and the Administration, as their masters. The analysis demonstrates interconnections between various roles and relationships, and shows that there are no contradictions within the system so presented. A Kond in Baderi village has relationships with other Konds in his community as an agnatic relative (he does not marry their daughters or their sisters and he has a common ancestry with them through male links); as a member of the same Earth congregation (if they pollute the Earth he is put into ritual danger, and vice versa); and as a member of the same political community (he fights to defend them, they fight to defend him, and there is no fighting between them). These roles are consistent with one another: they do not necessarily involve the actor in contradictory and inconsistent attitudes or actions towards other people of his community or towards people outside his community: and one role tends to reinforce another, as when a breach of the rule of exogamy pollutes the Earth, or as when political status is denied to those who are not agnates. These three institutions—warfare, agnation, and the cult of the Earth—define the group (the clan or the allied clans) and do not set up relationships between clans which might blur the loyalty of the members towards their own political community. Such an analysis identifies groups by the fact that several institutions are associated with one another in defining behaviour within the group and towards outsiders. We are satisfied with the analysis because we have identified political, ritual, and kinship functions for the group, and have shown that these are consistent with one another (i.e. they contribute towards the 'unity' of the group) and that this kind of relationship does not pass out beyond the group, and so blur the exactness of the structure.

A structure of social relations is *in the end* a statement of the absence of contradiction between different ways of behaving. But in order to present such a system it is necessary to hold 'other things equal', to postulate ideal conditions for the maintenance of the relationships which make up the structure. One necessary precondition of the tribal political structure was an appropriate ratio between population and land within each community. The system would work in the coherent way in which we presented it, if conditions were appropriate. But because the population grows too big for the land, or becomes too small to protect its territory, or for other reasons, there arise conflicts. Behaviour in fact does not conform to the abstract perfection which we have described.

As soon as we see the structure in action, we have ceased to hold some 'other things' equal, and we have to present not a static structure but a dynamic system which is not isolated but is affected in its working by 'outside' factors.

We continue to use the idea of structures, but we no longer present a static chart of groups and their inter-relationships. We try to identify the process which make groups and inter-relationships become similar to the chart, but which in fact never succeed in reaching its finality and perfection. Several words have been used to describe this process. The relatively mild disequilibrium set up by death and growth, countered by succession and inheritance, has been termed 'social circulation'.[1] The actors are conceived of as passing through various positions in a structure. More serious disequilibria, as when there is an imbalance of land and population followed by migration, fission, and subsequent accretion, have been called 'repetitive equilibrium'.[2] The word 'repetitive' means that we see instance after instance of the same *type* of relationship: the group which migrates either joins another group or sets up on its own in exactly the same *kind* of relationships which it previously had. Such a system is 'fluid but unchanging'. In order to take in the dynamics of the system we have had to introduce 'outside' factors—in this case birth and death rate, the amount of land under cultivation, and so forth. Without these we have no means of explaining why all relationships are not of the kind found on the static chart of structure which guides the analysis. These 'outside' factors clearly deserve to be called by that adjective, for they cannot be connected into the structure in the same way as, for instance in the Kond structure, the Earth cult is connected with agnatic kinship. They are not part of the system, but they affect it from outside.

In the chapter 'The Konds and their Dependents' I introduced a second structure of political relationships, of quite a different type from those which characterize the tribal system. Once again understanding of this structure is achieved by demonstrating the consistency of its different parts, by showing that the ritual, economic, and political relationships of, for instance, the PANS towards the Konds, all coincide and reinforce one another. This too, just as the

[1] G. and M. Wilson, 1945, p. 58. Radcliffe-Brown distinguishes between 'structure' and 'structural form' (1952, pp. 190-3).

[2] M. Gluckman, 1942, p. 244.

R

tribal system, can be viewed in action, and the factors which set it in motion are the same—for instance, too many people to be supported by the resources which the group commands—and the process by which a return to equilibrium is achieved are the same: migration and the assumption in the new home of ties exactly similar to those which were held in the old location. (There are, of course, other factors—quarrels, pressures from outside, and so forth—which set the structure in motion and I have chosen to consider only one particular set of them.)

The Kond-PAN relationship is not in the same system as the Kond-Kond relationship. Both can be described as complete structures in themselves without reference to the other, so long as we confine the description to the static chart of groups and their inter-relationships. At that level these are two separate structures. The role of clan member and the role of master of clients are neither consistent nor inconsistent with one another: they are merely separate: it is possible to be both and a full enjoyment of one role does nothing to detract from or add to the full enjoyment of the other. In a *static structural analysis* these roles neither reinforce nor contradict one another: for instance the Earth cult is neither consistent nor inconsistent with the relationship between a Kond master and his PAN client, nor do the rituals of subservience between the master and client have anything to do with the master's relationship with other Konds. But as soon as we begin to describe *structures in action*, then it may be necessary to bring in one set of relationships in order to complete our description of the working of the other set of relationships. When there is a ritual crisis in a Kond house, the Kond makes use of his PAN clients to help him in his tasks. Some of these tasks consist of entertaining other Konds who are related either as agnates or through uterine or affinal ties, and the Kond may only be able to fulfil his obligations towards other Konds with the help of his PAN clients. By making use of his relationships to the PAN, the Kond is able to further his purposes in the system of Kond-Kond relationships. Again Ponga's rivalry with Liringa in the Kond system of relationships affected the role which Ponga played in the dispute with the Baderi PANS (Case 35: p. 128). We may choose to regard the rivalry between the two Konds as an outside factor affecting the course of the dispute and the return to equilibrium in the system of Kond-PAN relationships, just as the growth of population is an outside factor. In reality, as the examples show, the two types of relationship may affect one another, and it must be counted a weakness of a 'one-structure' analysis that it cannot take account of this fact, except by treating the relevant relationship as something intruding from outside the system.

In his third role the Kond is brought into political relationships with Oriyas, and I have discussed this in the Chapter 'The Konds and their Masters'. This structure too may be presented as something complete in itself: and political, ritual, and economic ties can be interconnected so as to show their consistency. But in this case the gap between the structure and reality is much wider than in the other two cases. The only way of presenting this as a structure is to pretend that the Konds were reduced to a position of dependence similar to that of their own PANS. In fact they were not. We may present the system as an equilibrium point towards which relationships tended, but in fact the 'self-sealing' mechanisms, so apparent in the tribal system, are here scarcely discernible. The Oriya system of political relationships is not only different from the tribal system, but is contradictory. This contradiction may be seen at the level of conflict between groups, in which the Konds tried—initially at least—to extrude, even to exterminate, the Oriyas. Oriyas could not be fitted into the Kond political structure because they would not become relatives. The Oriyas tried to bring Konds into the Oriya political structure, which can incorporate persons who are not only unrelated but even are of different cultures. They did not in fact succeed in doing so because they were too few in number to subjugate the Konds. The contradiction can also be seen in roles, in that allegiance to the Oriya Sirdar may conflict with loyalty to the clan: clanship ties demand that Kond outsiders should be admitted to the clan territory only if they take on agnatic responsibilities: but the Sirdar demands that allegiance should be to him, and admits people who do not take on clanship ties. The role of clan member may be in direct contradiction to the role of retainer to an Oriya chief, when both these roles claim to give an exclusive right to the same piece of territory. There can be no self-sealing mechanisms in the Kond-Oriya political system, because there is no such system. There are two systems in contradiction, and an analysis of Kond-Oriya political relationships as a single integrated structure must await the elision of one or the other systems, at least in so far as they are political.

R*

We need to shift our analysis away from the interconnections of a structural analysis and the demonstration of one whole coherent system towards the analysis of an area of social action in which these different systems impinge, towards the exploration of a social field. The effort should not be to hold other things equal, and invite the reader to grant a gentleman's agreement to disregard 'outside' factors, on the ground that they manifestly belong to a different system, but to concentrate on those 'outside' factors. This is what I have tried to do in this book. I have given first a static structural description: I have then transformed this into a dynamic analysis, showing how the structure (if I may reify in order to be brief) copes with disturbances set up by 'outside' factors; and in the third part of the analysis I have tried to show that some of these 'outside' factors are themselves part of other systems of relationships, and that in order to describe adequately any field of social relationships we need to describe not only the structures which are found in that field, but also what might be called the 'bridge-actions' between those structures. Liringa's action in making use of the Manda-Goneswaro relationship to further his ends in his own village is an example of a 'bridge-action'. It is not part of the village structure: it is one of those 'outside' factors which keeps the structure in motion. Nor is it part of the caste and Administrative structure in which Manda and Goneswaro are interacting. It is a bridge between these systems. We cannot understand the motives of the actors, nor judge the outcome of any dispute or conflict, nor assess its importance, unless we concentrate on these bridge-actions.

The Individual and Choice

As the analysis has passed into more complicated stages, I have focused attention more and more on individual actors. In the individual actor, more often than in a group, the different systems meet, if I may put it that way. It has, of course, long been recognized that no individual has but a single role to play: a man who is a father in one family may at the same time be a son in another family: the farmer may also be a ritual expert; and so forth. By and large structural analysis consists of pointing out that these roles do not contradict one another, or, if they conflict, that there is some means of settling such conflicts without altering the type of social relations which are characteristic of the system. In the Kondmals there are several political systems. There is one system governing relationships about land between Konds. There is a different system governing relations between Konds and PANS and distributing not the land, but the produce of the land, between them. There is a third system, similar in intention (if I may put it that way) to the Kond-PAN system, governing the relationships over land between the Konds and the Oriyas. I am not here concerned with the fact that there may be different structures concerning ritual and kinship and politics, and that these may not add up into one grand system,[1] but rather with the fact that there are at least three distinct political systems, and that every Kond has a role in all three of these, as well as the roles he may play in kinship and ritual. The three political systems all have the same 'aim-content',[2] and the individual cannot operate in all three at once but must choose between them.

A *static* structural analysis does not have anything to do with choice: it presents either the norm in the moral sense—what a man ought to do; or the norm in the statistical sense—what most men do; and it does not take account of the fact that some men do not do what is expected of them. But within the *dynamic* analysis of a single structure there must be elements of choice: the Damanikia people can join either Balimendi or Gondrimendi (Case 14: p. 49). These are the kind of problems which 'social structure' cannot meet, and which must be considered by 'social organization' or some similar concept.[3] Choice at this level is one of the things which it is agreed to 'hold equal' so that a structural or systematic analysis can be made. When we consider a man as a locus of several roles which occur in different systems, all of which claim to do the same job, we must take into account choice. In the examples I have given, particularly in Chapter 8, I have stressed the element of choice by comparing the way different people acted, and by showing that they could have acted differently if they had wished to do so. Ponga and Nrusingh seemed to have an unspoken agreement not to involve their relationship as seller and buyer of turmeric in the tax dispute. Manda could have acted in several ways in his dispute with the Sirdar, but he

[1] S. F. Nadel, 1957, p. 153.
[2] S. F. Nadel, 1953, p. 77.
[3] R. Firth, 1951.

preferred to stress his role as a *proja*, as a subject of the Sirdar, and to leave it to others to point out that he also had rights as a citizen of India, and that as a member of the Baderi community and the Balimendi clan he could call on the united support of a large group of Konds. Sociologically speaking he was free to choose between these different roles and to select that which he thought might be the most effective.[1] The choice is not unlimited: the actors are, so to speak, creatures of their social environment: neither side, for instance, could gain its end by force: but within set limits of possible action the actors were, sociologically speaking, free to choose what they would do, according to their abilities to gauge the course which would best achieve the ends they had in view.

In some cases this element of choice is not going to affect the continuance of a social system. Whether the Damanikia people joined Balimendi or Gondrimendi, the result is the same from the point of view of the continuance of the system. The choice is within the system and not between systems. They were not choosing between different types of relationship, but between the persons with whom they would have a relationship which was already set for them. But where the choice lies between different types of relationship, the continuance of a social system may be affected. The more often Nrusingh chooses to behave as a man of affluence towards Goneswaro, the more does he erode his role as a *proja*. The more people like Manda in similar situations stand upon their rights at law, the more is their role as a *proja* diminished. In the example I have frequently quoted, the more people choose to join a territorial group by buying land and not by joining the clan which owns the land, the more is the political role of clan membership diminished. People can, so to speak, when there are several systems of political relationship between which to choose, opt out of one system and into another. This is the process by which the clan lost its political function to the *mutha*. Where systems contradict one another, it is choice which allows the more 'efficient' system to drive out the others.

---

[1] To an investigator in another science, his decision to act the humble part might have been explicable in terms of his upbringing, or of something else, and in that sense he might not have been exercising a free choice: but, sociologically, we must treat Manda as if he had the choice of several roles in this situation.

But the analysis of change simply by identifying and describing the structure towards which, and the structure out of which, a particular society is moving is jejune and unsatisfactory. It seems too far removed from reality. It is an advance to be able to indicate that the society one studies is not to be considered as one single political structure. But the hypothesis of a past structure and a future structure, although they help us to understand the broad picture of what is going on, does not do justice to the complexity of the present or the subtlety with which choice can be made between the different systems. Nor can the allocation of a particular action to a future structure or to a past structure help us to see *how far* the society has moved from one structure to another. This can be done only by examining a series of disputes and conflicts, which have a diagnostic value for the study of social change.

CONFLICT AND SOCIAL CHANGE

Besides focusing attention on the single actor, I have also been much concerned with conflict, dispute, and competition. Competition underlies the whole analysis, for my whole conception of an actor is as a person (or group) trying to gain his ends against other people who would prevent him or would gain the same end for themselves. Sometimes this competition takes place within the one system of social relations, and although the outcome of it may be a victory for one side or the other, the result of the conflict is not a change in the *type* of social relationships. At other times the actor may play upon the roles which he has in different systems of social relationships, so as to win for himself the support of more effective allies. These 'bridge-actions', which occur in situations of conflict, may be divided into two kinds: those which are symptomatic of social change and are the process through which change takes place, and those which are not. In Case 35 (p. 128) Ponga treated himself to a few mild aspersions on Liringa's ineptness in handling the Baderi PANS. This is a bridge-action through which Ponga scored a point over Liringa in their rivalry for leadership in the village. None of these actions are symptomatic of social change: the actors remain aligned in their groups, and the use which Ponga was able to make of the PANS and the fact that they became his unwitting allies, did not mean that a new group consisting of Ponga and the PANS was emerging as a structural unit in the village society.

But in the same case the PANS were able to draw on outside alignments in order to modify their position in the village. They make part of their living outside the village economy: they are identified with the 'Harijans' of Bisipara. The Baderi PANS did not make overt or spectacular use of these ties, and did not seek to dramatize their alignment with these outside groups and their consequent independence of the Konds. But these new alignments are none the less real, and it is likely that in the future the Baderi PANS will use these alignments to make themselves more independent in Baderi village, in just the same way as the Bisipara PANS are in their village. The use of these alignments is a bridge-action, and it is one which leads to social change. The PANS are able to opt out of the Baderi Kond-PAN group, and to join the wider group of Harijans. The traditional caste-relationships of Baderi village, and the new relationships in the modern political system, in which the Harijan group operates, are in contradiction to one another. In this case a bridge-action detaches the PAN from one group and makes him a recruit in another: the bridge-action means the decay of one system and the growth of another.

A bridge-action may result in change when the appeal is from one system of social relations to another which contradicts it. Besides the example of the contradiction between the role of a village PAN and the role of a Harijan, I have also given the example of the role of a clan-member against the role of a *mutha*-member. These are two examples of a single process. This does not mean, however, that wherever there are bridge-actions between systems which are in conflict, there must inevitably follow the decline of one system and the growth of another. It depends (and here I cannot avoid reification) upon the relative strength of the two systems. In case 1 (p. 17) the man from Rupamendi attempted to use his role as a citizen of India and as a tax-payer, whose name appeared on the Record of Rights, to own and cultivate land in Baderi. His bridge-action was an appeal to a system of land-holding which was in conflict with the traditional land-holding system of the Konds. The latter lays it down that no-one who is not a member of the village community ought to hold land in the village. The Government system implicitly says that community-membership is irrelevant to the holding of land. But the bridge-action failed.

The Rupamendi man was forced to give up his land. The integrity of the Baderi community remained unbroken. This case shows that bridge-actions lead to structural change only when they are usually successful, and when the actor by directing his allegiance elsewhere gains his end.

It is often said that a dispute is a means of stating the rules of the structure and bringing home to the disputants the continued strength of those rules and so holding the society together. A breach of the rule, followed by corrective action, serves to strengthen the system. Disputes and conflicts are seen to have the same effect as ritual—stating publicly the right relationships within a given system. A dispute may have this effect: but it also may be a means of testing the efficacy from the individual's or the group's point of view of a particular system of social relations. The outcome of the dispute may not be to re-affirm the structure, but to make public the inefficacy of that particular structure as a means of gaining one's ends, and to demonstrate that some other form of social alignment is the more effective. This kind of dispute is, so to speak, a proclamation of social change.

In theory there is no difficulty in gauging change by this method. We have to examine a series of disputes which are connected in that they concern the same object—let us say control over land. History does not tell us how the dispute between Balimendi and Gondrimendi started, but let us suppose that a man from Manipara village began to break new land in the jungle to the north-east of his village (Case 14: p. 49). After he had begun the work he was impeded—or perhaps the field or the crops on it were seized—by a man from Tendriguda, the nearest village in the Gondrimendi clan. Each of the contestants could draw upon an ever-widening circle of people united to them as agnates: first their fellow-villagers, then their clans, and then the clans in alliance. Now suppose that the war between these groups continued for some time and reached a stalemate (and was not settled, as in fact it was, by the alliance of the migrant group from Damanikia with the Balimendi clan). Then it might occur to one side or the other that there were other social ties on which to draw. They might invite an Oriya chief, the head, for instance, of a large and powerful village like Bisipara, to intervene on their side, and he might win the war for them. If that happens, then the dispute is a public statement that an alliance with an Oriya chief is—in this case at least—an effective means of gaining land. Such incidents might become more and more common until it is widely known that the most effective alignment for validating a claim to land is that with the Oriya chief, and in the end the disputants might no longer bother to call on the clans in alliance, who for reasons of distance might be less effective allies than an Oriya chief who lived in the vicinity. Through a series of such cases the growing ineffectiveness of one alignment and the increasing efficacy of others are demonstrated.

In order to gauge social change we have in theory only to examine a series of such cases and show how men increasingly disregarded one alignment and increasingly invoked another *type* of alignment in order to gain a particular end. In practice it is very difficult to do this, because we do not have the material. Historical records in areas like the Kondmals are seldom full enough in the details of the social alignments of the various actors to let us present a case like this. I certainly have not been able to do so, except for the most obvious of alignments: for instance, it is clear from the records that war was once an effective means of validating a claim to land, that one's allies in such a war were the members of a clan, and that to-day this method is completly ineffective and that a man no longer needs the help of his whole clan in order to validate a claim to territory. Consequently there are to-day many people who belong to no territorial clan at all—like the people of Arapaju in Besringia,[1] or the people of Bandibari in Balimendi,[2] and the members of a territorial clan do not rely completely on one another's political support, so much as upon ties of other kinds.

But even this is too extreme. For in saying that the clan has lost its political functions, I am exaggerating. I am talking of what *may* be a future state of social relations, but what is not so to-day. The clan members no longer band together in the dramatic political activity of war: but clan ties may still be relevant politically. The clan still exists, through the system of internal recruitment,[3] as a corporate unit having kinship functions, and some ritual functions. It retains some overt political functions in that clan membership gives a right in the earth, and this may be relevant to migration.[4]

[1] See p. 74.   [2] See p. 69.   [3] See p. 83.
[4] See Case 16: p. 53.

It may also be possible, through a bridge-action, for an actor to make use of clan membership, especially by recalling explicitly or implicitly the former warlike functions of the clan. This is the import of Liringa's remark, 'We will show you and Nrusingh what it means to be Sirdar of Balimendi' (Case 38: p. 198). He implies that the Konds of Balimendi are the members of one clan: they cannot be bullied and cheated as can people in a heterogeneous *mutha* like Besringia: they will stand together against the Sirdar. Liringa does not specify the means that they can employ, but it would be possible, for instance, for them to write a petition against the Sirdar and have it signed by the whole clan. He asserts—and probably truly—that in Balimendi loyalty to the clan takes precedence over loyalty to the Sirdar.[1]

I have called these bridge-actions in situations of competition 'diagnostic'. But it must be remembered that these are not prognoses so much as *post mortem* examinations. We can only identify change retrospectively. Continuing the metaphor and looking at the situation from the point of view of the tribal system of land-tenure, the bridge-action of the Rupamendi man (Case 1: p. 17), who used his status as a citizen of India to acquire land in Baderi, is a malignant symptom. But we have no means of telling from this action alone whether the body-politic will survive and cure itself, or whether it will die. After the event we can be wise. In fact Baderi got rid of the outsider. Similarly it is only after the event that we can say that fission in the clans has led to a decline in clan-membership and the emergence of the *mutha*. In other words, we need to have seen a large number of patients die of the disease, before we can say, on diagnosing the first symptom, that the disease is likely to prove fatal.

POLITICAL MOTIVATION

At the opening of this book I made a fundamental assumption about human nature: that the individual's motive in giving or continuing to give his allegiance to a political group is that in this way he expects to gain his ends and retain or achieve command

---

[1] In concentrating on bridge-actions and on a social field we cannot throw overboard the idea of structure. It would be impossible to understand the power behind Liringa's threat to invoke the clan to help Manda, if we did not also know of the structure of the clan, and the ties of kinship and ritual, and the way these ties reinforce one another.

over men and resources. In this way I postulate a 'political' man. 'Political man' is as much a sitting target as 'economic man' has been. There are close analogies between these two concepts, although I would not wish the same value ideas of utilitarian philosophy to be attached to 'political' man. It will be instructive to see how close my 'political man' comes to the assumptions of late nineteenth-century economists about the housewife who maximizes her utility undeterred by social obligations and other external factors. Must we assume a 'free market' and perfect competition in politics, as once was assumed in economics? Would it help my enquiry to do so? Have I in fact done so? Can my whole analysis be brought to the ground by showing that motivation is not the simple thing postulated in the first sentence of this paragraph?

Viewed in this way the factors which make for imperfect competition in politics, to continue the metaphor for the moment, are loyalties to various groups, which cause a man, knowingly or unwittingly, to sacrifice his own self-interest. It would be foolish to deny that men are swayed by loyalties of this kind, and there are often considerable social pressures urging a man towards self-sacrifice, and publicizing any act of this kind. Secondly there is the factor of ignorance: even if a man is resolutely self-interested, he may be incapable of assessing the best means of gaining his end. If therefore my analysis is based on the assumption of the political equivalent of 'perfect competition' and perfect knowledge of the 'political market', then clearly it is wrong. But in fact I have assumed nothing of the sort: I have assumed only the existence of the political equivalent of the entrepreneurs—of some individuals who are out to maximize their political utility, and who know how to set about doing it.

The dichotomy of 'self-interest' on the one side and 'group loyalty' on the other side poses a false problem—at least in so far as it concerns the Kondmals material. The opposition of these two concepts seems to give several suggestive openings, but in my opinion most of them are blind alleys. For instance, at first sight the number of men whose acts are self-interested against those who are still bridled by the traditional loyalties seems to give a measure (ignoring the enormous difficulties of measurement) of integration, of the persistence of the structure, or of the stability of the society.

But it is a mistake, I think, to oppose self-interest to group loyalty. Rather loyalty to one group is opposed to loyalty to another, and self-interest is equally present or absent in both. Those observers who see one system as right and good and who see change as bad[1] distort the situation by labelling a man's loyalty to the first system as 'group loyalty' or 'selflessness' or 'public spirit' and reserve the term 'self-interest' for the act of taking on new loyalties. Those who make the opposite estimate of the value of the two systems may reverse the procedure.[2] But from a position which is neutral one must assume that self-interest is equally present or equally absent in both. In short the opposition of group loyalty to self-interest is useful only in tracing the downfall of one particular structure or system: I have not found it useful in studying social changes from one structure to another, for in this situation 'integration' is not a characteristic of a whole society, but a measure of the pervasiveness of one structure in that society.

My description of political motivation is not a comprehensive assessment of human nature. It is only a brief way of saying that those who transfer their allegiance from one group to another, or who choose to follow one rule rather than another, expect that by doing this they will achieve some end, which they would not have done otherwise. It is a statement about 'political entrepreneurs', not about everyone.

THE DOMINANT CASTE

The caste system of India has lent itself more frequently to evaluation than to analysis. It is either condemned as an affront to human dignity, or it is praised as a remarkably mature and intelligent solution to the problems of living in a plural society.[3] An emotive description is seldom an exact description, and those who find the caste system to their taste have exaggerated the harmony

[1] V. Elwin, 1943, p. 13. 'The souls of the people are soiled and grimy with the dust of passing motor-buses. The village has ceased to be a living community; it is now an aggregate of isolated units,' *et passim.*

[2] G. S. Ghurye, 1943, p. 216. 'Tribal sections on joining Hindu society develop an internal organization of the caste pattern, and thus have the regulating and controlling power within themselves.'

[3] J. S. Furnivall, 1948, p. 308. J. A. Dubois, 1906, p. 28.

with which the system works, by stressing the degree of inter-dependence between the different castes. Interdependence means that everyone depends on everyone else: it means reciprocity. From this it is easy to slip into ideas of equality: because men are equally dependent upon one another, they are assumed to be equal in other ways. Equality of rank is so manifestly false when applied to a caste system that the final step in the argument is seldom taken, and the exposition rests upon a presentation of mutual interdependence, and the hint that, because one caste could bring the system to a standstill by refusing to play its part, castes do in fact use this sanction to maintain their rights against the rest. In fact, of course, the system is held together not so much by ties of recipro-city, but by the concentration of force in one of its parts. The system works the way it does because the coercive sanctions are all in the hands of a dominant caste. There is a tie of reciprocity: but it is not a sanction of which the dependent castes can make easy use.

Power is concentrated in the hands of the dominant caste. The main features of this system are well known and have been for many years. The administrators who had to deal with the caste system, as distinct from the writers who merely thought about it, could not afford to miss so important a feature as the dominance of one caste.[1] One caste has direct control over economic resources and it alone has a corporate political existence: the other castes derive their living by a dependent relationship upon the dominant caste, and in themselves they have no corporate political existence. Their political relationships are as individual clients of a master in the dominant caste. Political ties run vertically in the system and not horizontally: political and economic rank tends to be con-sistent with ritual rank: the dependent castes are not all of equal rank but are organized in several grades, and this is apparent in ritual usage.

These are the main features of caste seen as a political system. But as soon as this picture is put against reality, it becomes obvious that this is an abstraction of a high order. Many facts have to be discarded or accounted for before we can make use of the model. In Bisipara I identified the WARRIOR caste as dominant. But the WARRIORS did not own all the land: they had less than 30 per cent of it. On the other hand the PANS who as a dependent caste should have no land at all, had over 20 per cent of the land. The WARRIORS

[1] D. Ibbetson, 1883, p. 174.

as a group owned more land than any other group, but their income per head was smaller than that in several other castes. Persons of other caste were not dependent upon the WARRIORS for making their living. Although the WARRIORS dominated the village council, since they were by far the largest single group among the clean castes, who alone were eligible to sit on the council, they were far from being able to use an economic sanction, which is one of the bases of the system, to control the other castes. Nor could they make use—at least overt use—of the other basic sanction in the system, force, since this would have been against the law. Lacking both economic and political dominance, in the sense which the ideas about a dominant caste seem to demand, the WARRIORS were in an ambiguous position in the ritual hierarchy. They claimed to be second only to the BRAHMIN: the same claim was made by two other castes, the MERCHANT and the DISTILLER. None of these castes would accept food or water from one another. The case of the MERCHANT was not important since there was only one household in Bisipara: but the rivalry with the DISTILLER caste was continually breaking to the surface of village life in one form or another. WARRIORS took water from the HERDSMAN caste (and so did the BRAHMIN), but they refused it from the DISTILLERS, thus implicitly placing them below the HERDSMEN in the scale of ritual precedence. The HERDSMEN naturally agreed with this, and while they accepted not only water but also cooked food from the WARRIOR, they refused both from the DISTILLER. But the DISTILLERS themselves accepted food and water only from the BRAHMIN, thus claiming for themselves the second place in the hierarchy, which most people allotted to the WARRIOR caste.

The picture so presented does not fit with the postulate of WARRIOR dominance. Are we then to do away with the concept of a dominant caste? Before doing this, one ought to examine the system again, not this time as something static, but in its dynamic aspects. All the variations from the ideal pattern might be comprehensible in terms of a system in motion, just as the presence of sister's sons and outsiders of various kinds can be fitted into the dynamic analysis of the Kond agnatic groups within a village.[1] It might be possible to reconcile the evident disagreement about positions in the hierarchy, by supposing that this is a temporary disequilibrium caused by some outside factor, and that the system

[1] See pp. 27–40.

is moving all the time towards an equilibrium structure of one dominant and several dependent castes.

The activities of the DISTILLER caste become partly comprehensible on this hypothesis. As a result of 'outside' events they have been enriched, and their former lowly status in the ritual hierarchy (alcohol being polluting) did not match the economic power which they wielded nor their position as landowners and men of substance. The system consists of the correspondence of ritual, economic, and political power, and we can then envisage the claims and assertions of the DISTILLERS as evidence that the system is, so to speak, asserting itself, and bringing ritual status into line with political and economic status.

This has allowed us to save that part of the hypothesis in which ritual, political, and economic status are said to correspond. But it has not brought reality any nearer the concept of one dominant caste controlling other dependent castes. Neither the WARRIORS nor the DISTILLERS are dominant, one over the other: and if this is a movement towards the postulated equilibrium, it seems to have got stuck at a point short of the abstract model. There is not one dominant caste, but two castes, who stand towards one another not in relations of ordination, but of equality as rivals. Their mutual ritual 'abhorrence' symbolizes not ordination, but equality.

The events in Bisipara[1] are not part of any repetitive equilibrium, but are a sign of change. This is clear in the case of the PAN untouchables, in Baderi to some extent, and strikingly so in Bisipara. These PANS, in conflict with the clean castes and in particular with the dominant caste, are opting out of the caste system, in so far as it is political, and are entering a wider political arena. In terms of groups, they are exchanging their vertical allegiances within a village for a horizontal political allegiance towards their own caste, and they are becoming a corporate political group.

The concept of a dominant caste *in a village* is becoming one which is useful only as a datum line from which to measure social change. Although struggles and conflicts may still take place within the village between caste-groups (a 'caste-group' consists of members of the same caste who live in one village), nevertheless the political allegiances which are effective at the present day no

[1] F. G. Bailey, 1957, Part III.

longer are confined within the village, but embrace a much wider political arena.

The concept of the dominant caste has been used to describe not only the political system of a village, but also of some larger unit, which we may call a region. In large areas of north-western and north-central India the Rajputs are, or were, a dominant caste; Nayars were dominant on the Malabar coast; the WARRIORS were dominant throughout the Kondmals; Okkaligas and Lingayats are dominant in different parts of Mysore; and so forth. In what sense is dominance used in these cases, and is the concept the same as when it is used with reference to a village? I shall try to answer these questions with reference to the situation in the Kondmals before the coming of the Administration, and to the situation at the present day.

In one sense, to talk about a regional dominant caste is simply an abbreviated way of saying that the dominance-dependence pattern is found not in one village, but in all, and secondly that the same caste is dominant in all the villages. This is the traditional regional dominant caste. Political relations within this caste are segmentary in one form or another. In a primitive region like the Kondmals the segments consisted of villages and nothing larger: in the more sophisticated Malabar the segments were kingdoms and chiefdoms. But, whatever the complexity of political organization, the political system admitted competition mainly within the dominant caste. The WARRIORS fought with one another, with the help of their several dependent castes, and they tried to conquer territory, or perhaps to win Kond allies from one another. Political cleavages were within the dominant caste alone.

This does not, of course, mean that in any given stretch of territory there was one and only one dominant caste. In the Kondmals before the coming of the Administration, there were two dominant castes, each dominant within separate systems. In the Kond hills the WARRIORS were dominant in enclaves within a larger area of Kond dominance.

The situation in Mysore to-day, where the two most numerous castes, the Lingayats and the Okkaligas, compete for power, and where each has localities in which it is dominant, is reminiscent of the situation in the Kondmals before the coming of the Administration. Competition takes place between castes and not within a single caste. But there are also differences. Force is—theoretically at least—irrelevant: and the power that counts is voting power. Although many of the old allegiances persist and the master's clients tend to vote according to his wishes, nevertheless the dominant castes cannot call invariably upon the support of their dependent castes, as could the WARRIORS in their struggle against the Konds. These dependent castes themselves are likely now to have corporate identity as political units, and to be organized on a horizontal system of allegiances and not a vertical system. They are no longer dependent, although they may be politically allied: they might be termed, metaphorically, 'subordinate allies' rather than dependents.[1] There is a third difference between the 'dominant caste' in the traditional system and the 'dominant caste' in the modern political scene. Although there may be factions and conflicts within a dominant caste like the Okkaligas, or the Lingayats, or the Nayars, such a caste does not segment at the present day into institutionalized hostile groups (chiefdoms and Kingdoms) as it did in the past.[2] It co-operates as a single caste in opposition to other castes. There is, in other words, a radical difference in the structure in which the modern 'dominant caste' operates, from the structure in which the traditional 'dominant caste' operated.

Once again we must beware of the fallacy of thinking that change is once-for-all, abrupt, and radical. To identify a new structure in which a new kind of dominant caste is working does not mean that the old structure and the old type of dominant caste has vanished and that we no longer need to bother about it in analysing political relationships within a village. We need it as a datum line against which to measure political change. But it is required for other reasons as well. There are some elements in present-day behaviour which are incomprehensible unless we see them as part of the traditional caste system. We cannot, for instance make sense of the behaviour which symbolizes a difference in rank, unless we also know about traditional, political and economic rank. The fact that the WARRIORS refuse cooked food from HERDSMEN, while the HERDSMEN accept food from the WARRIORS, can only be understood as a means of symbolizing the dependence of the HERDSMAN upon the WARRIOR. This dependence existed in the traditional caste system. The ritual aspects of caste seem to diminish less quickly than does the political reality which it

[1] See p. 169.
[2] E. Miller, 1954, 415-17.

symbolizes. The ritual observances, which symbolize the HERDS-MAN's dependence, may continue as moral imperatives, even when the HERDSMAN is no longer dependent. Secondly, as is clear from my description of Baderi at the present day, in many villages the traditional system has held out against modern political allegiances, and political relations continue to be organized on the basis of dominance and dependence in a caste idiom. In other words there are still villages in which the abstraction of a caste system made up of one dominant and several dependent castes is near to reality, and Baderi is an example.

TRIBE AND CASTE

If 'caste' is an emotive word, 'tribe and caste' are doubly emotive. The debates about 'the tribal problem' have moved scholars to unscholarly anger, and produced rather pamphleteers than dispassionate observers. It is emphatically not my business to evaluate these two forms of social organization.

There is no single and accepted criterion by which to distinguish a tribe from a caste.[1] Yet at first sight the distinction is easily made. Tribal people live in the hills: they are not Hindus, but Animists: they are economically backward: they are autochthones: they speak tribal languages. But none of these criteria are in themselves satisfactory, and even taken together they will not include all the peoples who are labelled as tribes by the Administration or by ethnographers. The criterion of language begs the question, and runs counter to those accepted tribes who speak a dialect of one of the main Indian languages, such as the Mullu Kurumas, or the Muthuvans, or the Bhils. If we think not in terms of languages but of families of languages, then the results are even more surprising. The languages of the Gonds, the Konds, and the Oraons belong to the great Dravidian family of southern India, and if we accept this alone as the criterion of a tribe, then what is to be done with those who speak Tamil, Malayalam, Telugu, Kannada, and so forth? Nor is it satisfactory to say that the tribes are autochthones. Most tribes, including the Konds, believe that they came to their present territory from somewhere else, and displaced other people, who were the true autochthones. Economic status is equally unsatisfactory: the standard of living of many

[1] G. S. Ghurye, 1943, Chapter I.

people who are acknowledged to be tribal is no worse than that of peasants who are not tribal. Religion, too, is a fallible criterion: every tribal pantheon, in peninsular India at least, contains Hindu Gods; and many of the religious practices, particularly in the lower castes, resemble those of the tribes and are abhorred by high-caste Hindus, in many parts of modern India (though not in all). Finally the geographical criterion fails because if there were no other people beside the tribes living in the hills, there would be no tribal problem.

To decide who is and who is not an Adibasi is clearly an important question for the Administration, since there are privileges attached to Adibasi status: and the frequent complaints that large numbers of Adibasis have been excluded from the category shows that it is more than a mere academic question. But it is not my problem. I am interested in political organization, and I was able to get at least a *prima facie* distinction between the segmentary political system of the Konds based on agnatic kinship, and the Oriya political system which is characterized by ordination.

On closer examination this distinction conceals some difficulties. It is clearly a distinction between systems, which cannot be applied to reality without holding other things equal. The Konds, for their part, did not act politically only towards one another and only in a segmentary system of territorial clans: they also were the masters of PAN untouchables and of the other dependent castes, and in this respect they were a dominant caste in a caste system. In other words the Konds were both a caste and a tribe. Exactly the same can be said of the dominant WARRIOR caste: within this caste in the Kondmals there was a system of segmentary political relations based on territory, and at the same time the WARRIORS were the masters of numerous dependents of other caste. Where then, is the difference? Why have I called the political system of the Oriyas a caste system, while that of the Konds is a tribal system?

The only solution to this problem is to postulate a continuum, at one end of which is a society whose political system is entirely of the segmentary egalitarian type, and which contains no dependents whatsoever; and at the other end of which is a society in which segmentary political relations exist only between a very small proportion of the total society, and most people act in the system in the role of dependents. In the area of Orissa which I have surveyed, those Konds who were most remote from the influence of the Oriyas—say the Kuttia Konds—would be at one end of the continuum, while the small kingdoms of the Mahanadi valley and its surrounding hills, where political activity between equals lay only between a very small number of self-styled Rajput royal families, would be at the other end of the continuum. Just at what point on the continuum tribe ceases and caste begins it is impossible to say, but this way of envisaging the situation does provide a rough and ready way of distinguishing a region and saying whether it is (so far as political organization is concerned) a tribal region or a caste region. Since the Konds are a high proportion of the population of the Kondmals (five out of every eight persons at the present day and probably more in the past), and since they are typically about 80 per cent of the population in their own villages, with only a small proportion of dependents, the greater part of the population were politically active in the segmentary system of political relations, and the region may therefore be counted as tribal.

The methods of establishing whether a particular group is a tribe or a caste are the same. If they have direct command over resources, and their access to the products of the economy are not derived mediately through a dependent status on others, then they are to be counted as a tribe, providing they fulfil a further condition: that they are a relatively large proportion of the total population in the area. If they fulfil the first condition but are a small part of the population, then they are a caste.[1]

It is not so much the definition of tribe and caste that have interested people as the process by which those who are agreed to be tribal people are incorporated into the caste system, and whether or not this process ought to be hindered or helped forward. A tribe may become a caste in two ways. The one—the familiar 'conquest' theory—takes place when a small group of military adventurers conquer a large alien population, reduce it to dependence on themselves, and do not miscegenate or permit any form of political incorporation as equals. I mention this kind of development in passing, since it did not happen in the Kondmals

[1] These tests must, of course, be applied with caution at the present day, since a great part of political activity at the present day belongs neither to the caste system nor to a tribal system, but to the system of bureaucratic government and representative democracy.

s

because the military adventurers were not strong enough to effect a conquest. When the British first arrived in the Kond hills, the Konds began to lose their direct control over resources and to achieve a share in resources through a dependent relationship. For various reasons this process did not go as far in the Kondmals as it has gone in other parts of tribal India: the Kondmals were counted unhealthy: there was little rice-land for the taking; the Administration arrived quite late, and after a somewhat *laissez-faire* beginning became strongly paternalistic and protective towards the Konds. For these and other reasons the Konds did not lose their tribal identity and will never now become the dependents of immigrant Oriyas, because effective political allegiances are not now only in the local system but also in a wider arena.

Professor Ghurye—and administrators before him—made the point that many tribes held their own against immigrant Hindus, until the Administration appeared on the scene.[1] This is certainly true of the Kondmals, where the Konds were able to encyst the Oriya colonies apparently for several centuries. It is wrong to assume that caste is an automatic solvent of a tribal system. What is true is that a political system based on segmentary kinship can only 'adopt' people—that is, can only incorporate them as equals, or else extrude them entirely, whereas a caste system is adapted to incorporating dependents. But neither is in itself stronger, so to speak, than the other. What counts is the degree to which either people can make use of effective power, either naked force, or else by bridge-actions to outside systems. In the early period of the Administration the Oriyas could make most effective use of the Administration and they began to incorporate Konds as their dependents. More recently, through the paternalistic policies of the Administration, and later through Kond dominance in numbers in the representative democracy, the balance of power is shifting in favour of the Konds.

Politically at least the distinction between 'tribe' and 'caste' is ceasing to be a useful one. In the modern caste—the group which is politically active to the width of the linguistic region—both the tribe and the traditional caste are being merged.

[1] G. S. Ghurye, 1943, Chapter IV.

ISOLATION

The question of whether or not villages in India or in other relatively sophisticated peasant societies are sufficiently isolated to be studied as wholes in themselves is in many ways similar to my questions about the adequacy of the concept of a dominant caste in a village. Professor Redfield says that a village of peasants in an 'ancient civilization' cannot be isolated in the same way as a tribe which is presumed to be relatively untouched.[1] In abstracting a single social system for the village, the result is too far removed from the reality which it is supposed to represent.

There is no *a priori* answer to this question: it is primarily empirical. It is not even a question about particular *villages*. If the focus of interest is on ritual, for instance, it might well be possible to isolate a single, whole, and coherent social (not of course cultural) system within a village: but in the same village a political or an economic analysis might inevitably lead the enquirer to concentrate on ties which go outside.

Can Baderi be isolated as an object of political enquiry? If we are content to draw a static chart of groups and their normal interrelationships, this can be done. Baderi is a territorially segregated group of agnatic kinsmen who act together for political ends. But this is a meagre description. If we set the structure in motion, and begin to consider process, we must at once recognize that the village is a unit within a larger structure, and that there are individual ties and relationships going beyond the boundary of the village. The mere fact that this is a group of agnatic kinsmen means that brides must come from outside and leads us to describe a network of affinal and uterine relationships, which transcend village boundaries. The process of 'repetitive equilibrium' cannot be understood without taking into account relationships which go beyond both the village and clan. The agnatic structure of Baderi can only be understood as a part of the Balimendi clan, and in its turn the clan structure can only be seen as the product of movements and tensions over the total (Kond) society of the eastern Kondmals. So, in the tribal system alone, the unit of study is shifted from the village outwards to the clan, and from the clan outwards to the total society.

Exactly the same is to be said of the other type of political

[1] McKim Marriott, 1955, ix.

relationship within Baderi—that between the Konds as masters and other castes as dependents. Our ultimate unit for study is the whole group of villages between which the dependent castes may move, and only by taking into account this larger unit can we see how the system could work.

In studying the political relationships between Konds and Oriyas, it is clear that Baderi village is not the significant arena, since the only Oriyas present there are the politically insignificant Oriya HERDSMEN, and the only other Oriya who owns a field is the preceptor (Case 38: p. 197).

It might then be argued that although we cannot present an adequate picture of political life in Baderi village if we exclude all relationships which go beyond the village boundaries, we can still limit our analysis to Baderi and treat the external relationships as intruding into the system which we are describing. That is to say, we begin to consider them only at the point at which they cross the village boundary: we study their effects in the village but not the systems in which they originate. I have done this in Part II of the book for the tribal system of the Konds: I have recognized that this has been set in motion by various factors—differential growth of population, the Oriya invasions, and so forth—but I have considered only their effects in the tribal system. Is it always possible to treat outside events in this fashion? Can we always afford to cut them off at the point at which they enter the system which we have chosen to study?

There would be general agreement among anthropologists that outside events which intrude into the social system and originate in non-social systems, can be treated simply as intrusions. If the outside event is an epidemic, or a cattle plague, then we can study the effects of a large number of deaths among people or among cattle on the social system of the village or the tribe or whatever is our chosen unit, without making an excursion into medical etiology. It is not so easy to do this when these non-sociological outside events have themselves some sociological implications. It might, for instance, be necessary to make a study of medical facilities, if we are to understand why they have been patronized by some of the people in our unit of study, and why others have avoided them.

But when the external relationship is what I have been calling a 'bridge-action', then we are committed to making some kind of a study of the system to which these bridge-actions have reference, as well as of the relationships within our chosen unit of study. The rivalry between Liringa and Ponga is purely within the village and within the tribal system: yet to appreciate how each seeks to score over the other we need to know about the Kond-PAN system (Case 35: p. 128), and about the Kond-Oriya system (Case 38: p. 197). Ponga and Liringa are not simply passive: they are able to manipulate these two systems and the investigator needs at least as much knowledge of these systems as Ponga and Liringa have themselves.

We cannot study social change simply within the boundaries of a village. When bridge-actions lead to change, the system which we are studying may be changing to resemble the system to which the bridge-action appeals.[1] There is no understanding of the be-haviour of the Baderi PANS (Case 35: p. 128), if we look upon it simply as an act of defiance against the Konds. We will not know the strength or significance of their actions unless we also know about their modern economic affiliations, the Harijan movement, the wider political scene, equality before the law, and so forth.

Throughout this book the village of Baderi has been the starting point for an investigation into political systems which far tran-scend the village. I have found the village to be the best vantage point from which to survey these systems, and from which to analyse the way in which change is taking place. Events in the village provide a text, in the commentary upon which the wider systems are unfolded. The village is not an isolated whole in itself: in a political enquiry it has been merely a convenient field of observation, where several political systems can be seen at work and impinging upon one another.

TRIBE, CASTE, AND NATION

I have shown that tribe, caste, and nation are three different political alignments: three forms of allocating scarce resources, and of uniting to compete for those resources: three different kinds of arenas, in which are engaged three different kinds of groups. I have also shown that these three systems can be placed in a temporal order: that the caste system preceded the national system, and was itself preceded by the tribal system. This is the direction in which

[1] It is also, of course, possible that bridge-actions may result in anarchy.

political society is changing. But all three systems are still in existence and effective political action can be taken by making use of
ties in all of them, and by adroit bridge-action from one system
to another.

The village has remained an arena within which individuals
struggle with one another for power and the possession of land. In
a Kond village membership of the community and residence on
its territory still appear to be a necessary qualification for taking
part in the struggle. There still is, and always has been, a political
cleavage between individuals in the villages. What has changed is
the nature of outside alignments which are effective in this struggle:
these were, firstly, relationships with other Konds, within or outside the village; secondly relationships with local chiefs and headmen; and thirdly the use that can be made of the administrative
and judicial system.

The Kond clans are no longer primarily political units, engaged
in the struggle to validate a right to resources, although clan-
membership may still have political implications.[1] There is now no
competition for land between clans and the clan system has ceased
to provide the main political cleavage in the total society. There
have been four main cleavages: (i) individual against individual,
or faction against faction, within the village; (ii) Kond clan against
clan; (iii) clan or group of clans against an Oriya village and its
chief; and (iv) Oriya chiefs against one another. The first cleavage
continues to-day. The second and fourth are no longer of importance. The third cleavage continues, but it now tends to draw upon
wider alignments: it is being transferred, so to speak, to a larger
arena. There ceased to be cleavages only within small localities
between an Oriya chief and the surrounding Konds, and the
society developed a main cleavage between Konds and Oriyas.
This cleavage arose partly through the Government's insistence on
treating these two categories differently, partly in the manner in
which they are engaged in the modern economy, and partly
through such historical accidents as the fact that the first Administration was conducted not through the Kui language, but in
Oriya. As one would expect, with the improvement of communications—in the widest sense of the word—the struggle for control over resources can now be carried on by larger groups and
must take place in a larger political arena. Konds and Oriyas, who

[1] See p. 255.

in the Kond hills formerly were cultural categories, are now becoming political groups. 'Caste' (in the modern sense[1]) is replacing territory as the basis of political grouping.

The analysis of a political system as a logical model is a necessary first step to understanding political activity in the Kond hills: but it is not sufficient to stop at that point. In order to understand actual incidents, or in order to estimate what will be the effect of a particular social reform or a new technique, an analysis of this kind is virtually useless. In a field of activity as complicated as that of the Kond hills we need to emphasize complexity, and to look not for one political system, but for several. Secondly we need to see individuals not as passive creatures exhibiting for our benefit regularities in behaviour, but as actors who may not only choose between systems but may attempt to twist and amend these systems to their own advantage.

In this book I have largely been content to show that people do behave in this way: that there are several political systems: and that the actors pick and choose between them. Over the last hundred years in the Kondmals some courses of political action have been discarded and different political alignments have been taken up or are in process of being adopted, because they better serve the ends of the actors. To this extent there is regularity in choice: one particular choice begins to exhibit a statistical regularity, and so becomes part of a system: while another choice ceases to be exemplified, and with it dies a system. I have been able to show why particular choices are advantageous: what, for instance, is the advantage to a Kond of shedding Kond culture and taking on the manners and customs of the Oriyas: why clan membership is nowadays only of minimal political significance. I have also been able to show how the field of choice is itself delimited: why, for instance, the Bisipara PANS can make more effective use of the representative democracy than can the Baderi PANS; why force alone is becoming an ineffective means of gaining political ends, at least in relations between the larger groups. I have also been able to show why individuals have made certain choices in particular situations: why Ponga did not intervene in the Baderi PAN dispute (Case 35: p. 128); why neither Ponga nor Nrusingh brought in their commercial relationship (Case 38: p. 197); why Liringa chose to exacerbate an already difficult situation (Case 38:

[1] See p. 191.

p. 197). At this level I could also make prognoses, and I could suggest what Liringa or the other actors would do in similar disputes. But I have not proclaimed any 'principles' of social change: the only principle I have to offer is the heuristic one—to ask continually who profited and through what social alignments he did so.

REFERENCES

Calcutta Review.
Census of India, 1931, 1941, 1951.
Census of India, 1951: *District Census Handbooks, Orissa: Phulbani.*
Economic Weekly of Bombay.

BAILEY, F. G., 1957. *Caste and the Economic Frontier.* Manchester: Manchester University Press.
BARNES, J. A., 1954. *Politics in a Changing Society.* Cape Town: Oxford University Press. (Now Manchester University Press, 1958.)
BENDIX, R., and LIPSETT, S. M., 1954. *Class, Status, and Power.* London: Routledge and Kegan Paul.
CAMPBELL, J., 1861. *Narrative of Operations in the Hill Tracts of Orissa for the suppression of Human Sacrifice and Infanticide.* London: Hurst and Blackett.
COHN, BERNARD S., 1955. 'The Changing Status of a Depressed Caste' in *Village India,* edited by McKim Marriott, Chicago: Chicago University Press.
DUBOIS, ABBE J. A., 1906 (trans.). *Hindu Manners, Customs and Ceremonies,* translated by H. K. Beauchamp. Oxford: Clarendon Press.
ELWIN, VERRIER, 1943. *The Aboriginals.* Oxford Pamphlets on Indian Affairs. Bombay: Oxford University Press.
1948. 'Notes on the Juang' in *Man in India,* Vol. xxviii, No. 1.
EVANS-PRITCHARD, E. E., 1940. *The Nuer.* Oxford: Clarendon Press.
1949. *The Sanusi of Cyrenaica.* Oxford: Clarendon Press.
FIRTH, R., 1951. *Elements of Social Organization.* London: Watts.
1954. 'Social Organization and Social Change' in the *Journal of the Royal Anthropological Institute,* Vol. 84, pts. I & II.
1955. 'Some Principles of Social Organization', *ibid.,* Vol. 85, pts. I & II.
FORDE, DARYLL (Editor), 1954. *African Worlds.* London: Oxford University Press.
FORTES, M., 1945. *The Dynamics of Clanship among the Tallensi.* London: Oxford University Press.
FORTES, M., and EVANS-PRITCHARD, E. E., 1940. *African Political Systems.* London: Oxford University Press.
FRIEND-PEREIRA, J. E., 1904. 'Totemism among the Khonds' in the *Journal of the Asiatic Society of Bengal,* Vol. LXXIII, pt. III, No. 3.
FURNIVALL, J. S., 1948. *Colonial Policy and Practice.* London: Cambridge University Press.
GHURYE, G. S., 1943. *The Aborigines—'So-Called'—and their Future.* Poona: Gokhale Institute of Politics and Economics, Publication No. 11.
GLUCKMAN, MAX, 1942. 'Some processes of social change illustrated from Zululand' in *African Studies,* Vol. 1.
1955. *Custom and Conflict in Africa.* Oxford: Blackwell.

GOUGH, E. KATHLEEN, 1952. 'Changing Kinship Usages in the Setting of Political and Economic change among the Nayars of Malabar', in the *Journal of the Royal Anthropological Institute*, Vol. 82, pt. I.

GRIGSON, W. V., 1949. *The Maria Gonds of Bastar*. Bombay: Oxford University Press.

HOCART, A. M., 1950. *Caste: A Comparative Study*. London: Methuen.

IBBETSON, D. C. J., 1883. *Outlines of Punjab Ethnography*. Calcutta: Superintendent of Government Printing, India.

KABERRY, P., 1957. 'Malinowski's field-work methods' in *Man and Culture*, edited by Raymond Firth. London: Routledge and Kegan Paul.

LEACH, E. R., 1954. *Political Systems of Highland Burma*. London: London School of Economics and Political Science.

LLEWELLYN, K. N., and HOEBEL, E. A., 1941. *The Cheyenne Way*. Norman: University of Oklahoma.

LOWIE, R. H., 1927. *The Origin of the State*. New York: Harcourt Brace.

MACPHERSON, S. C., 1852. 'An account of the religion of the Khonds in Orissa' in the *Journal of the Royal Asiatic Society*, First Series. Vol. XIII.

MACPHERSON, W. (Editor), 1865. *Memorials of Service in India from the correspondence of the late Major Samuel Charteris Macpherson, C.B.* London: John Murray.

MARRIOTT, McKIM (Editor), 1955. *Village India*. Chicago: Chicago University Press.

MILLER, ERIC J., 1954. 'Caste and Territory in Malabar' in *American Anthropologist*, Vol. 56, No. 3.

NADEL, S. F., 1953. *The Foundations of Social Anthropology*. London: Cohen and West.

     1957. *The Theory of Social Structure*. London: Cohen and West.

O'MALLEY, L. S. S., 1908. *Angul*. Bengal District Gazetteers. Vol. XI. Calcutta. The Bengal Secretariat Book Depot.

RADCLIFFE-BROWN, A. R., 1952, *Structure and Function in Primitive Society*. London: Cohen and West.

RISLEY, H. H., 1891. *The Tribes and Castes of Bengal*. Calcutta: Bengal Secretariat Press.

ROY, S. C., 1912. *The Mundas and their Country*. Calcutta.

     1935. *The Hill Bhuiyas of Orissa*. Karachi.

SCHAPERA, I., 1956. *Government and Politics in Tribal Societies*. London: Watts.

SCHULZE, F. V. P., 1911. *Kuvi Grammar*. Madras.

     1913. *Vocabulary of the Kuvi-Kond Language*. Madras.

SRINIVAS, M. N., 1952. *Religion and Society among the Coorgs of South India*. Oxford: Clarendon Press.

     1955. 'Castes—Can they exist in the India of to-morrow?' in *Report of the Seminar on Casteism and Removal of Untouchability*. Bombay: Indian Conference of Social Work.

     1956. 'A Note on Sanskritization and Westernization' in *Far Eastern Quarterly*, Vol. XV, No. 4.

     1957. 'Caste in Modern India' in *The Journal of Asian Studies*, Vol. XVI, No. 4.

WILSON, GODFREY and MONICA, 1945. *The Analysis of Social Change*. London: Cambridge University Press.

WINFIELD, W. W., 1928. *A Grammar of the Kui Language*. Calcutta: Asiatic Society of Bengal.

1929. *A Vocabulary of the Kui Language*. Calcutta: Asiatic Society of Bengal.

INDEX

Adibasi, 4, 87, 184, 187, 191–2, 264; see also Harijan, Untouchable
Administration, 3, 5, 17, 20, 63, 70, 110–11, 113, 266; and the Konds, 180 ff., 239, 266; as a source of employment, 102, 183, 184
Administrative courts, 133; officials, see Dinobandu Patnaik, Ollenbach, Sirdar
Adoption, 92
Affines, 28, 29, 30, 37–8, 54
Agnates (and agnation), 22, 23, 25, 28, 37, 38, 41, 44 ff., 53–4, 58–9, 76–7, 89 ff., 167n., 267
Agriculture, see Axe-cultivation, Rice-cultivation
Allies, subordinate, 164, 166
Angul District, 181; regulations, 181–2
Animists, 4, 263
Assam, see Tea Gardens
Assembly, non-statutory, 132–3
Atonement, ceremony of, 21, 22, 79–80
Avunculocality, 30, 33, 37
Axe-cultivation, 4, 63–5

Baderi village, 3 ff. et passim; description of, 17 ff.
Balimendi clan, 22, 47 ff., 69 ff., 267; mutha, 3, 19, 47
Bendix, R., and Lipsett, S. M., 240n.
Bhils, 263
Bisipara village, 3 ff., 149 ff.
Bisoi, a service title, 162, 172
Boad, 16n.; Raja of, 150, 170, 171, 177, 181
Boycott, 135, 142
Bride-exchange, 29, 30
Bride-seizing folk, 28, 53, 57, 70
Bridewealth, 29, 30, 95
'Bridge actions', 248, 251, 252, 255, 269
'Brigandage, legal', 94–8
Brotherhood, 21 ff., 40, 50, 63
Buffaloes, sacrifice of, 51, 81, 83

Campbell, J., 26n., 172, 176–7, 183
Cash crop, 5; see Turmeric
Caste defined, 121n.; the dominant,

168–9, 191, 257–63; expulsion from, 42; groups, 169, 260; ranking, 159–60, see Sanskritization; readmission to, 42, 43; specialization and agriculture, 148; structure of Oriya villages, 168 ff.; and tribe, 173, 263–6
Castes, internal organization of, 121 ff.; BARBER, 168, 169; DISTILLER, 259–260; BRAHMIN, 150, 168, 169, 188; HERDSMAN, 122 ff., 168, 173, 262–263, Kond, 20, 121, 123–7, Oriya, 20, 121, 122–7; OUTCASTE, Boad, see PAN; PAN, vii, 47, 121, 127 ff., 251–2; Kond and Oriya, 121; POTTER, 121–2; SMITH, 20, 121, 125–7; SWEEPER, 152; WARRIOR, 3, 5, 116–17, 150, 168, 172, 258 ff.; WASHERMAN, 169
Cattle, 22, 125, 133
Change, social, 15, 88, 251 ff.
Clan, 47 ff., 69 ff., see Balimendi; exogamy, 50 ff., 84; founding, and immigrants, 78 ff.; territory, 47 ff., 71 ff.; totems, 42, 43
Clanship, dispersed, 52 ff., 84 ff.
Clients, 140
Climate, 3
Cohn, B., vii, 190
Colson, E., vii
'Conflict', 7, 239
'Contradiction', 7, 239
Courts, Government, 32
Crafts, 100
Cross-cousins, 29, 35, 36, 38
Cultivation, 4, 98 ff.; see axe-cultivation, rice-cultivation

Democracy, representative, 236, 242–3, 265n.; see also Legislative Assembly
'Diachronic', 8, 9
Dinobandu Patnaik, 71, 178, 181
Dowry, 30, 94
Dravidian languages, 4, 263
Dubois, J. A., 257n.
'Dynamic' analysis, 8, 9

276